Families in Cultural Context

FAMILIES IN CULTURAL CONTEXT

Strengths and Challenges in Diversity

Mary Kay DeGenova

University of New Hampshire

Mayfield Publishing Company
Mountain View, California
London • Toronto

Library of Congress Cataloging-in-Publication Data
DeGenova, Mary Kay.
    Families in cultural context : strengths and challenges in diversity /
Mary Kay DeGenova.
        p.   cm.
    Includes bibliographical references and index.
    ISBN 1-55934-581-0
    1. Minorities—United States.   2. Family—United States.   3. Ethnicity—
United States.   I. Title.
E184.A1D296   1997   96-34123
305.8′00973—dc20   CIP

Manufactured in the United States of America
10   9   8   7   6   5   4   3   2   1

Mayfield Publishing Company
1280 Villa Street
Mountain View, CA 94041

Sponsoring editor, Franklin C. Graham; production editor, Julianna Scott Fein;
manuscript editor, Betsy Dilernia; art director, Jeanne M. Schreiber; text designer,
Detta Penna; art manager, Susan Breitbard; manufacturing manager, Amy Folden;
cover designer, Donna Davis; cover image, Images © 1996 PhotoDisc, Inc. Quotation
on p. v: From Maya Angelou, *Wouldn't Take Nothing for My Journey Now* (New York:
Random House, 1993). The text was set in 10/13 Fairfield by Wilsted & Taylor
Publishing Services and printed on 50# acid-free Text White Opaque by The Maple-
Vail Book Manufacturing Group.

It is time for the preachers,

the rabbis,

the priests and pundits,

and the professors

to believe in the awesome wonder of diversity

so that they can teach those who follow them.

It is time for parents to teach young people early on

that in diversity there is beauty and there is strength.

We all should know that diversity makes for a rich tapestry,

and we must understand that all the threads of the tapestry are

equal in value no matter their color;

equal in importance no matter their texture.

Our young must be taught that racial peculiarities do exist,

but that beneath the skin,

beyond the differing features

and into the true heart of being,

fundamentally, we are more alike,

my friend,

than we are unalike.

—Maya Angelou

Contents

Preface

As the United States continues to become more ethnically diverse, family ethnicity is an increasingly important topic today. As educators, we are confronted with the demand to include more of a multicultural perspective in many of the courses we teach. While most family textbooks pay some attention to cultural diversity, the subject is rarely examined in depth and from a comparative perspective. This book was written with the primary objective of providing students with a comparable, comprehensive view of families from different ethnic groups. It explores cultural variations in family structure, life cycle, functions, and controls; discusses the impact of history, values, philosophies, and religions upon families; and examines changes and adaptations made by families following their immigration to the United States.

The focus of this book is on normative behaviors as opposed to social problems—which is usually the main topic of books and chapters on this subject. By centering on family structures that are primarily normative, this text provides an opportunity for students to examine the strengths inherent in, and the challenges of, normative families. This approach encourages students to strip away preconceptions about superficial cultural variations, to uncover similarities among groups, and to bridge the mental gap between "us" and "them."

To help make meaningful comparison possible, the chapters are intended to be consistent and follow the same basic structure. However, to confine each chapter to a rigid format, without allowing them to accommodate the variety of experiences and characteristics of each ethnic group, would do great harm to the book's multicultural focus, and would lose much of the richness of diversity. The chapter on African American families, for example, approaches the description of family structure from the perspective of socioeconomic status rather than from a thematic perspective; and the immigration history of American Indians, so different from that of the other cultures featured, necessitates a unique approach to the study of the American Indian family's heritage.

The book offers a wider range of ethnicities than other available books on family ethnicity. The eleven ethnic groups represented—American Indians, African Americans, Mexican Americans, Mormon Americans, Chinese Americans, Japanese Americans, Puerto Rican Americans, Asian Indian Americans, Cuban Americans, Arab Americans, and Hawaiian Americans—demonstrate the diversity of families among a variety of subcultures within the United States, and highlight cross-cultural similarities in family structures and roles. Individually, each chapter provides a concise overview of the family in a particular culture; taken as a whole, the book illustrates the complexity of the combination of cultures that contribute to the richness of the United States.

The inclusion of pedagogical aids should make the book more interesting and useful to instructors and students. To help students better understand the challenges families face, each chapter includes a section describing common misconceptions and stereotypes surrounding the ethnic group. Each chapter concludes with a personal interview with a member of the culture portrayed, increasing readers' empathy by adding a human face to the discussion. The personal interview is unique to this book and helps bring the subject matter to life. Questions for discussion, suggested readings and videos, and additional resources are listed at the end of each chapter. The questions for discussion challenge students to make comparisons between the groups, to draw conclusions, and to reflect on their own family patterns shaped by culture. A glossary at the end of the book defines terms that are boldfaced in the chapters.

The absence of a concluding chapter is deliberate. The book's intention is to challenge students to think about families that are different from their own. The objective is to open a pathway of exploration, not to provide a conclusion that could prevent students from having the opportunity to reach conclusions on their own.

This is very much an interdisciplinary text, drawing on a wide range of disciplines. The contributors represent many different fields of study and backgrounds. Most chapters were written by a scholar from that particular ethnic group. This approach provides a crucial combination of scholarly integrity and cultural sensitivity. By being interdisciplinary, normative in perspective, and following a developmental life-cycle approach, this book would serve well as a primary text in a family ethnicity course and as a supplemental reader to basic marriage and family texts.

Many people have contributed to the writing of this book. I would like to thank the reviewers: Douglas A. Abbott, University of Nebraska–Lincoln; Shirley L. Baugher, University of Nebraska–Lincoln; Timothy H. Brubaker, Miami University; Norma J. Burgess, Syracuse University; Ramona Marotz–Baden, Ph.D., Montana State University–Bozeman; Patrick C. McKenry, The Ohio

State University; and Paul C. Rosenblatt, University of Minnesota. I would also like to thank Frank Graham, editor at Mayfield Publishing Company, for his support, advice, and encouragement. I am indebted to Amy Voege, who, with her expert editorial assistance and good humor, made the editorial process manageable. I wish to thank Gerard DeGenova for his thoughtful contributions to the introductory chapter. Lastly, I would like to thank the contributing authors for their scholarship, patience, and flexibility. Without them the text would not have been possible.

Mary Kay DeGenova

The Contributors

Barbara C. Aswad, Ph.D., Professor of Middle Eastern Anthropology, Wayne State University, Detroit, MI, is the author of *Property Control and Social Strategies in a Middle Eastern Village*, editor of *Arabic Speaking Communities in American Cities* and *Family and Gender Among American Muslims*, as well as the author of numerous articles on Middle Eastern and American Arab women. She is Past President of the Middle East Studies Association of North America.

Hector Carrasquillo, Ph.D., born in Puerto Rico, is an Assistant Professor in the Department of Puerto Rican Studies and Director of the Center of Latino Studies at Brooklyn College, City University of New York. He earned his doctorate from Syracuse University, and his current work focuses on the family and Latino aged. Professor Carrasquillo's most recent publication includes a chapter on "The Puerto Rican Family" in *Minority Families in the United States: A Multicultural Perspective*, edited by Ronald L. Taylor.

Tamara Cheshire, M.S., is a Lakota Indian who studied Cultural Anthropology, Women's Studies, and Family Studies at Oregon State University. Her research focuses on the transmission of culture in urban American Indian families. She has been a part of the Oregon Coastal American Indian community since she was a young girl, and was coordinator of the OSU Native American Longhouse for two years.

Mary Kay DeGenova, Ph.D., is an Assistant Professor of Family Studies at the University of New Hampshire. She received her doctorate in Child Development and Family Studies from Purdue University. Her research interests include cross-cultural comparison of families, AIDS and the family, and regrets in later life.

Masako Ishii-Kuntz, Ph.D., is Associate Professor of Sociology at the University of California, Riverside, and Director of the University of California Tokyo Study Center. Her research interests include family and gender in cross-ethnic and cross-cultural perspectives. Her publications have appeared in, among others, the *Journal of Marriage and the Family, Journal of Family Issues, The Gerontologist, Sex Roles,* and *Sociological Perspectives.* She is the author of *Ordinal Log-Linear Models* and recently completed a study comparing Chinese, Japanese, Korean, and Filipino American families. Presently residing in Tokyo, Japan, she is studying Japanese dual-earner couples who share housework and child-care responsibilities.

Walter T. Kawamoto, Ph.D., recently completed his doctoral program in Family Studies at Oregon State University. His latest research, funded by a grant from the National Institute of Mental Health, focuses on stability and family problem solving in American Indian intermarried families.

James D. Lambert, M.S., is a doctoral student in Child and Family Studies at the University of Wisconsin–Madison. His current research interests include investigating the dynamics of father-child relationships, family policy, and family status differences in well-being. He has published on the effects of involved fathering, and health issues in later life families. He is currently serving as a consultant for both the Governor's Commission on Families and Children and the Lieutenant Governor's office, State of Wisconsin.

Hamilton I. McCubbin, Ph.D., is a Native Hawaiian, Dean and Professor, School of Human Ecology, University of Wisconsin–Madison; Director of the Center for Excellence in Family Studies and Director of the Institute for the Study of Resiliency in Families, both at the University of Wisconsin–Madison. His postdoctoral studies include Yale University, a Bush Fellow in Early Childhood Education at the University of Minnesota, a Mellon Fellow at the Center for Advanced Study in the Behavioral Sciences at Stanford University, and Fellow at the Radcliffe Public Policy Institute. He has recently coedited two books: *Resiliency in Ethnic Families, Volumes I and II*; and *Family Assessment Inventories: Stress, Coping and Resiliency.* His forthcoming books include *The Dynamics of Resilient Families: Qualitative Approaches* and *Promoting Resiliency in Families and Children at Risk: Interdisciplinary Perspectives.*

Laurie D. McCubbin is a Native Hawaiian and is currently a graduate student at Boston College in Counseling Psychology. She completed her undergraduate studies in Psychology at the University of Wisconsin–Madison, with master's graduate work in International Business at the University of St. Thomas, St. Paul, Minnesota. She has served as a research associate with the Family Stress, Coping and Health Project, the Center for Excellence in Family Studies, and the Institute for the Study of Resiliency in Families. She is a co-editor on the forthcoming book *Promoting Resiliency in Families and Children at Risk: Interdisciplinary Perspectives.*

Shobha Pais, Ph.D., is Clinical Director of Family Service of El Paso, Texas. She completed her doctoral training in Marriage and Family Therapy at Purdue University. She is originally from India, where she lived for over 20 years. Her research interests include the lives of women and children in India, exploring cultural variation in families, cross-cultural perspectives on the abuse of children, and ethical and legal issues for family therapists in the context of HIV/AIDS and risky sexual behavior. She is presently a member of the American Association of Marriage and Family Therapy and received the AAMFT dissertation research award in 1996.

Yolanda Sanchez, Ph.D., received her doctorate in Family and Child Ecology from Michigan State University. She has worked extensively in service delivery and program development with Latino communities in New Mexico and Michigan. From her experience stem her research interests of elder abuse and intergenerational relationships in Latino families. She is currently an Assistant Professor with the Department of Human Development/Family Studies at the University of Nevada–Reno, where she teaches Adult Development and Aging.

Zulema E. Suarez, Ph.D., received her doctorate from the University of Chicago School of Social Service Administration. She is an Associate Professor of Social Work at Wayne State University, where she teaches minority- and gender-sensitive interpersonal practice. Her primary research interests are in the areas of Latino health and poverty.

Gordon C. Thomasson, Ph.D., an anthropologist and historian with a master's degree in World Religions, teaches World History and Cultural Geography at Broome Community College, Binghamton, New York. He organized the American Academy of Religion Consultation on the Study of Latter-day Saint Religious Traditions, did fieldwork among the Kpelle of Liberia, and has published widely, including in the *Encyclopedia Britannica* and the *American Historical Association Guide to Historical Literature.*

Doris Wilkinson, Ph.D., is a Professor of Sociology at the University of Kentucky. She received her master's degree and doctorate in Medical Sociology from Case Western Reserve University and her master's degree in Public Health from Johns Hopkins University. She has been a Ford Fellow at Harvard University. She is coeditor of *The Black Male in America* and *Race, Gender, and the Life Cycle: The Afro-American Experience* and has published numerous articles in such journals as *Phylon, Journal of Marriage and the Family, British*

Journal of Sociology, Sociological Forum, Daedalus, and *Social Problems.* She has been elected President of the District of Columbia Sociological Society, the Society for the Study of Social Problems, and the Eastern Sociological Society, and has received the American Sociological Association's Du Bois-Johnson-Frazier Award.

Mary Kay DeGenova

Introduction

Imagine what it would be like if the whole world were populated by people just like you. In every way—appearance, habits, thoughts, ideas, clothes, skin color, inclination toward work, and so on—there would be no difference from one person to the next. Now imagine that the whole world is populated with people identical to a person from a culture other than your own. You will probably agree that neither of these scenarios would be ideal, and that it is important to have some diversity in our lives. If that is the case and diversity is desired, consider the following questions as you read this book:

▲ Why are many people uncomfortable in the presence of other human beings who are different from themselves?

▲ Why are we, when in a group, most prone to seek the company of others just like ourselves?

▲ If diversity is important and uniqueness is admirable, why are people uncomfortable when taken away from their familiar surroundings and friends and placed in situations where they know nobody?

▲ Why is it that people can understand and appreciate the uniqueness of themselves, but fail to appreciate difference and uniqueness in others?

The United States is a country that includes people from virtually all the world's cultures. This diversity is considered by some to be a source of strength and by others a source of weakness. If people allow themselves to learn about and benefit from diversity, the cultural makeup of the United States can be a significant strength. Consider the words of former U.S. President John F. Kennedy (1963):

Let us not be blind to our differences, but let us also direct attention to our common interests and to the means by which those differences can be resolved. And if we cannot end now our differences, at least we can help make the world safe for diversity.

Failing to honor Kennedy's request, many people allow ethnic difference to be a source of friction, misunderstanding, and conflict. Part of the reason lies in **ethnocentrism**, the belief that one's own ethnicity and its characteristics are superior to those of other ethnic groups. White supremacy and neo-Nazi movements are grounded in ethnocentrism. There is also an abundance of faulty negative stereotypes about different ethnic groups, and an unhealthy fear of difference in general. It would be beneficial if fear of the unknown were replaced by healthy curiosity to foster questions and discussion, but fear often leads to panic. The panic that arises when individuals are placed in an environment or a situation foreign to them—a different culture, a group of people with different skin color, a conversation in a foreign language—is a very real phenomenon, and people ease that panic by seeking out something comfortable and familiar. This fear of foreigners is called **xenophobia**.

To minimize these uncomfortable feelings, many people want to be associated only with others similar to themselves in color, belief, or language. Even among people who look like them, act like them, and dress like them, if they don't know anyone in the new group from previous experience, they are distinctly uncomfortable. So adamant are some people in their desire to be with only their own kind that tribal genocide, ethnic cleansing, and civil wars are now a way of life in many countries. One has to ask if this is the road to building a strong nation. What Greeley (1969) stated almost 30 years ago deserves reflection today: "Family, land and common cultural heritage have always been terribly important to human beings, and suspicion of anyone who is strange or different seems also deeply rooted in the human experience" (p. 21).

Defining Ethnicity

In this book, each chapter about a different ethnic group consists of expert knowledge that has been crystallized, after countless hours of research, down to a manageable length. In these pages, individuals are converted into ideas and classified into particular groups. For the purposes of discussion and comparison, people are stripped of their individuality and made to act as one. In this book, that "one" being is a concept referred to as an ethnic group. In the process of labeling and classifying, we have made generalizations that cannot possibly fit all people belonging to a particular group. For example, when we discuss the Arab American family, many Arab American readers will want to say, "I am not like that" or "My family does not value that." This is the problem that results from generalizing, but it is necessary for our purposes of discussion.

The term **ethnicity** has been defined by many scholars. Yinger (1976) defines it as

> a segment of a larger society whose members are thought, by themselves and/or others, to have a common origin and to share important segments of a common culture and who participate in shared activities in which the common origin and culture are significant ingredients. (p. 200)

Gordon (1964) believes that race, religion, national origin, language, or some combination of these are core categories defining ethnicity for most people. The attitudes, values, customs, lifestyles, and rituals of groups express ethnicity. The best definition of an ethnic group may be "those who share a unique social and cultural heritage that is passed on from generation to generation" (Mindel, Habenstein, & Wright, 1988, p. 5).

This book is about family ethnicity. In a general sense, **family ethnicity** can be thought of as the way people define themselves as part of a group through similarities in common ancestry and cultural heritage (race, religion, or national origin).

While many of the groups in the book are classified as minority groups, it is important to distinguish between ethnicity and minority. The sociological term *minority* is used to describe groups of people who are oppressed and do not share equally in the power base of society, although their actual numbers may indicate a majority (e.g., women). Because the word "minority" is sometimes associated with inferiority, *ethnic group* is a more appropriate term, and we use it throughout this text.

Culture and Values

Ethnicity and culture are not always the same thing, as culture can encompass many different ethnicities. For example, American culture is a mixture of the arts, beliefs, customs, and all other products of human endeavor and thought created by many different ethnic groups. Consider the following definition of **culture**:

> Culture is the sum total of ways of living, including values, beliefs, aesthetic standards, linguistic expression, patterns of thinking, behavioral norms, and styles of communication which a group of people has developed to assure its survival in a particular physical and human

environment. Culture and the people who are part of it interact so that culture is not static. Culture is the response of a group of human beings to the valid and particular needs of its members. It, therefore, has an inherent logic and an essential balance between positive and negative dimensions. (Hoopes, 1979, p. 3)

Lustig (1988) explains that values and cultures are linked inseparably. Each can be understood only when examining the other, because values form the basis for cultural differences. Values guide behavior and almost automatically dictate what is a good, proper, or moral way of behaving. In this sense, values shape culture and culture shapes values, and individual and family values develop within the context of culture.

If values are the basis of culture, then a careful examination of our own values and of how these values shape our behavior is necessary to more fully understand the values and behaviors of others. The intention is not to invoke change in another person's values, but to clarify, understand, and respect both our own behavior and that of others.

Assumptions about the world, and the behaviors and ideas we think are right and wrong, are buried deeply within us (Hess, 1994). They are reinforced continuously by our family, friends, and teachers. They are so much a part of us that most of the time we are not even aware our values are guiding our behavior. The more ethnocentric we are, the more likely we are to believe that our values are the only "right" values, the only "natural and normal" values, and that other people should adopt these "good" values.

By exploring cultural diversity, you may discover many values and behaviors that differ significantly from your own. In the process, you can critically examine the values governing your own behavior and that of others. For example, many people in the United States value individualism and independence over the pursuit of the common good. In this context, it would be understandable, for example, for people to move hundreds or thousands of miles from their families to pursue careers of their own choosing. However, in a culture that values the extended family over the individual, this type of behavior might be viewed as deviant or even immoral.

Assimilation and Acculturation

In contemporary usage, the terms assimilation and acculturation are often used interchangeably and irresponsibly. **Assimilation** is the cultural absorption of a smaller ethnic group into the main cultural body. Assimilation usually occurs gradually, as one group's set of cultural uniqueness is given up and the characteristics of the dominant culture are adopted (Kumabe, Nishida, &

Hepworth, 1985). Assimilation is the changing of one culture to make it similar to another. In the United States, members of ethnic groups outside the dominant culture are often expected to assimilate and to take on European American values, but European Americans are rarely expected to adopt, for example, American Indian values.

In contrast, **acculturation** is the process of different cultures in close contact adapting to each other. Acculturation occurs when minority and mainstream cultural characteristics are blended and exchanged (Kumabe et al., 1985). "Acculturation" is often used when "assimilation" is intended, but it is essential to clearly distinguish between the two. The accurate use of terminology should indicate the *exchange* of cultural characteristics between mainstream and ethnic groups, as opposed to the adoption by the ethnic group of the characteristics of the mainstream culture.

There once was a strong push toward assimilation into the mainstream. For example, when eastern European Jews began immigrating to the United States, the German American Jews who were already there tried to "Americanize" the newcomers, seeing their strange dress and speech as an embarrassment, and feeling that the more quickly the new immigrants became indistinguishable from the rest of America, the better (Mindel et al., 1988). Today in the United States, ethnic groups are becoming more readily recognized and valued and are developing pride in their own ethnicity by emphasizing their unique heritage. The question of whether this cultural revitalization has a positive or negative impact on the United States as a nation is hotly debated.

Prejudice and Racism

H. G. Wells wrote:

> Every one of these hundreds of millions of human beings is in some form seeking happiness. . . . Not one is altogether noble, not altogether trustworthy, not altogether consistent; and not one is altogether vile. Not a single one but has at some time wept. (p. 601)

Prejudice is a judgment or an opinion formed without closely examining the person or group you are evaluating. It is an attitude one holds about groups of people. **Racism** is an active expression of prejudice or **discrimination** based on inherited characteristics of ethnicity or cultural group membership. A person with a racist point of view believes that inherited differences, such as skin color and facial characteristics, make one race superior or inferior to another (McPhee & Rhodes, 1990).

Many of the ethnic groups featured in this book have been subjected to racial discrimination because of their skin color or other such inherited differences. When studying different ethnic groups, it is important to remember that race alone does not determine economic and educational success or failure (Steinberg, 1989), but it often does affect access to economic and educational opportunities and resources. Thus, many obvious differences in family characteristics are not determined by race or ethnicity, but rather by socioeconomic status.

Unfortunately, prejudice and racism are prevalent in the United States. People may be less likely to admit they are racist today than they were 30 years ago, but negative racial stereotypes continue to be accepted and maintained (Dovidio & Gaertner, 1986). For example, members of ethnic groups still have a difficult and even threatening time fitting into predominantly White universities (Fleming, 1984), and feelings of isolation, hostility, and insensitivity are reportedly common among ethnic students (Allen, 1985). While the obvious forms of racism, such as forced segregation in schools, have diminished, many racist attitudes are still expressed in less direct ways (Kinder & Sears, 1981). One of the first steps in changing racist attitudes is to admit to racist thinking. People must examine their racist attitudes and the reasons for them. We are taught to be racist; therefore, because racism is learned, it can be unlearned (Cole, 1990).

The Search for Similarity

There are many differences between various ethnicities. People look differently, smell differently, dress differently, eat differently, speak differently, pray differently, and raise children differently. Generally speaking, people can recognize differences more quickly than similarities when encountering people from other ethnic groups. However, no matter how many differences there may be, beneath the surface there are even more similarities. It is important to try to identify the similarities among various cultures. Stripping away surface differences will uncover a multiplicity of similarities: people's hopes, aspirations, desire to survive, search for love, and need for family—to name just a few. While superficially we may be dissimilar, the essence of being human is very much the same for all of us. Experience the paradox of human diversity: that "we are all the same but in different ways" (Billingsley, 1993).

People of various cultures differ in the ways they view the world and human behavior. Every human being is born into a culture whose values transmit to him or her a significant **social identity**. Each of us learns to perceive the world in specific ways, based largely on the culture from which we come. Our social identity can be thought of as a lens that colors how we see the world. For example, do you think males and females, Blacks and Whites, or rural and urban families see the world the same way? Do you see the world the same way as your parents, your sister, or your children do? All these characteristics are part of the social identity that shapes the way you view the world.

One of your tasks as you read this book is to try to view the world through the eyes of someone whose culture or social identity is different from your own. Become multicultural in your thinking by imagining what it would be like to be an Arab American or a Cuban American growing up in a mostly European American neighborhood.

Stereotypes

A **stereotype** is an oversimplified set of beliefs and generalizations about an individual or group of people. For example, a statement such as "All blonds are dumb" is a negative stereotype about people (usually females) with blond hair. Generalizing is unavoidable when discussing ethnic groups, but it is crucial to remember that not all individuals fit the generalization. While most of us have some stereotypical thoughts about groups of people, Adler (1991) cautions us that our stereotypes should incorporate the following criteria:

1. **Consciously held.** If you are engaged in stereotypical thinking, be aware that you are basing your judgment of an individual on generalizations about a group. Remember that there are exceptions to the stereotypes in all groups, and be open to finding those exceptions. Just as you don't like to be labeled by the color of your hair, your weight, or your occupation, other people don't like to be labeled based on your limited understanding of their ethnic group. Be conscious that you do engage in stereotypical thinking, and be prepared to have your assumptions challenged and changed.

2. **Descriptive.** When you engage in stereotypical thinking, your thoughts should be about describing people's behavior, rather than judging people's behavior. Oversimplified thinking doesn't consider the complexity of the motivation and reasoning behind human behavior. For example, you may think that Asian Americans are more intelligent than other ethnic groups because of their national math averages. But this kind of simplistic thinking overlooks the fact that Asian Americans place a very high value on education and pursue it with much discipline and seriousness. Asian Americans may do better overall at math than European Americans because of a difference in the value each group places on education, but it does not mean that one group is more intelligent than the other.

3. **Accurate.** Many people harbor faulty negative stereotypes about people from different ethnic groups about whom they know nothing and with whom they have never personally interacted. Make a conscious effort to determine whether the stereotype you hold is based on sound evidence.

4. **Modifiable.** Be prepared to modify your thinking about individuals and groups, based on new evidence you acquire. Modifications challenge oversimplified thinking by adding a new layer of complexity to human behavior. When you allow your simple thinking to become more complex, you often find just as much diversity within ethnic groups as you do between them.

Understanding without Judgment

Because the way I do something seems right and "normal" to me, it is easy for me to judge behavior that differs from mine as wrong. You may be surrounded by people who reinforce your belief that your behavior is "normal," but it does not necessarily follow that different behavior is "abnormal." It is important to believe in one's own "normalcy" and worth and at the same time to be open to learning about other cultures and accepting their different values.

We must separate worth from behavior when studying other cultures. The worth of a culture should never be questioned, and it is important to remember that the value placed on human behavior or achievement is formed differently among cultures (Billingsley, 1993). For example, when comparing 3- or 4-month-old infants in middle-class homes in Japan and the United States, Caudill and Frost (1974) found that European American mothers talked to their babies more, while Japanese mothers spent more time soothing their babies. The difference in parenting style reflects a difference in the value placed on certain behaviors.

By not viewing families through a judgmental or an ethnocentric lens, we can gain important insight into the multiplicity of family patterns and modes of behavior. Conversely, maintaining a narrow view of family and relationship patterns can easily mislead us into believing that family behavior and relationship patterns with which we are familiar are innate. However, by viewing the family patterns of other cultures, we discover that most family traits have variations (Queen & Habenstein, 1974). A good example is **polygyny**, the practice of a man having more than one wife at the same time. In most of the world, polygyny is legal and not considered deviant. Although it may not be a practice you feel comfortable about based on your upbringing, it is not outside the range of "normal" human behavior in many cultures.

The Standard by Which All Others Are Measured

There is an infinite variety of family forms, patterns, and experiences both between and within families. Among the diverse family forms that exist today, there is no single "ideal" or "appropriate" model. However, in the United States, European Americans are often the ethnic group against which all other families are compared. To believe that there is a single ideal family form is a narrow view of family relationships, and to assume European American family characteristics are better than those of other ethnic groups is clearly wrong.

The predominant influence of European American culture on ideas about the way a family should operate is undeniable. Some would argue that because of the strong influence of European American values, it is appropriate to describe those values as representative of the culture of the United States (Locke, 1992). However, demographics are changing. It is estimated that by the year 2050, European Americans will constitute approximately 53% of the population (down from 73% in 1990); Hispanics, 21%; African Americans, 16%; Asians/Pacific Islanders, 11%; and Native Americans, 1% (U.S. Bureau of the Census, 1990). As the demographics change in the United States, the influence of European American cultural values may weaken.

As is true for families in all ethnic groups, the European American family form has both strengths and weaknesses. Below are thoughts from the Dalai Lama (1991) on the European American culture. From the perspective of his interpretation, one can clearly question whether these are traits of an "ideal" culture. He states:

> Overall I have found much that is impressive about Western society. In particular, I admire its energy and creativity and hunger for knowledge. On the other hand, a number of things about the Western way of life cause me concern. One thing I have noticed is an inclination for people to think in terms of "black and white" and "either, or," which ignores the facts of interdependence and relativity. They have a tendency to lose sight of the grey areas which inevitably exist between two points of view. Another observation is that there are a lot of people in the West who live very comfortably in large cities, but virtually isolated from the broad mass of humanity. I find this very strange—that under the circumstance of such material well-being and with thousands of brothers and sisters for neighbors, so many people appear able to show their true feelings only to their cats and dogs. This indicates a lack of spiritual values, I feel. Part of the problem here is perhaps the intense competitiveness of life in these countries, which seems to breed fear and a deep sense of insecurity. For me, this sense of alienation is symbolized by something I once saw at the home of a very rich man whose guest I was on one of my trips abroad. It was a very large private house, obviously designed expressly for convenience and comfort, and fitted with every kind of appliance. However, when I went into the

bathroom, I could not help noticing two large bottles of pills on the shelf above the hand basin. One contained tranquilizers, the other sleeping pills. (p. 199)

Becoming a Pluralistic Society

As the United States becomes increasingly diverse, a better understanding among ethnic groups is extremely important. Today, we must be knowledgeable about different ethnic groups simply to be prepared for life (Higgenbotham, 1990) and to promote a more harmonious social environment.

Smith (1989) defines **pluralism** as "a social condition . . . in which several distinct ethnic, religious, and racial communities live side by side, willing to affirm each other's dignity, ready to benefit from each other's experiences, and quick to acknowledge each other's contribution to the common welfare" (p. 38). In a culturally pluralistic society, ethnic groups maintain characteristics that give them a unique identity and yet remain members of the larger society (Gonzalez-Mena, 1993).

A truly pluralistic society sees ethnic diversity as a strength and works toward understanding, acknowledging, and appreciating it. In this book, you will read about groups of people who may seem different from yourself, yet who in many ways are very similar. Try to see the world through their eyes. Be aware that you are reading generalizations and that there is tremendous individual variation within groups. Acknowledge that you may have preconceived stereotypes about certain groups, and allow those stereotypes to be challenged and changed. Finally, work toward understanding other peoples' values and behaviors without placing judgment on that which is different. It is through these individual mechanisms that we can work toward a more pluralistic society.

Questions for Discussion

1. How would you feel if you had to assimilate? Is assimilation too high a price to pay to fit in?

2. What are some of your stereotypes about different ethnic groups? Are these fair assumptions? Where do they come from?

3. Why is it important to have some diversity in the world? In the United States?

4. When have you been in a situation in which you felt uncomfortable because everyone appeared different from you? How did you respond? How would you like to have responded?

5. What current events or political controversies are you aware of in the news that attest to Greeley's comments?

6. What is different about you and someone from another culture? What is similar?

7. Give an example of how you can become multicultural in your thinking.

8. Define ethnicity in your own words. To what ethnic group do you belong?

9. The text stated that while direct expressions of racial hostility, such as forced segregation, have declined over the past two decades, many racist values have merely been rechanneled into less direct forms of expression. Do you agree with this statement? Why or why not?

10. Can we create a pluralistic society? Is it in our best interest as a nation to be pluralistic?

11. How would you respond if English were your second language and people became impatient with your accent?

Suggested Resources

Readings

Hayden, C. (1992). *Venture into cultures.* Chicago: American Library Association.

Hess, J. D. (1995). *The whole world guide to culture learning.* Yarmouth, ME: Intercultural Press.

Kohls, R., & Knight, J. (1995). *Developing intercultural awareness.* Yarmouth, ME: Intercultural Press.

Videos

Ogami, N. (Producer). (1987). *Cold water.* (Available from Intercultural Press, P.O. Box 700, Yarmouth, ME 04096)

Schrank, L. (Producer), & Phyfer, D. (1995). *Valuing diversity: Multicultural communication.* (Available from The Learning Seed, 3450 Engle Road, P.O. Box 446, Middleville, MI 49333)

References

Adler, N. A. (1991). *International dimensions of organization behavior* (2nd ed.). Boston: PWS-Kent.

Allen, W. R. (1985). Black student, white campus: Structural, interpersonal, and psychological correlates of success. *Journal of Negro Students, 54,* 134–147.

Billingsley, R. (1993). Fostering diversity: Teaching by discussion. *The Teaching Professor,* February, 3–4.

Caudill, W., & Frost, L. (1974). A comparison of maternal care and infant behavior in Japanese-American, American, and Japanese families. In W. Lebra (Ed.), *Youth, socialization, and mental health: Vol. 3 of Mental health research in Asia and the Pacific* (pp. 3–16). Honolulu: University Press of Hawaii.

Cole, J. (1990, May). Melange: Commencement 1990. *Chronicle of Higher Education, 25,* B2.

Dali Lama. (1991). *Freedom from exile.* Scranton, PA: Transaction Publishing.

Dovidio, J. F., & Gaertner, S. L. (Eds.). (1986). *Prejudice, discrimination, and racism.* New York: Academic Press.

Fleming, J. (1984). *Blacks in college: A comparative study of students' success in Black and White institutions.* San Francisco: Jossey-Bass.

Gonzalez-Mena, J. (1993). *Multicultural issues in child care.* Mountain View, CA: Mayfield.

Gordon, M. (1964). *Assimilation in American life.* New York: Oxford University Press.

Greeley, A. M. (1969). *Why can't they be like us?* New York: Institute of Human Relations Press.

Hess, J. D. (1994). *The whole world guide to cultural learning.* Yarmouth, ME: Intercultural Press.

Higgenbotham, E. (1990). Designing an inclusive curriculum: Bringing all women into the core. *Women's Studies Quarterly, 18,* 7–23.

Hoopes, D. S. (1979). Intercultural communication concepts and the psychology of intercultural experiences. In M. Pusch (Ed.), *Multicultural education: A cross-cultural training approach* (pp. 3–33). La Grange Park, IL: Intercultural Press.

Kennedy, J. F. (1963, June 10). Commencement address, American University, Washington, DC.

Kinder, D. R., & Sears, D. O. (1981). Prejudice and politics: Symbolic racism versus racial threats to the good life. *Journal of Personality and Social Psychology, 40,* 414–431.

Kumabe, K. T., Nishida, C., & Hepworth, D. H. (1985). *Bridging ethnocultural diversity in social work and health.* Honolulu: University of Hawaii, School of Social Work.

Locke, D. C. (1992). *Increasing multicultural understanding: A comprehensive model.* Newbury Park, CA: Sage.

Lustig, M. W. (1988). Value differences in intercultural communication. In

L. Samovar and R. Porter (Eds.), *Intercultural communication: A reader* (5th ed., pp. 25–61). Belmont, CA: Wadsworth.

McPhee, S., & Rhodes, G. (1990). *Facing difference: Living together on campus.* Louisville, KY: University of Louisville Press.

Mindel, C., Habenstein, R., & Wright, R. (Eds.). (1988). *Ethnic families in America: Patterns and variations.* New York: Elsevier.

Queen, S., & Habenstein, R. W. (1974). *The family in various cultures* (5th ed.). Philadelphia: Lippincott.

Smith, D. G. (1989). *The challenge of diversity.* Washington, DC: George Washington University, School of Education and Human Development.

Steinberg, S. (1989). *The ethnic myth, race, ethnicity, and class in America* (2nd ed.). Boston: Beacon.

U.S. Bureau of the Census. (1990). *Statistical abstract of the United States* (110th ed.). Washington, DC: U.S. Government Printing Office.

Wells, H. G. (1931). *The outline of history.* Garden City, NY: Garden City Publishing Company.

Yinger, M. (1976). Ethnicity in complex societies. In O. Larson and L. Coser (Eds.), *The uses of controversy in sociology* (pp. 197–216). New York: Free Press.

Walter T. Kawamoto

Tamara C. Cheshire

American Indian Families

Historical and Cultural Background

American Indian tribes flourished long before the invasion of the Americas by European immigrants. The complex civilizations of the indigenous peoples featured advanced architecture, sophisticated agrarian systems, and effective herbal medicinal cures. Each American Indian tribe had a distinctive language, spiritual belief system, and history, which were transmitted from generation to generation in oral or sometimes written form.

Creation stories document in great detail the existence of American Indians in the Americas. For instance, the Iroquois tell of a tree on a floating island that needed more soil to live. Swimming animals such as the beaver, the otter, and the turtle, dove under water in attempts to bring up more earth for the tree. The turtle succeeded and became the base of the earth. The Navajo (or Diné) tell a different creation story, one that features five worlds, each a different color: black, blue, yellow, white, and red. People originated as misty beings in the black world, and eventually moved through the blue, yellow, and white worlds. Ultimately, they arrived in the red world, where they found an abundance of land on which they could live peacefully together. These stories reflect ideologies about nature and about the existence of humans, animals, plants, society, and culture. Many of these stories focus on finding a balance among the spiritual, natural, and physical aspects of existence.

The natural environment played a major part in American Indian religions, philosophies, and value systems. Contact with other tribes through trade led to the realization that most American Indians shared many common values, including respect for others and the environment, the sharing of resources, and

We wish to thank Frank Merrill for the personal information he shared. He is a respected elder in our community.

generosity. These values, along with traditions, spread as tribes continued having contact with each other.

The arrival of European immigrants in the Americas negatively affected American Indian cultures. The immigrants not only inflicted their social and religious values and economics on Indian people, but they also brought and promoted disease in an attempt to annihilate the indigenous population. The introduction of disease affected cultural transmission and retention by destroying the indigenous population's sources of oral history—its elders—and its prospects for the future—its children (Colley, 1992).

As Europeans established governments and stole territory from the indigenous people, they institutionalized a series of barriers to prevent American Indians from continuing their traditions. The European immigrants' complete disregard for the complex civilizations already existing in the Americas was both disrespectful and dehumanizing.

By taking over tribal homelands and forcing the inhabitants to migrate to distant reservations, the U.S. government uprooted Native peoples from a primary source of their cultural identity—their natural environment. In order to survive in the inhospitable surroundings of the newly formed reservations, tribes had to abandon some traditional ceremonies, rituals, and ways of life and develop new resources and cultural patterns in order to survive. Cultural cohesion was further subverted when the U.S. government refused to recognize the tribes as distinct, autonomous, self-governing entities, forcing them instead to adapt to the political and legal systems of the European immigrant culture (Pevar, 1992). Government policies that ultimately resulted in genocide placed enormous strain on the traditional ways of life of the American Indians. Eventually they were forced to submit to a paternalistic system that necessitated their reliance on the federal government for their physical survival.

Despite changes dictated by these drastic upheavals, American Indian culture has proved both dynamic and resilient. Tribal Elders have worked to preserve their peoples' distinctive heritage by passing down language, traditions, stories, and oral histories from generation to generation.

Forced Migration

In addition to their different philosophy regarding the abuse of the land in the New World, European immigrants believed they had the right, and perhaps even the responsibility, to own the land. They claimed huge tracts of territory in the names of their monarchies, arguing that it was their God-given "manifest destiny" to bring "civilization" to the Americas. For their personal gain, they set about abducting and enslaving both the land and its Native inhabitants.

Entire tribes were forced to move from cultural homelands they had inhabited for thousands of years to tracts of land designated by the invaders to serve as reservations. The reservations were, generally, the bleakest and most inhospitable areas of the country, and the tribal communities were hard-pressed to survive in these areas. Additional methods of assimilation attempted by the new European American government included the kidnapping and en-slavement of thousands of American Indian men, women, and children. Government-sponsored boarding schools, run by various European religious groups, physically separated children from their families and homes in the hope of assimilating them into White society. Large numbers of American Indian men, women, and children died from abuse, depression, and disease.

With their ability to earn a living essentially denied them on the reservations, American Indians were forced into dependence on the federal government for subsistence. The government, in turn, demanded that the tribes assimilate into the dominant culture (Pevar, 1992). A degree of assimilation was inevitable, but American Indians kept their cultures alive by passing down their languages, ideologies, oral histories, and spiritual traditions through the generations.

Traditional and Emerging Family Systems

The characteristics of American Indian families are extremely diverse. Recognizing that all ethnic communities have their challenges, this chapter is primarily about normative families. The available literature on normative American Indian families is understandably light because of the tendency of researchers to focus on *problems* in human behavior. However, the need to address normative families is essential in order to counteract the stereotypical misconceptions of the drunken, abusive, impoverished, ignorant Indian savage.

Diversity within the American Indian community takes many forms. Geographic and cultural characteristics make the various American Indian tribes and regional groups very distinct, and individuals see themselves more commonly as members of specific tribes, bands, or clans (Lakota, Diné, Umatilla, Turtle, etc.). In addition, although a growing majority of American Indians live in urban areas, the community is basically split between rural reservations and urban centers. At the same time, American Indians from diverse backgrounds have created a contemporary "pan-Indian" identity necessitated by common bonds such as sweeping oppression, majority culture misconceptions about all Indians being the same, and intertribal urban communities.

These are just a few of the ways in which one can see the incredible diversity in the American Indian family. Because of this diversity, a complete account of all American Indian communities in the context of a single chapter is impossible.

Although most tribes have adopted the patrilineal structure of the majority culture, a few still hold important their lineage through the mother. In the northeast, southeast, and southwest, women historically held much power within the family. The family structure in these areas was usually matrilineal and matrilocal. American Indian women had control over their bodies, behaviors, children, and personal property obtained before and during marriage. The inheritance of personal property was traced through the women of the family as well (Green, 1992a).

Conjugal relationships and **consanguineal relationships** vary in importance among American Indians. In close-knit communities with aunts, uncles, and grandparents living nearby, consanguineal ties take on extreme importance. This closeness is based on the historic **kinship systems** of many tribes, which consider family membership the most important group membership a person can have. In many American Indian communities, belonging to or aligning with the right family determines community status, economic opportunity, or even political power.

For American Indians who are separated from their families due to death or relocation, **fictive kin** provide a support system. The whole community may share in the raising of a child and assist with child care, food, or money while the parents (or parent) work or go to school. In intertribal communities with few elders, kinship roles are expanded, and elders serve as grandparents to all the children in the community. Unlike some Mexican Americans who have godparents (*padrinos*) and Hawaiians who refer to fictive kin as "Uncle/ Auntie," many American Indians call their fictive kin by name or even "Mom/ Dad" or "Grandmother/Grandfather."

Household Size and Composition

Most American Indian households are small, primarily because of the limitations imposed by economics and by a lack of living space. Urban families, facing a high cost of living, gravitate toward small living spaces, which cannot accommodate large numbers of people. In rural areas, tribal-supported housing is usually designed for nuclear families. In spite of their cramped quarters, however, many Indian families take in neighbors, friends, and members of the extended family as temporary or permanent additions to the household.

As in many ethnic groups, American Indian single parents look to their communities for support. Elders often take in young parents and their children, especially in rural Indian communities where family members are readily available. In urban areas, families often find support from contacts made in intertribal community groups. With the passage of the Indian Child Welfare Act in 1978, which calls for American Indian children to be adopted by American Indian families, adoptive families have become an important tool in the preservation of American Indian communities. Nuclear family structure is still the norm, although typical family size varies from region to region.

Population, fertility, and mortality rates in American Indian communities are dynamic. In Oregon, for example, there are conflicting population estimates. One statewide statistic suggests that the majority of American Indians in the state are older (D. Hutchinson, personal communication, February 1994). However, in another Oregon Indian community, the Confederated Tribes of Siletz report that the majority of its members are younger (Retasket, 1994).

The Socialization of Children

Socialization practices in American Indian communities are similar to those in the majority culture, partly because of the pervasive policies of cultural indoctrination to which Indians have been subjected, and partly because Indian families share certain values common throughout the world—such as respect for elders, the treasuring of children, and the acknowledgment of strong bonds within the family. Although in some cases American Indians have adopted European American **gender roles**, in many important ways the culture has preserved its traditional patterns of socialization.

Many contemporary expectations placed on American Indian boys are rooted in tradition. The most obvious connection between history and modernity lies in the role of the male warrior. In addition to a man's position in the American Indian family and community, in times of conflict he served the tribe as a warrior. Today, men who serve their community or their country—from the tribal leaders who fight for recognition and autonomy, to the Navajo code talkers of World War II, to the veterans of Desert Storm—are among the most respected in Indian Country.

In addition to soldiering, Indian men traditionally worked with their hands—hunting, fishing, or building. This was profitable when jobs in commercial fishing, logging, construction, and ranching were plentiful. But today, most jobs that pay a decent wage require training that has traditionally been unnecessary for American Indian boys. Some male college students feel that their families and communities do not respect or understand the purpose of a job that does not involve making or fixing something.

The roles of warrior and manual worker are closely associated with traditional gender roles of males in Western society and with European American stereotypes of Indian males. But American Indian boys are also encouraged to pursue careers in such helping professions as teaching, law, child care, health, social work, and alcohol and drug treatment. An appreciation for these vocations can be traced to traditions such as the medicine man's use of herbs and faith, to long-held beliefs that fathers are often the best people to teach young boys how to be men, and to the storyteller who taught everything from how the planet was made to why children should respect their elders.

Another significant difference between the socialization of boys in many American Indian families and in the majority culture centers on the principle of competition. Many Indian traditions celebrate teamwork and commitment to the good of the community, in contrast to the dominant culture's emphasis on personal achievement. American Indian boys are instilled with a sense of pride in their family, clan, team, or tribe. They are also taught to respect the dignity of their adversaries; in many Indian communities, it is considered unnecessary to humiliate an opponent by winning by too great a margin.

The merging of modern expectations with ancient traditions is often less disruptive for American Indian girls than it is for boys. Modern Western society adheres to a dichotomy in which girls are socialized to be dutiful wives and mothers and/or career women. This modern expectation is directly in line with earlier American Indian concepts regarding the roles of girls and women.

American Indian girls have traditionally been taught that women have primary responsibility for the family, including elders and sometimes younger siblings. Historically, this responsibility was greatly respected by the community. In some tribes, women were responsible for choosing the tribal chief, and in others, all family property except the father's personal effects belonged to the mother.

Today, in the face of the many stressors affecting Indian families, girls are taught that the maternal role is more important than ever. Indian mothers, especially in the early stages of their children's lives, are regarded as the primary familial source for socialization and cultural transmission (La Fromboise, Heyle, & Ozer, 1990). However, girls today are also encouraged to pursue an education and to be leaders in the service of their community. Green (1992b) put it best when she described the multiple roles of Wilma Mankiller, former Principal Chief of the Cherokee Nation: "She is all those converged together. Like all of us can be. Warrior, peacemaker, mother, father, Beloved woman, the white and the red merged together, to take our story back" (p. 516). Relatively high percentages of Indian women go to college and take jobs and positions of responsibility in their tribes.

Parents and the community at large both demonstrate tremendous respect for children. One unique indication of this respect involves the way in which many families use the cradleboard to prop up Indian babies so that they can see the people around them and be on a more even level with the rest of the household. Another way adults demonstrate respect is by letting children learn independently, helping to boost their self-confidence. At other times, parents employ moments of silence in ways unique to their communities to communicate with their youth.

In many ways, the parenting of American Indian youth is not gender-specific. Children are taught that men and women may have different roles, but that both are to be respected for their contributions to the family. This long-standing attitude is very different from the lack of respect many Western women may feel they are shown relative to their role in the family.

American Indians also work to foster creativity in their children. Many boys and girls are involved in the creation of, and care for, their pow-wow regalia; also, their participation in traditional ceremonies often affords them the chance to create music, to engage in dance, and to produce art. American Indian poets, artists, writers, and musicians are celebrated today as they have been for centuries.

Balance is an important factor in the socialization of boys and girls. The need to balance masculine and feminine characteristics, such as developing compassion in boys and strength in girls, is seen as vital to personal wholeness. Traditionally, this emphasis on balance has been demonstrated in the special place of honor reserved in some communities for homosexuals, whose intimate perspective on both genders is acknowledged as an unusual gift. European influence, however, has contributed to a shift in focus; valuing homosexuals for their unique perspective is not as prevalent as it once was.

Intimate Relationships

Assimilation into mainstream Western culture has brought about many changes in American Indian courtship and wedding rituals. In most Indian communities today, dating begins in adolescence and follows the pattern typical of the dominant culture.

Fragments of tribal customs have, however, been retained and reinterpreted in light of changing circumstances. For example, in many traditional American Indian cultures, a young man was permitted to marry only when his elders felt he was ready to do so—after he had accumulated sufficient goods or resources to support a family, or had successfully negotiated a certain rite of passage. Although young people today have much more freedom to choose when they will marry, families still play a major role in the process, and an individual's readiness for marriage is dictated more by emotional maturity than by chronological age.

While acutely aware of the atrocities committed against their ancestors in the name of God, many American Indians find Indian spirituality and Judeo-Christian religion entirely compatible. Accordingly, a significant number of American Indians choose to marry in traditional European American style, with a church service, an ordained minister, and an elaborate wedding cake. Other couples prefer to celebrate their union in the manner historically observed by their tribes. Most Indian weddings, however, are hybrids of the two cultures. Traditional Indian ceremonies usually still include a cake, while classical Western services may feature an Indian give-away, the presentation of gifts to close extended family members.

This merging of cultures is not successful in all aspects of mate selection. Perhaps the biggest source of frustration is the series of messages regarding sexuality and desirability to which today's Indian youth are exposed. Most of the images of ideal beauty and sexuality in contemporary American popular culture are blond, blue-eyed icons such as Pamela Anderson and Brad Pitt, in sharp contrast to the dark skin, hair, and eyes of most American Indians. Partly due to this pervasive cultural definition of attractiveness, and partly because American Indians are exposed to non-Indians regularly at work, in school, or at home, the tendency toward intercultural marriage has grown steadily (Sandefur & McKinnell, 1986).

The impact of intermarriage on American Indian society is the subject of a great deal of debate. The loudest critics fear the loss of traditional culture as Indian families move farther away genealogically from the tribe, and the loss of opportunities as family members with diminished genetic ties are deemed ineligible for various services guaranteed to tribal members (Wagner, 1976). Others recognize these fears, but point to such concerns as family violence and substance abuse, arguing that the emotional and financial stability of a mate is, ultimately, more important than cultural background. These same critics also point out that some of the most effective Indian education programs are in urban areas, created by and for intermarried families. In fact, many intermarried families are quite active in preserving cultural traditions precisely because they fear the dilution of American Indian culture (Kawamoto, 1995).

Scholars are concerned about the impact of intermarriage on issues such as divorce rates (Chu Ho & Johnson, 1990). Preliminary research suggests that both intermarriage and cultural heritage affect family functioning and should be taken into account, along with other characteristics such as socioeconomic status and education (Kawamoto, 1995). More research is needed to determine the exact nature of the relationship between intermarriage, culture, and the functionality of American Indian families.

Contemporary American Indian attitudes and practices regarding intimate relationships have been shaped largely by the dominant culture and by demographic variables. However, in some respects American Indians have retained traditional values or rituals associated with intimate relationships. To women in many tribes, for example, the onset of the first menstrual cycle has long been an important sexual rite of passage. Many still refer to it as the onset of their "Moon Cycle." When it occurs, many Indian women have a "coming out" at a local gathering, such as a pow-wow, where the girl is presented, usually dressed in a new set of traditional regalia, as an adult member of the community. The family usually has a give-away to commemorate the significance of this event.

Over time, there has been a marked change in the customs surrounding intimate relationships, mostly resulting from majority culture oppression. While other ethnic groups have had the opportunity to adjust gradually to American society, many American Indians were forced to give up their customs and adopt Western ones. One of the most effective strategies of this forced change was the system of boarding schools set up by a combination of government and religious institutions, which separated generations of children from their families. The effect is still felt, because those who went to boarding school often knew little of traditional parenting customs. However, the more recent trend toward Indian professionals serving Indian families has eased the conflict between modern expectations and historic traditions (Red Horse, 1980). One example of this trend can be seen in the tribal colleges, which focus on education, health, law, and social service programs. Also, boarding schools are often now staffed with people who are Indian and/or sympathetic to the need to respect and celebrate American Indian communities. Sometimes these schools serve as safe houses from poverty, drugs, and crime at home.

Work Relationships and the Family

Like other ethnic families in the United States, most American Indian families cannot survive on only one income. It is important to distinguish between minority families and majority culture families, who often require a second income to maintain a middle-class to upper-middle-class lifestyle. Like most dual-earner families, Indian couples strive to share household tasks and child-care responsibilities, although at least one study suggests that mothers in Indian families may spend more time than fathers do on these tasks (Kawamoto, 1994). In American Indian communities, neighbors and/or family members often assist with day care; also, Head Start programs are active in many urban and reservation communities, often staffed by Indian professionals.

There is a wide range of incomes in American Indian communities. A recent socioeconomic survey conducted by the Confederated Tribes of Siletz provides a picture of the employment characteristics of one Indian community (Retasket, 1994). This community is a "representative" American Indian group in that it reflects trends common to many contemporary American Indian cultures. For example, only recently has the federal government rescinded its official "termination" of recognition of the group. Another feature of the group that is typical of American Indian communities is its composition: an amalgamation of several tribes. The community is moving toward self-determination by establishing innovative education, economic, and service-oriented programs.

The survey showed that a large majority (72%) of the group's members are employed, actively seeking work, or retired. The four occupations with the most respondents were vocational trades (26%), labor/factory (18%), clerical (14%), and management/business (12%) (Retasket, 1994). All these occupations require a level of skill drastically different from common perceptions of American Indians as uneducable and unemployable. The income and education levels of the respondents, although slightly skewed on the lower end, range from a few years of school and very little money to doctorates and very respectable incomes (Retasket, 1994). Taken as a whole, the report suggests that this one American Indian community, while by no means wealthy or highly educated throughout, does have a strong middle class that pervades all sectors of the community. The majority of families have earners in a skilled or professional occupation and/or multiple earners in lower-paying jobs to meet the needs of the family.

Life-Cycle Transitions

Only about half of American Indian households consist of traditional "two-parent biological" families (Reddy, 1993). Life-cycle transitions such as divorce, single parenthood, and remarriage occur for Indians at levels the same as, or greater than, the national average. These transitions affect the family system in terms of changing the family structure and causing a loss of resources. However, maintaining strong support systems in the community and the family helps ease the burdens of such changes.

While majority culture demographics show large numbers of elderly and small numbers of youth to support them, many ethnic communities—especially American Indians—have small numbers of elderly and large numbers of youth. This makes it easy for Indian communities to honor long-held traditions that revere and treasure elders. Often when an elder is no longer able to care for himself or herself, family members (usually daughters) provide the care.

Many American Indian communities refer to death as "going over to the other side." This image suggests that few think of it as an ending, but rather as another transition in the life cycle. This concept is evident in the practice, observed by many tribes, of looking at life in the context of seven generations: making decisions based on the best interests and wishes of the three preceding generations, one's present generation, and the three succeeding generations. In other words, one asks, "What would my great-grandparents and great-grandchildren think of what I am about to do?" In this light, one is responsible for one's actions; and the actions of one's ancestors, as well as the actions of one's children and grandchildren, affect and reflect on the self, the family, the community, and ultimately the tribe/nation. Thus, an individual's responsibilities do not end with physical death.

Family Strengths and Challenges

We survive war and conquest; we survive colonialism, acculturation, assimilation; we survive beating, rape, starvation, mutilation, sterilization, abandonment, neglect, death of our children, our loved ones, destruction of our land, our homes, our past, and our future. We survive, and we do more than just survive. We bond, we care, we fight, we teach, we nurse, we bear, we feed, we earn, we laugh, we love, we hang in there, no matter what. (Allen, 1992, p. 43)

Assimilation and annihilation are the two major tactics of European immigrants against which American Indians have struggled. After enslaving the tribes and seizing control of much of their land, the federal government enforced a "blood quantum" regulation in order to monitor Indian bloodlines. At the time the Indians were moved to reservations, incomplete and inaccurate attempts were made to register them by tribe and blood quantum with the Bureau of Indian Affairs (BIA). The BIA set stringent rules prohibiting individuals with less than a certain, specific percentage of Indian blood from participating in federal programs designed to aid American Indians. This policy has two possible outcomes: (1) the technical extinction of the Indian people as a race because, after several generations of intermarriage, there would be no one left with sufficient Indian blood to qualify for BIA registration; and (2) the view of the protection of tribal resources for the few "true Indians," which in itself has divisive outcomes for Indian families and communities.

Attempts have been made since colonial times to assimilate American Indians into the European-based culture. In the case of the boarding schools, Indian children were told that their families or even their entire tribes had died of disease to keep them from trying to escape; and they were severely beaten, maimed, or even killed if they were slow to adopt the behaviors, language, and religion of the European immigrants. Suicide, illness, and fatal attempts at escape inflated the mortality rates among these Indian children to 50% or higher. Even those who survived the horror of the boarding schools and returned to their tribes had often been so fundamentally changed that their people rejected them. Like Japanese Americans in the internment camps, and African Americans on the slave plantations, many American Indians had their culture altered through forced governmental action.

The 1950s and 1960s saw a large-scale mandated migration and relocation of American Indians to urban areas, where they had been promised training and job opportunities by the government. In the 1970s, however, many American Indians returned to their tribal reservations, frustrated by the tremendous pressure they felt to assimilate in the dominant culture and by the promise of jobs that ceased to exist upon arrival in urban areas. A growing number of Indians began demanding that the government reinstate many smaller tribes it had ceased to recognize during previous decades.

American Indians' primary concern today is that their heritage and cultural traditions will die out as the European American–based society lures their children from the reservations to cities. For example, language is an issue, from not being able to speak English to a frustration with not being able to speak their own language in their communities because of years of suppression. Indian children seem to be caught in a vicious cycle in which their schools and the media teach them to hate their Indianness. Poverty, domestic violence, and drug and alcohol abuse prevalent on the reservations are consequences of these negative messages. Few opportunities for education and employment are available to them unless they leave their homes and their culture behind. In the face of these stressors, many Indian children and teenagers attempt to commit suicide (D. Hutchinson, personal communication, February 1994).

American Indian families work to save their children and to keep their culture and heritage alive. They work to find a balance between tradition and change. This is seen today in many Indian Education programs throughout the United States, and in the way modern drug and alcohol treatment techniques are being combined with a respect for different tribal traditions at places like Canada' a Nechi Institute.

Misconceptions and Stereotypes

The government and society have the power to dehumanize a race or even to declare it nonexistent; the U.S. government has often used this power in times of war to dehumanize the enemy, which is frequently composed of people of color. The federal government was created by European immigrants with the specific intention of expanding its hold over North American land and enslaving the Native peoples of the Americas, as it did people from Africa, to promote greed and to amass wealth for European Americans. Intentionally created laws, policies, and procedures inherent in governmental structure continue to oppress people of color today.

One method of dehumanization that is particularly effective is the dissemination of negative stereotypes regarding Indians. Some misconceptions about American Indians can be heard in such comments as "There aren't any more 'real' Indians, they are all dead"; "American Indians are lazy and a burden to the taxpayers"; "American Indians on the reservation have a defeatist attitude—why don't they just get over it and get a job?"; and "Why do Indians always bring up the past? We can't do anything to change it, and they are just whining." These comments and others like them reflect commonly held stereotypes.

In fact, there are still "real" Indians in the United States. There are 510 federally recognized tribes in existence, and 1.5–2 million American Indians alive today (D. Hutchinson, personal communication, February 1994). One of the reasons people believe there are no more Indians is that media coverage of American Indians has for decades been limited or nonexistent. What little attention is paid to American Indians by the media tends to focus on negative stereotypes. American Indians have been rendered essentially invisible by society and the government. When visible, they play a historic, nostalgic role during the time when the country was young.

American Indians are not living at the expense of the rest of the nation. The federal government owes recognized tribes, and many others that are still not recognized today, money and resources promised in treaties for the continued survival and existence of Indian people forever. The Northwest Ordinance of 1787, ratified by Congress in 1789, ordained: "The utmost good faith shall always be observed towards Indians; their land and property shall never be taken from them without their consent" (quoted in Pevar, 1992, p. 3). Consent was often obtained through deadly force against an individual, a family, or an entire tribe. Money paid to American Indians today comes from forced agreements with the U.S. government in the form of prior treaties, ceded land, and land in trust. These are monies and resources owed in return for what Indians were forced to give up long ago.

Another complaint by paternalistic government bureaucrats about American Indians is that they are "childlike" and "need to be in the care of the government so that they don't hurt themselves or others." This belief is based on the misconception that American Indians are less civilized or less intelligent than European Americans and cannot care for themselves. This stereotype is clearly false and is a ploy used to gain power and control not only over the race, but over individual American Indians' decisions and resources.

While it is true that American Indians have high rates of alcohol and drug addiction relative to the rest of the nation's population, the vast majority of Indians are not alcoholics or drug addicts, nor have they ever been. Different forms of alcohol and drugs used by American Indians in ceremonies prior to European contact were subject to traditions and limitations, so that overuse or addiction was rarely a problem. When the European settlers introduced their alcohol and drugs, there were no traditions associated with these, so addiction was a possibility, especially when European settlers pushed the alcohol on American Indians as a valued trade item.

Stereotypes are also abundant in regard to gender and emotion. Simple words such as "squaw" and "redskin" underlie strong forms of oppression and negative stereotypes. *Squaw* is an Iroquoian term for a woman's vagina. Many frontiersmen and soldiers used this term for Indian women, leading to the adoption by White men and society of the belief that American Indian women are good only for sex and menial work. The term *redskin* comes from a time when bounty was paid on every "human" American Indian skin that was turned in. Throughout history, American Indians have been portrayed as solemn, stoic, or emotionless, leading people to believe that they do not have feelings and therefore are not human. They are something less than human—something worthless. These stereotypes have taken a toll on American Indian men, women, and children's self-esteem and identity.

One other damaging stereotype effectively creates a cage around American Indian women. They are seen as either exotic, submissive, and beautiful, only good for sex; or as fat and ugly, only good for work. These are two extreme stereotypes that, when used together, create a set of standards that are unrealistic and undesirable to any human being. Such stereotypes negatively affect the self-esteem and confidence of American Indian women and can limit their aspirations.

In their acceptance of stereotypes, many European Americans fail to recognize diversity within the American Indian population. One example of this diversity, both now and in the past, can be found in the various tribes' religious beliefs. Not all American Indians have the same religion. Many have Christian beliefs mixed with their own tribal traditions, while others harbor animosity toward Christianity for its role in the oppression of their communities. Still other tribes maintain strong spiritual beliefs not tied to a specific religious doctrine.

All tribes, bands, and clans are different. Not all indigenous people of the Americas lived on the plains in tipis and hunted buffalo. Not all heads of tribes were known as chiefs, nor were they all men. The leaders of the different nations were known to represent the people, not their own interests. Although traditional values are still strong both on reservations and in urban Indian communities, it seems that today, European immigrant values, such as placing the individual before the community, are becoming apparent.

Many American Indians see striking similarities between historical oppression and current government policies. Institutionalized disempowerment has understandably led many Indians into despair and pessimism. Although the effects of generations of oppression cannot be reversed, the need is clear: to change the views and actions of society and government as a whole. To change the future, we first must understand the wrongs of the past. The truth about the heritage of American Indians has been usurped by the version of history to which the public has access—the history written by European immigrant settlers. This history only reflects biased European stereotypical views about the diverse cultures already present in America. One cannot readily rely on writings by non-Indians regarding the truth about American Indian life and culture. But American Indians are beginning to write about themselves, and these writings are certainly more accurate and valid.

Personal Interview

Frank (FM) is from the Karuk tribe of Northern California. He was born and brought up on Indian lands with a family of 14 in a house that measured about 20 feet by 20 feet.

What do you think are some similarities or differences Indian families might have compared to other families you've seen?

Frank Merrill: We don't have as much greed or respect for money as other people do. With the money I make I buy groceries and keep up the house, but if there's somebody on the street or anybody that comes into town that doesn't have a place to live they can stay at my house a week or two until they find a place. Some nights when I've got a lot of frybread left over after an outing, I take it around to the neighbors and give it to them, but I hardly ever get to see them [non-Indian neighbors]. The non-Indian people don't visit like the Indians. That's how we also keep our relationship alive. These are the things I see as the common bond of Indian people. These are the reasons why I go to pow-wows and travel around to different programs that I don't have in my own neighborhood. It makes me feel good when I go to places and see how people welcome you and talk to you and respect who you are.

What are the most important challenges facing Indian families today?

FM: Not to lose respect for who they are is probably one of the main things that I see, and

that we continue to bring our young ones up to where they believe in and respect themselves. Also, to continue to hold on to our traditional ways that have been slipping through our society a little at a time, especially our language. When my Mom went to boarding school, she was brainwashed into thinking the only way to talk and learn was the White man's way. I lost my native language and now my kids and grandkids want to learn it, but I have no way I can help. I can only understand it, not talk it.

The other societies are moving forward at a fast rate, but the Indian families are moving at a much slower pace. They know that if we don't turn back to the circle, and not the straight line—what [non-Indians] believe in, we have no place to go and the end is near. This is why I think it is important that we hang on to what we have had for 500 years. An important part of Indian life is to stick it out and hold on to what we've got and to keep our own and teach amongst ourselves.

What are some ways you see families dealing with these challenges?

FM: What I see in Indian people is that we respect our elders because the elders are the ones that have the knowledge of keeping us in line with respect and the knowledge of what comes from an Indian's heart. Once we lose that respect for our elders and go into non-Indian society, we won't have that. Non-Indian society would rather lock their elders in a home with all the knowledge that they have locked away. I get my knowledge from my elders. I follow whatever my elders tell me. They keep telling me these things over and over—what to respect, what to look for, and how to act. And so all of these things have to be kept sacred amongst our people, otherwise we'll lose what we have. I can't teach you stuff that an elder hasn't taught me yet. I'm learning every day. Every day I go out into society I learn something different, and all the knowledge I have I'm passing onto the kids below me. By the time you get my age, people will be looking to you for answers.

Can you talk about the pow-wow as a family event?

FM: That's a learning point. Each time we go to a pow-wow, we always hear the emcee or the people showing their respect, talking about respect, and continuing with the culture that we were brought up in. The little kids who are one, two, or three years old hear this too, and even if they can't speak it out, they're taking it in. This is how the tradition of the circle of knowledge keeps repeating itself over and over. We need to have more outings, and we need to have more people because a lot of our families have moved away from the reservation. They were brought up in the White school system so they need to come to pow-wows to have knowledge of the Indian culture. I listen to young people and to Moms and Dads when they come to me and say, "You know, I learned so much at today's pow-wow. And I wish I went to more when I was younger, but I didn't see it as an important event."

Tell us about your family.

FM: When I was brought up, my grandparents did most of my disciplining. The grand-

parents are usually the ones who end up being the teachers. I think that is where the respect for the elders came in a long time ago. They used to set me down if I did something wrong, and a lot of times they'd tell me stories of how to gather my food if I was alone, and if I was playing around when I was supposed to be working, they'd tell me coyote stories, about how this coyote didn't do his work and the outcome would be where we learned the lesson.

I have my granddaughter living with me, and I have uncles and nephews that come stay with me. We stick together and are responsible for one another. My second-oldest daughter is 35 years old, and she's still living at home. I have some non-Indian families come over and say, "Kick em out, kick em out." Well, I can do that, but because of respect for my family and the tightness of the family circle, you don't do these things among Indian families.

And that's why it's so hard, like the other day when my nephew passed away. The school didn't want to give me time off because it wasn't "immediate family." To me it was immediate family. I mean, he stayed with me, he lived with me. They couldn't see the closeness. They have their rules and regulations about immediate family to mean grandparents, wife, husband, and kids.

Talk about diversity within the Indian community.

FM: The way I see it, each and every one of the tribes is different. We have our own religions, languages, beliefs, and ceremonies. So when I go into a different tribe, they invite me in to share their culture. They may have things similar to my people, yet treat them in a different manner. Respecting diversity is important amongst Indian people. If you go to another tribe, you go there as a guest, and you don't take away from that tribe what is theirs. When I leave, I leave with a lot of knowledge behind me. I can go to Siletz, and a lot of times I don't know how to act because they have different ways, and their tribe does things that my tribe may do in another way.

What do you think about intermarriage in Indian families?

FM: To me, there is no good or bad about it. A lot of the tribes want to hold on to federal guidelines of keeping the bloodlines. I believe that any Indian who has any proof of Indian blood can be a member of that tribe; even if he's only got one drop, he's still a member. I believe this strongly because I am married to a non-Indian and have grandkids. It's getting down to the borderline now where the federal government won't recognize them by quota degree. After my grandkids get married, if they intermarry one more time, their kids will not become a member of my tribe. That's very wrong, because they *are* a member of my tribe. I talk to people that believe in the full bloodline, and then I say, "Do you have a grandson that's not full?" Almost every one of them will say, "Yeah."

Are there any concluding statements you want to make?

FM: Well, if I was out here for the first time and never knew about Indians, I would ask the Indians themselves what makes them an Indian. I always answer that question based on how I believe, what I feel, how I act, and how I present myself to people. The way I look at it is that Indian people have a gift that they use when they share, care, and respect things. It's not because I'm brown skin, it isn't because I have lived on a reservation, it isn't because I eat eels or acorns—it's not all of that, but because our spirituality has to be everyday living. It's so confusing when we talk about spirituality amongst non-Indian people because they want to know which church I belong to. I say, "It's not a church, it's how you believe in yourself and it's how you act and conduct yourself."

Questions for Discussion

1. What are some of your stereotypes about Indian people, and where did they come from?

2. What did you learn from school about American Indians? Compare what you know with the ideas in this chapter.

3. Discuss your ethnic background and how it relates to your family. How does it relate to the way American Indian heritage was discussed in the chapter?

4. What are some values in society today? Is society more individually based or community based? What are some issues or problems neighborhoods

are facing today because the families in those neighborhoods are not community based?

5. What are the different ideologies about ageism and the elderly in the dominant society and American Indian society? What are the impacts on the different societies?

Suggested Resources

Readings

Journals

American Indian and Alaska Native Mental Health Research. The Journal of the National Center. University Press of Colorado. P.O. Box 849, Niwot, CO 80544.

Journal of American Indian Education. Center for Indian Education. College of Education, Arizona State University, P.O. Box 871311, Tempe, AZ 85287.

Historical Accounts

Avery, S., & Skinner, L. (1992). *Extraordinary American Indians.* Chicago: Children's Press.

Brown, D. (1970). *Bury my heart at Wounded Knee: An Indian history of the American West.* New York: Holt.

Josephy, A. M. (1992). *America in 1492: The world of the Indian peoples before the arrival of Columbus.* New York: Knopf.

McLuhan, T. C. (1971). *Touch the earth: A self-portrait of Indian existence.* New York: Promontory Press.

Pevar, S. L. (1992). *The rights of Indians and tribes: The basic ACLU guide to Indian and tribal rights.* Carbondale and Edwardsville, IL: Southern Illinois University Press.

Contemporary Stories

Brave Bird, M. (1991). *Lakota woman.* New York: Harper Perennial.

Brave Bird, M., & Erodes, R. (1995). *Ohitika woman.* New York: Harper Perennial.

Neihardt, J. G. (1992). *Black Elk speaks: Being the life story of a holy man of the Oglala Sioux.* Lincoln: University of Nebraska Press.

Shkilnyk, A. M. (1985). *A poison stronger than love: The destruction of an Ojibwa community.* New Haven, CT: Yale University Press.

Wall, S. (1992). *Wisdomkeepers and wisdom's daughters: Conversations with women elders of Native America.* New York: Harper Perennial.

Children's Books

Crum, R. (1994). *Eagle drum: On the pow-wow trail with a young grass dancer.* New York: Four Winds Press.

Dorris, M. (1992). *Morning girl.* New York: Hyperion.

Dorris, M. (1994). *Guests.* New York: Hyperion.

Hirschi, R. (1992). *Seya's song.* Seattle: Sasquatch Books.

Videos

Apted, M. (Director). (1992). *Thunderheart.* (Available from FACETS Media, 1517 W. Fullerton Avenue, Chicago, IL 60614)

Margolin, S. (Director). (1994). *Medicine river.* (Available from Academy Entertainment, 9250 Wilshire Boulevard, Suite 404, Beverly Hills, CA 90212)

Pal, L. (Director). (1991). *Journey to Spirit Land.* (Available from Academy Entertainment, 9250 Wilshire Boulevard, Suite 404, Beverly Hills, CA 90212)

Pittman, B. (Director). (1989). *Where the spirit lives.* (Available from Hollywood Home Entertainment, 6165 Crooke Creek Road, Suite B, Norcross, GA 30092)

Public Broadcasting Services (Producer). (1990). *Winds of change: A matter of promises, a matter of choice.* (Available from FACETS Media, 1517 W. Fullerton Avenue, Chicago, IL 60614)

Wyss, A. (Producer), & Wacks, J. (Director). (1989). *Pow-wow highway.* (Available from Videofinders, 425 E. Colorado Street, Suite 10B, Glendale, CA 91205)

References

Allen, P. (1992). Angry women are building: Issues and struggles facing American Indian women today. In M. Anderson & P. Collins (Eds.), *Race, class, and gender: An anthology.* Belmont, CA: Wadsworth.

Chu Ho, F., & Johnson, R. C. (1990). Intra-ethnic and inter-ethnic marriage and divorce in Hawaii. *Social Biology, 37,* 44–51.

Colley, C. (1992). Personal communication, Summer 1992.

Green, R. (1992a). Culture and gender in Indian America. In M. Anderson & P. Collins (Eds.), *Race, class, and gender: An anthology.* Belmont, CA: Wadsworth.

Green, R. (1992b). *Women in American Indian society.* New York: Chelsea House.

Kawamoto, W. (1994, February). *Maternal involvement and marital satisfaction in American Indian and non-Indian families.* Paper presented at the annual conference of the National Council on Family Relations, Baltimore, MD.

Kawamoto, W. (1995). *Stability and process issues in intermarriage: A study of marital satisfaction and problem solving in American Indian intermarried and European American endogamous families.* Unpublished doctoral dissertation, Oregon State University.

La Fromboise, T., Heyle, A., & Ozer, E. (1990). Changing and diverse roles of women in American Indian cultures. *Sex Roles, 22,* 455–476.

Pevar, S. (1992). *The rights of Indians and tribes: The basic ACLU guide to Indian and tribal rights.* Carbondale and Edwardsville: Southern Illinois University Press.

Reddy, M. (1993). *Statistical record of Native North Americans.* Detroit: Gale Research.

Red Horse, J. (1980). Family structure and value orientation in American Indians. *Social Casework, 61,* 462–467.

Retasket, T. (1994). *1993 Socio-economic and health survey of the Confederated Tribes of Siletz.* Portland, OR: Planning Department, Confederated Tribes of Siletz Indians.

Sandefur, G., & McKinnell, T. (1986). American Indian intermarriage. *Social Science Research, 15,* 347–371.

Wagner, J. (1976). The role of intermarriage in the acculturation of selected urban American Indian women. *Anthropologica, 18,* 215–229.

Doris Y. Wilkinson

3

American Families of African Descent

Historical and Cultural Background

The African American family, as a system closely interconnected with its past and with economic and political institutions in American culture, has needed objective documentation and interpretation for decades. In studying the family, scholars have used various conceptual models. Overall, composition and form have constituted the principal units of analysis. Most social science descriptions of African American families have been comparative and have emphasized structure rather than cultural history and psychological functioning (Allen, 1978; Nobles, 1978; Wilkinson, 1978b). Because of the unique record and cultural origin of the African American family, a special approach is required.

In the latter part of the twentieth century, there have been significant changes in the characterizations of African American family life. However, a paucity of research has been devoted to an examination of the forces that have shaped parenthood, spousal relationships, patterns of child rearing, dating, mating and marriage, and the interplay of familial and work roles within the context of socioeconomic status. Before the classic work by Andrew Billingsley, *Black Families in White America* (1968), which, along with others in the 1970s, highlighted strengths and healthy adaptations, positive marital relationships, and effective parental role performance, the African American family had not been viewed constructively. Instead of objectively reviewing historical and economic influences on family functions and transitions, social scientists have primarily studied lower-class family formation, lifestyles, and problem behaviors.

This chapter emphasizes the historical, demographic, political, and cultural events and processes that have framed the African American family. Pertinent sociological findings, beginning in the 1970s, demonstrate that family organization, child-rearing practices, parental role expectations, patterns of control, husband-wife interaction, life-cycle episodes, intergenerational continuity, and support among kin are directly linked to social antecedents—including economic and educational ones. Comparative appraisals of the family institution by ethnic group have failed to grasp the essence of traditional African American values and customs within a caste-based context that has given rise to distinctions between them and all other immigrant families (Allen, 1995; Asante & Mattson, 1991; McAdoo, 1993). The husband's occupational status and the labor-force participation of wives and mothers by ethnicity have been among the foremost indicators of these dissimilarities (Dill, 1979; Wallace, Datcher, & Malveaux, 1980; Wilkinson, 1991).

African Americans have a family and cultural heritage grounded in rural folkways. Their roots are attached to the soil, where farming in the countries of origin was once the fundamental way of life before their forced migration across the Atlantic to the New World. In the distant and culturally varied African countries from which they originated, family rites, rituals, and ceremonies were integrated with tribal villages and clans. Life revolved around hunting, gathering, food production, and child rearing. Men—the heads of their clans, tribes, and families—tilled the soil and were skilled hunters and craftsmen. Extraordinary artistic and building skills were refined in the old country. In addition to helping with planting and harvesting crops and gathering food, women performed the universal tasks of mothering, caring for children, preparing meals, and providing a place for the elderly. With respect to the latter, maintaining intergenerational continuity has always been intrinsic to African culture. Traditional African customs and values emerged from a rich agrarian environment.

Before Africans arrived in the Americas, religious ceremonies and activities characterized their way of life. Especially important were ancestor worship and the belief in "a spirit world" (*African Americans: Voices*, 1993). When folk medicine practices did not produce desired outcomes (Wilkinson, 1987b), religious rituals offered meaning and answers to the mystery of sickness and death. Village singing, dancing, and chanting were the foundation of religious expression. Men served as the commanding leaders and liaisons to the spirit world. Rites of passage from adolescence into adulthood, as well as family life-cycle crises, were intricately tied to religious ceremonies. Indigenous tribal observances among African slaves carried a central meaning in their lives in the Americas (*African Americans: Voices*, 1993; Andrews, 1984; Smith, 1988).

One aim of this discussion is to present and summarize studies of African American family life, kin networks, gender differences in socialization, dating and mating habits, work-family linkages, and life-cycle transitions. Family strengths and challenges will be explored. The major focus underscores historical precedents and socioeconomic status variations among traditional and emerging families, cultural biographies, and modes of adaptation within this country's racially framed and gendered status configurations. Ideas relevant to understanding the general character and special arrangements of the family as reflected in the status of women are incorporated.

The African American family cannot be logically described nor understood without cataloguing the unique background of displaced Africans in seventeenth-, eighteenth-, and nineteenth-century America. This radical transference to unfamiliar and unsought surroundings resulted in extensive changes in family organization, indigenous values, **consanguineal relationships**, mate selection, parenting, and socioeconomic status determination. Many of the transplanted Africans in the Americas came from the proud tribes of the Ashanti, Dahomey, and Mende, among others, on the African continent. Before being sold into European-dominated slavery, they lived free in strong families in countries such as Senegal, Gambia, Sierra Leone, the Congo, the Ivory Coast, and Liberia. In spite of the far-reaching consequences of the dissolution of their essential primary unit, under the European slave trade, African women succeeded in maintaining a modicum of stability for their families. The histories and lives of African Americans have been anchored in the meaningfulness of family unity.

The Slave Legacy

The African American family has a social past that differs substantially from that of all other ethnic immigrant families. Of particular interest are its roots in the United States, the economic and ideological forces that have shaped the family, and its adaptive processes as well as its strengths. Because of the harsh and brutal experience of violent uprooting and being placed in captivity, the duties of parents and grandparents were molded by a slave identity and later with domestic service. The socioeconomic status of families of African descent was thus established. Estimates vary regarding the numbers of Africans who were bought and sold in the United States, South America, Latin America, and the West Indies. The calculations range from 10 million to 20 million between the sixteenth and mid-nineteenth centuries.

In 1518, the first cargo of African slaves came to the West Indies directly from Africa (Bergman & Bergman, 1969). Between 1502 and 1600, nearly 1 million African slaves were imported to Latin America to harvest crops, build, and work on the sugar and tobacco plantations. They were shipped under extraordinarily inhumane conditions to the United States and other countries. Those transported to Brazil were primarily from the Guinea Coast, Angola, and the Congo Basin. "Each group had a distinct culture, and tribal groups were sought for their special skills. Later slaves came from Guinea and the Western

Sudan" (Bergman & Bergman, 1969, p. 3). Not long after the first Africans arrived in Jamestown, Virginia, in 1619, slavery was introduced in both the North and the South, in such states as New York, Connecticut, Maryland, Delaware, Virginia, and the Carolinas.

Corresponding with a legacy of bondage, political and economic pressures over the centuries molded the form, structure, and functioning of African American families (Allen, 1995; Billingsley, 1968, 1969; Blackwell, 1991; Blauner, 1972; Davis, 1981). The ancestors of families of African heritage who were brought to the United States in the seventeenth and eighteenth centuries entered the country as slaves. A large proportion came from tribes in West Africa, where Arab and European traders had capitalized on the small-scale practice of enslaving indigenous peoples, usually violating family mores, village customs, and tribal laws. Although slavery was institutionalized in other countries, only in the United States did it reach widespread prominence and relative permanence until the Emancipation Proclamation and the Civil War (Still, 1970). The tragic relocation caused families and cultures of people of African descent to be altered in ways that differed significantly from those of other ethnic populations. Therefore, any model used for analyzing African American families must be contingent on their unique history and contemporary experiences. One cannot speak rationally of "an immigration experience" for slaves or their descendants (Allen, 1978; Douglass, 1986; Wilkinson, 1978a).

The unrestrained act of dissolving the African family by European American slaveholders violated the sacredness of this institution as the link to rural African culture. Ironically, enslavement did not completely crush marriage or the primary nurturing unit. Unexpectedly, "the institution of slavery only acted to reinforce the close bond that had already existed between mother and child in African society" (Ladner, 1971, p. 279). On the other hand, racial customs and historically circumscribed economic colonization gave rise to distinctive social experiences for African American grandparents and their offspring that are reflected in their philosophies today (Bennett, 1984; Billingsley & Greene, 1974; Blassingame, 1979; Fitchett, 1941; Frazier, 1948; Gutman, 1976; Wilkinson, 1995).

In the United States, before the Civil War, the privilege to establish enduring bonds and lasting marriages differed from plantation to plantation, depending on the receptiveness of slaveholders (Blackwell, 1991; Genovese & Roll, 1974). To illustrate this, I will briefly sketch my own family heritage. In contrast to other states, in Kentucky, the birthplace of my maternal and paternal grandparents' families of origin, African Americans were closely connected to the White families who owned them. There were not merely residential linkages, but kinship ties as well (Brodie, 1974; Graham, 1961; Thomas, 1977). Slaveholders fathered children by women they bought and sold. This was mutually understood and frequently acknowledged by the slaveholders themselves. My own paternal great-great-great-grandfather was a White slaveholder and the ancestor of my father's family and relatives (Wilkinson, 1984).

The kinship connections between African slaves and European slaveholders created a divisive prestige system among African Americans based on color, socioeconomic status, and opportunity. In 1850, 13 years before the Emancipation Proclamation, my paternal great-great-grandfather and his wife were free and listed in the census as mulattoes. They were granted their freedom by their slaveholding fathers. Ambivalent about my great-great-grandfather's identity, upon seeing the wife and children, the census taker erased "W" for White and replaced it with "M" for mulatto. From the 1850s through the early 1900s, my father's grandparents were allotted property that they in turn willed to their heirs down through the generations.

Such consanguineal linkages between slaves and those who owned, bought, sold, and exchanged them prevailed throughout the slave communities in the South, as well as in the historically border states (Allen, 1995; Bennett, 1984; Brodie, 1974; Graham, 1961). Socioeconomic status and special privileges were based on these kinship connections, which distinguished slaves from the free Americans of mixed African and European ancestry. This differentiation was founded on paternity, land, and property. In his will, out of deep affection for my enslaved paternal great-great-great-grandmother, her slaveholding master, with whom she lived and by whom she bore children, granted her property and land. Similar practices occurred in the other southern states, as well as in Haiti, Brazil, and the islands (Wilkinson, 1984).

Throughout the South where slavery was entrenched in the mores and the laws, African Americans carried the names of their owners, who were in most cases their biological fathers. Both first names and surnames verified direct consanguineal bonds. It was common practice for African American slave women, like Sally Hemmings, to give birth to children fathered by their masters (Brodie, 1974; Gutman, 1976; Haley, 1976; Hine & Wittenstein, 1981; Wilkinson, 1978a). Notwithstanding the indignity of forced sexual intimacy, the mistresses of slaveholders were obligated to their own households and dedicated to the survival of their own biological families (Davis, 1971). Unlike my father's family's lineage, my mother's grandmother was born into slavery and her father was the direct descendant of African slaves and Indians. The majority of Americans of African descent share similar family narratives (Davis, 1971; Delany & Delany, 1993; Hill-Lubin, 1991; Watkins, 1939).

During the establishment of the system of slavery, with its far-reaching economic, political, and ideological repercussions, African women had multiple domestic and work roles. They maintained their own homes and those of their masters and later domestic-service employers, giving rise to the contemporary myth of "the strong Black woman" (Bell, 1974; Hine & Wittenstein, 1981; Kane & Wilkinson, 1974; Mack, 1971; Marks, 1993; Wilkinson, 1978a).

In spite of being in captivity, there were innumerable courageous and skillful women like my great-great-great-aunt Patsy Riffe, the daughter of a prominent White political figure and an African slave. A school and a street were named after her. Although she was freed before her husband, she worked, saved, and struggled for more than a decade to purchase his freedom.

Intimacy and mate selection were forced on women of African descent by European American slaveholders, often with the knowledge of their own wives and older children. Under the slave regime, women were also coerced into living with male slaves for whom they had no feelings of love. Denied choices, enslaved African women in America in many instances had to select husbands based on the economic and psychological motives of plantation owners. Being subjugated, male slaves lacked the power or the "right" to protect their daughters, wives, or mothers from dishonor and unrelenting abuse. As the American racial order was gradually transformed, "ex-slave women [continued to confront] a legacy that viewed them as dependent sexual objects" (Gutman, 1976, p. 390). The far-reaching psychological impact of sexual indignities on ex-slaves and their descendants pervades family legends of the past (Hine & Wittenstein, 1981; King, 1973).

With the reconstruction of the U.S. economy as it evolved from an agricultural to an industrialized one, the norm of **patriarchy** endured as a relative constant in the family, and mothers, older daughters, grandmothers, and aunts retained traditional housekeeping and caretaking roles. Following the termination of legal slavery, women of African ancestry continued to work in the homes of European Americans as domestic servants. Their occupational positions, like those of their husbands and fathers, were virtually entrenched in the unskilled service and laboring sector (Wilkinson, 1991). During the war years and following World War II (1939–1945), as indicated earlier, they supported two households and cared for their elderly parents. As societal changes emanating from international conflict, rapid urbanization, new laws, and social norms unfolded, like the White American family, those of African heritage were also being radically transformed (Staples, 1971).

Traditional and Emerging Family Systems

The scope and character of family life contrast intrinsically according to socioeconomic level. Parenthood, work and family relationships, the organization of households, socialization practices, and adjustment to life-cycle transitions are framed by socioeconomic status and by the social forces in the larger economic and political culture. Femininity and masculinity, and the associated expected male and female behaviors, are precisely differentiated in African American families and communities, with minimal variations according to education or income. Family rituals that support appropriate **gender-role behaviors** offer insight into the characteristics of a group of people that has a precisely defined and conventional division of labor.

Gender-role training and status distinctions within the family mirror an African cultural past, despite conversion to European American norms and lifestyles. Reluctant but necessary adaptation was inevitable because of the powerlessness of male slaves. With the historical transference of kinship traditions, aunts and uncles became principal participants in the extended family system. Despite being inevitably shaped by changes in the larger society, this nurturing unit acted to preserve intergenerational succession. Basically, caring for elderly parents is normative in African American culture, regardless of socioeconomic status. And although its structure has been modified dramatically since its beginnings in the United States, the African American family has thrived as an essential communal network of sharing, support, protection, emotional reinforcement, and adaptation to the regularity of change.

Following **Reconstruction, Jim Crowism**, and the Civil Rights era, men and women developed effective coping strategies for themselves (Beal, 1970; Davis, 1981). Despite discrimination, racial barriers, the closing of the system of opportunity in housing, education, employment, and health care, and other impediments to the durability of family life, parents and grandparents carried out their sanctioned roles along strictly circumscribed gender lines. Parenting and spousal relationships have always blended with established norms for male and female behavior. In addition, the economic and political contexts from which present African American families evolved, albeit with variations in form and socioeconomic history, have resulted in a special bridge between a woman's family role and her work role (Wallace et al., 1980). Likewise, the immense difficulties Black women have experienced have generated a "personality that is rarely described in the scholarly journals for its obstinate strength and ability to survive" (Ladner, 1971, p. 280).

The regional relocation of African American families within the United States exerted a profound influence on their organization and functioning. The one constant has been that all family members, regardless of background, have experienced social, employment, and educational discrimination. Socioeconomic status distinctions have persisted since Reconstruction (1867–1877) and the mass migration to the northeastern urban regions during the early part of the twentieth century. This internal movement reassembled entire communities. Prior to this vast movement, most African American families resided in the South (e.g., Alabama, Georgia, Louisiana, Mississippi). But after 1900, the southern part of the country was no longer the preferred residence of the descendants of slaves and free men and women (Bergman & Bergman, 1969). Family composition and the rituals, beliefs, and values compatible with an agricultural way of life began to be reshaped by urban customs and White workers' responses to African American men and their skills and employment potential. The purposeful geographic emigration in search of a better quality of life was aligned directly with hopes for the family.

At the time of Reconstruction and up to the Civil Rights activism of the 1960s, two-parent households prevailed in African American communities in both the North and the South. Even as the 1980s unfolded, a majority of the estimated 6.4 million Black families were two-parent households; nearly two-fifths were female-headed. Since World War II, however, census data disclosed growing numbers of households headed by women (U.S. Bureau of the Census, 1978, 1995). On the other hand, the nuclear family, with strong kinship alliances and a philosophy of caring for elderly parents, has lasted as a standard model in the African American community.

In 1990, the majority of African American families were married couples. However, more and more children are growing up without fathers. This trend is contrary to the ancestral roots and fundamental structure of the traditional African family. In 1994, an estimated 47.9% of African American families had a female head of household with no spouse present (U.S. Bureau of the Census, 1995).

The diminishing of a rural way of life and the problems of adjusting to urban conventions have been the prominent catalysts for transforming the structure and functioning of African American families. These changes have been manifested in spousal relationships, family formation, the socialization of children, and techniques of coping with dissolution, especially divorce. Other systemic developments included a devaluation of the skills of workers whose experience and craftsmanship in the agrarian South were no longer in demand in the racially conscious and competitive North. With the "great migration" to urban centers, husbands and fathers encountered skill devaluation along with chronic housing and job discrimination. Also, given the disproportionate representation of sons, husbands, and fathers of African descent in two world wars and the Korean War (1951–1953), the family was predictably reconfigured by their absence. Similarly, sociodemographic processes such as the embedding of a color caste system, property ownership in the South, geographic resettlement, the gradual cessation of farming, rising unemployment rates, and escalating industrialization altered the occupational prospects of husbands and fathers (Staples, 1982; Wilkinson & Taylor, 1977; Wilson, 1978).

Since emancipation, modifications in the status hierarchy have consolidated class distinctions among families within the African American community. Historically, lacking the financial support of male wage-earners, women have been active participants in the labor force (Almquist, 1975; Wallace et al., 1980; Wilkinson, 1991). Similarly, unlike ethnic immigrant families, those of African lineage are unevenly affected by national crises and shifts in the economic structure. Today, families of African ancestry tend to be seriously threatened by cyclical changes in the national economy. Aligned with recessions, inflation, and employment discrimination, the skill devaluation of male workers has had far-reaching consequences for the effective functioning of African American families. But in spite of these occurrences, effective parenting does take place.

Families in Poverty

American families of African heritage that are impoverished and female-headed have vastly different histories, parenting behaviors, and expectations from those in the working, middle, and upper classes (Brewer, 1988; Bryant, 1971; Simms, 1985). Having two parents, unifying family customs and kinship rituals, the mother's positive feelings about child rearing, high educational attainment, an employed father, a small number of children—all of these vary according to socioeconomic status (Billingsley, 1969; Comer & Poussaint, 1975).

In the United States, poverty is systemic and thus predictably high among African Americans residing in urban and rural areas. Nearly one-third of these families were below the poverty level in 1994 (U.S. Bureau of the Census, 1995). Perpetual unemployment, discrimination, lack of access to adequate housing, an increase in the divorce rate, cultural changes, and a decline in the two-parent household have given rise to a distinct population of poor families and single-parent households. According to the U.S. Bureau of the Census (1995), in 1994 there were an estimated 3.8 million African American female heads of households with no spouse present. About 43% were never married, 20% were married with spouse absent, 13% were widowed, and 23% were divorced; 18% had children under 18 years of age living in the household.

Families that are poor with absent fathers and unemployed mothers experience endless complications in fulfilling their basic needs. Single mothers, who are usually teenagers, spend considerable time searching for a place to live—a process made difficult, if not impossible, by a lack of money. As would be expected, family functioning is shaped by the economic position of the female head, who is a product of a long history of social forces (Brewer, 1988; Bryant, 1971; Simms, 1985, 1991). As a result of the relative permanence of the family's plight, parenting is difficult and children's development and aspirations are impeded. Rules for dating and mate selection are not firmly outlined. It is from this group that many children of poverty flourish in the streets and the juvenile courts. The vast organizational, value, and cultural differences between poor single-parent households, especially female-headed units, and families in other socioeconomic levels are fixed in a racially and class-based stratification system.

When possible, and if the resources are available, fatherless families in the "working poor" class may have grandmothers and siblings who participate in the child-rearing process. One vestige of the African heritage is the **extended family**, which reflects the value placed on maintaining contact with kin (McAdoo, 1975; Martin & Martin, 1978). The custom of sharing among relatives creates a support network for unemployed and working-poor families with or without fathers in the home. When there are strains in the economy, siblings, relatives, and grandparents may not always be able to provide economic assistance, but they may be able to help with child care. The intergenerational transmission of loyalty and the emotional strength gained from strong consanguineal relationships sustain families under stress (Hill, 1972).

Families of lower socioeconomic levels, in which one or both parents are employed, have different viewpoints from those of the chronically unemployed and the impoverished. Public assistance creates obstacles for mothers who want to work. Generally, if they get a job, their welfare payments are reduced, making it nearly impossible to pay rent or buy food, clothes, and schoolbooks for their children. Moreover, mothers who are poor tend to have more children than they can support on what they might earn from unskilled labor.

As the 1970s were ending, approximately 50% of the 2.1 million Black female heads of families were in the labor force, employed mostly in low-paying jobs that required low levels of skill (Wallace et al., 1980). Of these, almost half had not graduated from high school, and the majority were under the poverty level at the time. Unexpectedly, data indicate that notwithstanding the problems faced in meeting fundamental needs, mothers—and fathers, when present—in impoverished homes have definite hopes for their children (Billingsley, 1969; Wilkinson, 1984). With the sole authority for child rearing, mothers do the best they can in parenting.

Appropriate behaviors for male and female children are expected. Virginity for girls is valued, especially in the working, middle, and upper classes. Early sexual relationships and public displays of affection in these families are frowned upon.

Regardless of life-cycle experiences and the family's financial position, the health and economic needs of the children are primary concerns. Understandably, in a single-parent household, because of her educational level, segregation in the job market, and struggles with a welfare existence, the mother may be unable to participate in her children's schooling or take an active role in community affairs. Involvement in a church has a paramount place in employed and unemployed poor female-headed households, as well as in the lives of those in the working, middle, and upper classes. Historically, the church and religious expression have supported and supplemented African American family and community life (Andrews, 1984; Smith, 1988).

The Non-Poor Working Class

Families in the non-poor working class differ in composition and functioning from those that are below or at the poverty level, especially female-headed households. Working-class families are two-parent households with both spouses employed, each usually earning an annual income of at least $10,000–$25,000 (Billingsley, 1992; Massaquoi, 1993). The employment of both parents is necessary and indicates the financial situation of the family. Because the husband may be unskilled and therefore hold a low-paying job, the wife must work to help meet the needs of the family. Since neither parent will likely have an advanced college degree, the family will not be economically secure unless the wife contributes as a wage-earner. Although these women share certain similarities in child rearing and gender-role socialization with middle-class mothers, working outside the home is imperative for wives of the non-poor working class.

African American husbands and wives in working-class families do not have the educational achievements of middle-class men and women. Even if working-class mothers and fathers are high school dropouts, they generally desire more education for their children than they have achieved themselves (Wilkinson, 1978a). Solidarity and internal strength are intrinsic features of the non-poor working class, and family life is characterized by a constant effort to retain its fragile economic security. The persistent preoccupation with the family's financial condition affects the opportunities for and aspirations of children. Nevertheless, special comfort accrues from children and the hopes that mothers and fathers hold for them. Parents hope their children will go to college and become constructive participants in society. Billingsley, a pioneer in the study of the African American family, views the non-poor working class as the "backbone of the Black community."

Maternal relatives hold a meaningful place in non-poor working-class families. They can serve as role models, and, when available, they can cooperate in a system of joint assistance in times of family crisis. Typically, husbands have service jobs or those that require physical labor, and they regularly work long hours. As a result, they may not have the time to engage in family activities or participate directly in the upbringing of their sons and daughters. This clearly distinguishes them from middle- and upper-class fathers.

Within the stable working-class family, strictly gendered parenting and work responsibilities shape conjugal relations and parenting tasks. Traditional spousal and parental duties provide continuity and regularity in role functioning. Working-class mothers, fathers, and their children make up a closely knit unit that sequesters its members from external social and health crises and economic stresses. Reflecting an embedded cultural foundation, mothers are central in the non-poor working-class household (Hale, 1977; McAdoo, 1980; Staples, 1971). Fundamentally, they and the fathers are accountable for instill-ing family values, integrating beliefs, and modeling appropriate codes of conduct.

In implementing their customary roles, women may aspire to the middle-class value of egalitarianism. Although male dominance is paramount, they count on their husbands to assist and support them when necessary with child rearing, especially with the upbringing of sons. To retain uniformity in family role allocation, the male head in the secure working-class family has a domi-nant place (Massaquoi, 1993; Staples, 1971). In cases where the mother is ab-sent as a result of divorce or death, the father may be found acting to keep the family intact. In the United States in 1994, an estimated 238,000 families had a male head with his own children under 18 years of age present in the home (U.S. Bureau of the Census, 1995). This form reflects familial solidarity, al-though single male heads of households have been rare (Lyons, 1993).

The Upwardly Mobile Middle Class

During the latter part of this century in the United States, along with the expansion of a sizable impoverished population, a well-educated and economi-cally secure middle class has flourished (Giles, 1994; McAdoo, 1978; Landry, 1987; Wallace et al., 1980). Contemporary socioeconomic differences among African Americans, as stated before, are outgrowths of dissimilar ancestral and economic histories. Perceptions of the African American family as a **matriar-chy** have a political and social basis that reveals an adaptive response to a harsh and disruptive history.

Wives and mothers in middle-class families have spousal and parenting ob-ligations, as well as work lives, that are quite divergent from those of women in poor single-parent households, and even from those in the non-poor working class. Mothers in the middle class are more likely to be married and to have come from intact nuclear families, a characteristic they share with non-poor working-class wives and mothers. However, their modes of child rearing di-verge from those who are economically deprived (Billingsley, 1968; Comer & Poussaint, 1975). Like other African American wives, mothers, and grand-mothers, they participate in intergenerational exchange (Taylor, Chatters, & Jackson, 1993). Yet "middle-class values are more compatible with a nuclear than an extended family" (Martin & Martin, 1978, p. 76).

Characteristically, men in upwardly mobile middle-class families are the principal authority figures, although decision making and task allocation are based on precisely defined gender roles. Marital interaction and sharing in de-cision making reflect socioeconomic status, with education and occupation being the basic determinants (Rutledge, 1980). With respect to employment status, both husbands and wives customarily work. In this connection, history shows that "well-educated Black women have learned how to balance the demands of the work environment and the demands of their home" (Wallace et al., 1980, p. 101). In the middle-class home, teenage and sometimes young adult children reside with both parents. Fathers are effective authority figures. By holding a job to augment family income, mothers act as occupational role models for their daughters.

Salespeople, waiters, postal workers, and public school teachers have usually comprised the African American middle class. Today, with increased education and especially college training, changes have taken place in the occupations that make up this socioeconomic group. In keeping with the beliefs of middle-class culture, family expectations include education for children, deferring gratification including saving for the future, respecting parents and grandparents, attending Sunday school or church, and interacting with and dating young people who are in the same socioeconomic group.

Middle-class families tend to live in suburban areas (Hatchett, 1995; Randolph, 1992; Wiese, 1993). They participate in church activities, and wives and mothers are engaged in social clubs as well as community voluntary organizations. When children attend the heterogeneous public schools, family values that have been instilled are expected to remain. Children in the African American middle class may "feel under pressure not only from the expectations family members have of them, but sometimes from what is expected in the Black community" (Martin & Martin, 1978, p. 78). Discipline and decision making are joint parental responsibilities, especially when the latter involves major expenditures such as buying a home or car or sending the children to college, or controversial mate selection issues such as interracial dating or choosing mates outside their socioeconomic group (Downs, 1975).

Since middle-class families tend to provide for elderly parents when the need arises, grandmothers and aunts typically play auxiliary roles. In middle- and upper-class families, maternal and paternal grandparents adhere to the same goals, reinforcing those in the family of origin. During the formative child-rearing years when the mother is employed, support from grandparents and other relatives, usually aunts, is invaluable (McAdoo, 1975). As in the working class, kin are fundamental when the family confronts a disaster or is modified by divorce or death.

Parents in the upwardly mobile middle class anticipate that their children will sustain the values that they have acquired during childhood and adolescence. One of the primary expectations of both parents is that their children will attend college and obtain secure professional positions. Essentially, African American middle-class families are characterized by the following:

▲ A sufficient family income.

▲ Conformity to American norms of morality.

▲ The close supervision of children.

▲ The dual employment of husband and wife.

▲ At least one spouse with a college education.

▲ A belief in upward mobility.

▲ A close attachment to and involvement with their children's goals and lives.

▲ The expectation that children will look to their parents as role models. (Wilkinson, 1984)

The Established Upper Class

The number of upper-class African American families is small but growing. This group has different family structures, values, behaviors, and cultures than those of the poor and working classes. Removed from the inner cities of urban communities, upper-class families live in integrated suburban neighborhoods, and the mothers may or may not be employed. A great deal of the wives' energies are applied in the home—maintaining the house, setting standards for family behavior, and supporting their husbands' efforts outside the home (Wilkinson, 1990). Children, who are virtually always planned for, are the foundation of family life and its genealogical continuity.

Dual-career marriages are also frequent in the upper class. While egalitarianism is an expectation in spousal relationships, child rearing is a key dimension of the mother's role. Like the working and middle classes, women tend to have principal authority in this domain. As children grow up and leave the home, if the mother is not employed, she is likely to be affiliated with social clubs and civic and voluntary associations. Women may serve on corporate boards of directors, and the majority have earned professional degrees. Their children often attend quality private schools that usually have few African Americans.

Like their European American counterparts, upper-middle and upper-class African American women are college-educated and have fewer children at a somewhat later stage in the life cycle than women in the non-poor working and lower-middle classes. Also, similar to upper-class White families, upper-class African American families may consist of three or more children. Whatever the family composition, rules are strictly outlined, and children are ordinarily well-behaved.

Within the context of particular customs and parenting behaviors, mothers and fathers in upper-class homes are an integral part of the lives of their grandchildren. Family members act to sustain long-standing traditions. As the family life cycle progresses, parents rely on their college-educated children for advice, especially if they are doctors, lawyers, or college professors (Beeler, 1988). Caring for elderly parents, when possible, is not uncommon in the upper-middle and upper classes.

Upper-middle and upper-class African American families, headed by fathers who are lawyers, physicians, owners of real estate, high-level administrators, publishers, or corporate executives, have a legacy in this small but notable socioeconomic level. In 1968, when his classic study *Black Families in White America* was published, Billingsley noted that the "new upper class" families contrasted with those in the established upper class. The established upper class was

> much more likely to be highly educated for the professions, to have reached the peak of their fame at older ages than the new upper classmen, more likely to be light in complexion, and to have grown up in nuclear families with strong fathers. (Billingsley, 1968, pp. 129–130)

Generational cohesiveness in the upper-middle and upper classes is demonstrated in enduring values, a belief in higher education, exceptional parental role-modeling behaviors, and children's ambitions. Kinship bonds are essential. Siblings and relatives—aunts, uncles, and cousins—are always a part of family rituals and ceremonies such as births, holidays, graduations, and marriages. The extended family, a meaningful support network in times of sickness and death, provides a legacy that pervades African American culture and is one of its cardinal strengths.

Upper-middle- and upper-class African American women are also integral contributors to service organizations and to their sororities, churches, and communities. Their civic commitments frequently emanate from the social contacts of their husbands. However, appointments to boards of directors and local and national committees may also be the result of their own achievements.

Upper-class families reside in the best homes in suburban neighborhoods or rural-urban fringe areas (Randolph, 1992; Wilkinson, 1990). Like stable and well-educated middle-class families, they are viewed as members of an elite.

In the late 1940s, African American social scientists documented the convictions, viewpoints, and customs of African American families in the upper socioeconomic levels (Drake & Cayton, 1945; Frazier, 1948). Several of their findings are relevant in the 1990s. As early as the post–World War II years, family heritage and property ownership empowered African American couples and their children to imitate lifestyles that coincided with those of a "wealthy leisure class." Using ethnographic approaches and oral histories, the sociologists found that upper-class African American families accepted the norm of sharing in decision making. Despite the tendency of wives not to work, they still assumed a fundamental participatory role in family decisions. Today, even if the wife is financially dependent on the husband, she is a significant contributor in determining how family income is distributed, how the household is to be organized, and how the children are to be raised (Wilkinson, 1984).

Intimate relationships in African American upper-middle- and upper-class families are based on gender-role specificity, conservative attitudes toward premarital sex, and a strong belief in the value of monogamous relationships. Other characteristics of this socioeconomic group are:

▲ Inherited wealth or ample financial security.

▲ Home ownership, typically in a racially integrated suburban neighborhood.

▲ A history of intergenerational family stability.

▲ A background with both spouses having been born in the middle or upper class.

▲ A premium placed on organizational memberships.

This small stratum of the African American population shares the manners and lifestyle of the wealthy White population. If wives are employed, they occupy high-status jobs as doctors, lawyers, and teachers (Wilkinson, 1984). In the upper-middle and upper classes, mothers have the education to help their children and grandchildren with schoolwork and the free time to participate in community activities.

Family Strengths and Challenges

The traditional values and customs of African American families have produced a solid foundation for generating the strength they need to face economic and other external challenges. In working-, middle-, and upper-class families, grandparents and older extended family members are especially conscientious about maintaining family continuity. Changes in family form and in spousal and parenting roles are directly related to economic and sociodemographic processes. In addition, national displacements after slavery and events during the post–Civil Rights era have created patterns of exclusion in employment. Likewise, normative changes, such as transformed conceptions of gender roles and societal modifications in behavioral standards, have permeated the African American family. Because racial prejudice remains systemic, African Americans invariably face discrimination in both the social sphere and the workplace (Blauner, 1972; Cade, 1970; King, 1988; Wilson, 1978).

The racial and socioeconomic history of African Americans is reflected in images of them in folklore and cultural artifacts. For transplanted Africans, slavery and later economic subordination in the United States created disequilibrium in previously wholesome family lives. The European portrait of a matriarchy was in essence an outcome of the historical willingness of slaveholders to free African women before men. While serving as a pragmatic adaptation to subjugation, the chronic unemployment of men, job discrimination, and restricted economic opportunities for husbands and fathers, the growth of female-headed households has embellished this notion. Biased portrayals of African American men and women between the nineteenth and mid-twentieth centuries have been a main feature of national racial socialization (Jordan, 1968; Wilkinson & Taylor, 1977). The imposed and actual family roles of African American mothers have been linked to a domestic "Mammy" figure that became embedded in American fiction and even in children's toys, games, and dolls up to the late twentieth century (Wilkinson, 1987a).

In the United States, the family remains the central nourishing, supportive, and economic unit in the lives of African Americans. While their families are identified with a history in which the mother has been a pivotal figure, correlations between matriarchy and socioeconomic status vary. Aside from the disparities and escalating problems associated with poverty, mothers and fathers, as well as extended kin, have fixed roles in family organization. What is not often documented in the literature is that although the family is changing in the larger culture, it is still the most fundamental institution in African American life.

African Americans have faced economic and political challenges with extraordinary strength and adaptability (Billingsley, 1981; Blackwell, 1991). For example, regardless of their income and educational achievement, parents maintain high goals for their children. However, although more frequent among families of African descent, the legacy of poverty in all ethnic groups tends to be intergenerational, thereby contradicting the underlying American ethos of equal opportunity (Billingsley, 1981; Blauner, 1972; Brewer, 1988; Wilkinson, 1995).

Finally, although single-parent households and dual-career families have increased, the nuclear family, with reinforcing kinship bonding, has lasted. Strong families have empowered Americans of African ancestry to survive slavery, Jim Crowism, and pervasive discrimination in education, housing, employment, and health care for centuries. Through family nurturing, consistent values, beliefs, customs, and legends, African Americans have met and coped with innumerable obstacles. Coping strategies have included the involvement of grandmothers and grandfathers in the life of the family, emotional and economic protection, maintaining family loyalty, parent-child solidarity, kinship exchange in times of need, collective identification with significant symbols, regular rites of passage, and filial responsibility. While the interconnections between family and work roles created tension in the past, the sense of unity and shared pride among immediate and extended family members has enabled African American families to endure.

Personal Interview

Alice (not her real name) is an upper-middle-to upper-class, highly intelligent woman of African descent in her fifties in a dual-career marriage. Having a master's degree in English, she is a public school teacher. Her husband is a key administrator in public education and a leading member of the community. Alice and her husband live in a spacious three-story home in an integrated suburban neighborhood. Along with one of their sons and his family, they are among the few African Americans in the area. Alice and her husband have two married sons and four grandchildren. Their older son has a medical degree, and the younger one has a bachelor's degree in social work. Their daughters-in-law also have college degrees. Each son has two children.

When I first telephoned Alice, I asked if she were busy, and if so, when I should call back.

Alice: I am helping my 10-year-old grandson with his homework. He is a fifth-grader and is using posterboard for a school project. I often help my grandchildren with their work and pick up my 9-year-old granddaughter from school.

In their formative years, who was primarily responsible for child rearing, and who set the rules for the children's behavior?

Alice: I did. I gave orders for the behaviors of children. My sons knew that I was the mother and could get away with a lot. However, I never had any trouble with my children. Their father was a strong male role model in the family. Now, both sons are strong fathers and husbands.

Briefly, tell me about your sons' gender-role socialization and mate selection.

Alice: They started dating about age 15 or 16. I was concerned about some of the girls at the teenage stage. But I am very satisfied with the mates they have chosen.

Describe family strengths and parent-child relationships in your family.

Alice: I feel that my children have been my friends. We take our vacations together. We enjoy one another. We go to Las Vegas together—both sons and their wives. I have a strong relationship with my sisters.

I would like to ask about the local school system as it relates to the family. For example, what are some of the challenges that your children face in the public school system?

Alice: Basically the challenges have involved teachers dealing with (my) middle-class grandchildren. My 9-year-old granddaughter's teacher was more concerned about how she looked and what she wore than with teaching her anything. When my son would go to the school to discuss the matter, the teacher would never recognize him. Also, my grandson was never recognized. He was never Student of the Month, nor was his birthday recognized (like that of the other children). He is a middle-class Black child. Most of the others in his class were and are in public housing.

How do you explain this unfair and unequal treatment of middle- and upper-middle-class African American children?

Alice: This is a prejudiced school system. Some of the teachers have just "arrived" themselves, and they are threatened by middle-class Black kids.

Since you are very fair and it is virtually impossible to know your ethnicity, have you encountered problems related to this? And if so, have they affected the family in any way?

Alice: I have listened to people saying things. They didn't know I was Black. I let them know that I am African American. When the family is nurturing, you can deal with those kinds of things.

Questions for Discussion

1. Why and how was the immigration experience for African Americans different from that of all other ethnic families in the United States? How does it compare to the American Indian experience?

2. Describe how African American families have been influenced by traditional West African culture.

3. How did slavery and forced transfer to a new country affect the African American family over the generations?

4. Describe the meaning of the extended family and kinship relationships as strengths of African American families.

5. Why is socioeconomic status such an important variable in the examination and analysis of African American family structure, composition, and functioning?

6. What are the historical and cultural differences among African American families according to socioeconomic status, and how do these enable them to meet challenges?

7. What comparisons can be made between the African American family and the American Indian family regarding acculturation and assimilation?

8. What underlies the challenges many African American families face? How does this compare to your family's challenges? How does it compare to the challenges of the American Indian family? What accounts for the similarities and differences between these two groups?

Suggested Resources

Readings

African Americans: Voices of triumph: Perseverance (Vol. 1). (1993). New York: Time-Life Books.

An American dilemma revisited (1995, Winter). *Daedalus, 124* (entire issue).

Hine, D. C. (Ed.). (1993). *Black women in America: An historical encyclopedia* (Vol. 1). New York: Carlson.

Hughes, L., Meltzer, M., & Lincoln, C. E. (1983). *A pictorial history of Black Americans.* New York: Crown.

Lee, G. (1991). *Inspiring African Americans: Black history makers in the United States, 1750–1984.* Chapel Hill, NC: McFarland.

Low, W. A., & Clift, V. A. (Eds.). (1981). *Encyclopedia of Black America.* New York: Da Capo Press.

Phelps, S. (Ed.). (1995). *Who's who among Black Americans.* Detroit: Gale Research.

Videos

Donahue, P. (Director). (1990). *Daughters of the Black revolution.* (Available from Films for the Humanities, P.O. Box 2053, Princeton, NJ 08543)

Public Broadcasting Services (Producer). (1992). *W. E. B. DuBois of Great Barrington.* (Available from Videofinders, 425 E. Colorado Street, Suite 10B, Glendale, CA 91205)

Public Broadcasting Services (Producer), & Frost, D. (Director). (1996). *General Colin Powell: What I have learned.* (Available from Videofinders, 425 E. Colorado Street, Suite 10B, Glendale, CA 91205).

References

African Americans: Voices of triumph: Perseverance (Vol. 1). (1993). New York: Time-Life Books.

Allen, S. D. (1995). More on the free Black population of the southern Appalachian mountains: Speculations on the North African connection. *Journal of Black Studies, 25,* 651–672.

Allen, W. (1978). The search for applicable theories of Black family life. *Journal of Marriage and the Family, 40,* 117–129.

Almquist, E. M. (1975). Untangling the effects of race and sex: The disadvantaged status of Black women. *Social Science Quarterly, 56,* 129–142.

Andrews, D. (1984). The African Methodists of Philadelphia, 1794–1802. *The Pennsylvania Magazine of History and Biography, 108,* 471–486.

Asante, M. K., & Mattson, M. T. (1991). *The historical and cultural atlas of African Americans.* New York: Macmillan.

Beal, F. (1970). Double jeopardy: To be Black and female. In T. Cade (Ed.), *The Black woman: An anthology* (pp. 90–100). New York: New American Library.

Beeler, J. (1988, September 8). Exhibit portrays early Black doctors. *The Lexington-Herald Leader,* p. B2.

Bell, D. (1974). Why participation rates of Black and White wives differ. *Journal of Human Resources, 9,* 465–479.

Bennett, L. (1984). *Before the Mayflower: A history of Black America.* New York: Penguin.

Bergman, P., & Bergman, M. (1969). *The chronological history of the Negro in America.* New York: Harper & Row Publishers.

Billingsley, A. (1968). *Black families in White America.* Englewood Cliffs, NJ: Prentice-Hall.

Billingsley, A. (1969). Family functioning in the low-income Black community. *Social Casework, 50,* 563–572.

Billingsley, A. (1981). Black families in White America: A challenge for the 80's. *Black Family, 1,* 14–18, 22–23.

Billingsley, A. (1992). *Climbing Jacob's ladder: The enduring legacy of African American families.* New York: Simon & Schuster.

Billingsley, A., & Greene, M. (1974). Family life among the free Black population in the 18th century. *Journal of Social and Behavioral Science, 20,* 1–17.

Blackwell, J. E. (1991). The Black family in American society. In James Blackwell (Ed.), *The Black community: Diversity and unity* (pp. 81–116). New York: HarperCollins.

Blassingame, J. (1979). *The slave community: Plantation life in the Antebellum South.* New York: Oxford University Press.

Blauner, R. (1972). *Racial oppression in America.* New York: Harper & Row.

Brewer, R. (1988). Black women in poverty: Some comments on female-headed families. *Signs, 13,* 331–339.

Brodie, F. M. (1974). *Thomas Jefferson: An intimate history.* New York: Norton.

Bryant, W. C. (1971). Discrimination against women in general: Black southern women in particular. *Civil Rights Digest, 4,* 10–11.

Cade, T. (1970). *The Black women. An anthology.* New York: New American Library.

Comer, J. P., & Poussaint, A. (1975). Black child care: How to bring up a healthy Black child in America. New York: Simon & Schuster.

Davis, A. (1971). Reflections on Black women's role in the community of slaves. *The Black Scholar, 3,* 2–15.

Davis, A. (1981). *Women, race and class.* New York: Random House.

Delany, S. L., & Delany, A. (1993). *Having our say: The Delany sisters' first 100 Years.* New York: Dell.

Dill, B. T. (1979). The dialectics of Black womanhood. *Signs, 4,* 543–555.

Douglass, F. (1986). *Narrative of the life of Frederick Douglass, an American slave.* New York: Penguin. (Original work published 1845)

Downs, J. (1975). Black/White dating. In D. Wilkinson (Ed.), *Black male/White female: Perspectives on interracial marriage and courtship* (pp. 159–170). Morristown, NJ: General Learning Press.

Drake, S. C., & Cayton, H. R. (1945). *Black metropolis.* New York: Harcourt, Brace.

Fitchett, E. H. (1941). The origins and growth of the free Negro population of Charleston, South Carolina. *Journal of Negro History, 26,* 421–437.

Frazier, E. F. (1948). *The Negro family in the United States.* New York: Citadel Press.

Genovese, E. D., & Roll, J. (1974). *The world the slaves made.* New York: Pantheon.

Giles, D. (1994). Summer resorts: Black resort towns are enjoying a renaissance thanks to buppies and their families. *Black Enterprise, 25,* 90–91.

Graham, P. N. (1961). Thomas Jefferson and Sally Hemmings. *Journal of Negro History, 44,* 89–103.

Gutman, H. (1976). *The Black family in slavery and freedom, 1750–1925.* New York: Pantheon.

Hale, J. (1977). The woman's role: The strength of Black families. *First World, 1,* 28–30.

Haley, A. (1976). *Roots: The saga of an American family.* New York: Doubleday.

Hatchett, D. (1995). The Black flight to the "burbs." *The Crisis, 102,* 30–33.

Hill, R. (1972). *The strengths of Black families.* New York: Emerson Hall.

Hill-Lubin, M. A. (1991). The African American grandmother in autobiographical works by Frederick Douglass, Langston Hughes, and Maya Angelou. *International Journal of Aging and Human Development, 33,* 173–185.

Hine, D., & Wittenstein, K. (1981). Female slave resistance: The economics of sex. In F. C. Steady (Ed.), *The Black woman cross-culturally* (pp. 289–300). Cambridge, MA: Schenkman.

Jordan, W. (1968). *White over Black: American attitudes toward the Negro, 1550–1812*. Chapel Hill: University of North Carolina Press.

Kane, P., & Wilkinson, D. (1974). Survival strategies: Black women in *Ollie Miss* and *Cotton Comes to Harlem*. *Critique: Studies in Modern Fiction, 16*, 101–109.

King, D. (1988). Multiple jeopardies, multiple consciousness: The context of a Black feminist ideology. *Signs: Journal of Women in Culture and Society, 14*, 42–72.

King, M. C. (1973). The politics of sexual stereotypes. *Black Scholar, 5*, 12–23.

Ladner, J. (1971). *Tomorrow's tomorrow: The Black woman*. New York: Doubleday.

Landry, B. (1987). *The new Black middle class*. Berkeley: University of California Press.

Lyons, D. C. (1993). Mr. Moms: Black men shatter stereotypes by taking on dual roles. *Ebony, 48*, 102, 104, 106.

Mack, D. (1971). Where the Black matriarchy theorists went wrong. *Psychology Today, 25*, 86–87.

Marks, C. (1993). The bone and sinew of the race: Black women, domestic service and labor migration. *Marriage and Family Review, 19*, 149–163.

Martin, E. P., & Martin, J. M. (1978). *The Black extended family*. Chicago: University of Chicago Press.

Massaquoi, H. J. (1993). The Black family nobody knows. *Ebony, 48*, 28–31.

McAdoo, H. (1975). The extended family. *Journal of Afro-American Issues, 3*, 291–296.

McAdoo, H. (1978). Factors related to stability in upwardly mobile Black families. *Journal of Marriage and the Family, 40*, 761–776.

McAdoo, H. (Ed.). (1980). *Black families*. Newbury Park, CA: Sage.

McAdoo, H. (Ed.). (1993). *Family ethnicity: Strength in diversity*. Newbury Park, CA: Sage.

Nobles, W. (1978). Toward an empirical and theoretical framework for defining Black families. *Journal of Marriage and the Family, 40*, 679–688.

Randolph, L. B. (1992). Browning the suburbs. *Ebony, 47*, 36–39.

Rutledge, E. (1980). Marital interaction goals of Black women: Strengths and effects. In L. F. Rodgers-Rose (Ed.), *The Black woman* (pp. 145–159). Newbury Park, CA: Sage.

Simms, M. (1985). Black women who head families: An economic struggle. *Review of Black Political Economy, 14*, 141–152.

Simms, M. (1991). Wanted: A few good men. *Black Enterprise, 21*, 41.

Smith, E. D. (1988). *Climbing Jacob's ladder: The rise of Black churches in eastern American cities, 1740–1877*. Washington, DC: Smithsonian Institution Press.

Staples, R. (1971). *The Black family: Essays and studies*. Belmont, CA: Wadsworth.

Staples, R. (1982). *Black masculinity: The Black male's role in American society*. San Francisco: Black Scholar Press.

Still, W. (1970). *The underground railroad*. Chicago: Johnson Publishing Company. (Original work published 1871)

Taylor, R. J., Chatters, L. M., & Jackson, L. S. (1993). A profile of familial relations among three generations of Black families. *Family Relations, 42,* 332–341.

Thomas, G. C. (1977). *Casey County, Kentucky: 1806–1977*. Casey County, KY: Bicentennial Heritage Corporation.

U.S. Bureau of the Census. (1978). The social and economic status of the Black population in the United States: An historical view, 1700–1978. *Current population reports*. Special Studies, Series P-23, No. 80.

U.S. Bureau of the Census. (1995). *Statistical abstract of the United States* (11th ed.). Washington, DC: U.S. Government Printing Office.

Wallace, P., Datcher, A., & Malveaux, L. (1980). *Black women in the labor force*. Cambridge, MA: MIT Press.

Watkins, W. M. (1939). *The men, women, events, institutions and lore of Casey County, Kentucky*. Louisville, KY: Standard Printing.

Wiese, A. (1993). Places of our own: Suburban Black towns before 1960. *Journal of Urban History, 19,* 30–54.

Wilkinson, D. (1978a). The Black family, past and present: A review essay. *Journal of Marriage and the Family, 40,* 829–835.

Wilkinson, D. (1978b). Toward a positive frame of reference for analysis of Black families: A selected bibliography. *Journal of Marriage and the Family, 40,* 707–708.

Wilkinson, D. (1984). Afro-American women and their families. *Marriage and Family Review, 7,* 125–142.

Wilkinson, D. (1987a). The Doll exhibit: A psycho-cultural analysis of Black female role stereotypes. *Journal of Popular Culture, 21,* 19–29.

Wilkinson, D. (1987b). Traditional medicine in American families. *Marriage and Family Review, 11,* 65–76.

Wilkinson, D. (1990). Afro-Americans in the corporation: An assessment of the impact on the family. In R. Hanks and M. Sussman (Eds.), *Corporations, businesses and families* (pp. 115–129). New York: Haworth Press.

Wilkinson, D. (1991). The segmented labor market and African American women, 1890–1960: A social history interpretation. *Race and Ethnic Relations, 6,* 85–104.

Wilkinson, D. (1995). Gender and social inequality: The prevailing significance of race. *Daedalus, 124,* 167–178.

Wilkinson, D., & Taylor, R. (Eds.). (1977). *The Black male: Perspectives on his status in contemporary society.* Chicago: Nelson-Hall.

Wilson, W. J. (1978). *The declining significance of race.* Chicago: University of Chicago Press.

Yolanda M. Sanchez

4

Families of Mexican Origin

Historical and Cultural Background

Mexicans and individuals of Mexican origin, commonly referred to as Mexican Americans, are distinguished from other Hispanics by their culture's long-established roots and presence in the United States, dating back to the early 1600s. The Hispanic population, as a whole, has experienced tremendous growth, and it is expected to become the largest ethnic group in the United States by the year 2020. Mexicans and individuals of Mexican origin now account for 62% of the entire Hispanic population, and it will continue to grow (Ortiz, 1994). Furthermore, this growth will be fueled by a continuous flow of migrants from Mexico to the United States, a trend that will continue to contribute a unique cultural dynamism to the Mexican American population (Baca-Zinn, 1994d).

Historically, researchers have focused on **Hispanics**, a word used by the U.S. government to categorize a large homogeneous group that includes people of Spanish or Latin American origin or background. In this chapter, "Mexican American" and "Mexican origin" are used interchangeably to refer to groups of people who have a Mexican or Mexican American heritage. There are many subgroups of Hispanics, and researchers have often failed to focus on differences in values, beliefs, behaviors, and patterns of interaction among the various subgroups. This misperception has fostered stereotypes that, until recently, have gone unchallenged. Current studies seek to move away from these stereotypes toward a deeper understanding of the complex interactions that take place within Mexican and Mexican American families.

When we consider Mexican American culture, it is important to distinguish between sociocultural patterns inherited from the Mexican past and those that are currently evolving in the United States. Many of the interactions within Mexican and Mexican American families have been viewed by researchers as maladaptive; however, Hayes-Bautista (1989), in a study of Mexican immigrants in the Los Angeles area, argues that these immigrants often arrive in the United States with strong families. Initially, they demonstrate high rates of family formation and labor-force participation, and low levels of dependency on welfare. As Mexican American families grapple with the same social and economic conditions that affect all families and that are compounded by adjustment to life in the United States, these positive family characteristics appear to weaken over time and in successive generations. Baca-Zinn (1994a) argues that these shifts in lifestyle reflect the Mexican American family's ability to adapt to changing circumstances and, as such, should be viewed as strengths.

Mexicans and Mexican Americans are often credited with enjoying large extended family and close kinship ties. **Familialism**—a collective term for a strong and persistent family orientation, widespread and highly integrated extended kinship systems, and a consistent preference for relying on the extended family for support as the primary means of coping with emotional stress—is a defining characteristic of Mexican-origin families (Baca-Zinn, 1994c; Ramirez & Arce, 1980).

Initially, familialism was believed to be a cultural pattern handed down through the generations; however, research supports the perspective that it was, in part, a response to historical conditions of economic deprivation (Alvirez & Bean, 1976). In one study, Hoppe and Heller (1975) found that among lower-class Mexican Americans, familialism is a positive form of social organization that facilitates adaptation to marginal existence. Furthermore, the use of kinship networks in migration to the United States has been found in studies by Macklin (1976) and Wells (1976), demonstrating how Mexicans use a process of **chain migration** in which kin help each other find housing and employment. The extent to which familialism is maintained in Mexican American and Mexican-origin families is an area that needs further investigation.

In addition to the family and home, religion has always been central to individuals of Mexican origin. Each subgroup of Hispanics has a distinct form of worship and a belief system reflecting the unique history and presence of the church in the homeland. However, **religiosity**, or extreme religiousness, is often formed throughout the processes of assimilation and adaptation of private religious practices. Religious instruction is usually the responsibility of the women in the family.

The overwhelming majority of Mexican and Mexican-origin individuals are Catholic. For many of these families, Catholicism is rooted in folk beliefs and practices, as evidenced by the use of Spanish herbal remedies and faith healing performed by folk healers, curers, or *curanderos(ras)*. These methods combine folk religious beliefs with a knowledge of medicinal herbs to restore physical and mental health (Klor de Alva, 1988).

Curanderos, or folk healers, use the forces of good and evil to remedy just about any human ailment. Women often perpetuate the healing tradition. They can cure a child of *ojo* (the effects of someone's covetousness) or *susto* (fear) and can help with other ailments. One cannot merely decide to become a *curandero* or *curandera*, and it is not like a recipe one can learn. Rather, one must be born into a family of healers and at a very early age begin the process of mentoring by a predecessor. The relationship enables the novice to be taught through many informal experiences. In this relationship, the *curandero(ra)* learns the secrets of the herbs and the balance that exists in the natural order of things. All *curanderos(ras)* work their healing differently from one another, but they share the faith that a greater power is working through them. A *curandero(ra)* who summons evil forces is technically a *brujo* or *bruja* (witch), using his or her tools to bring harm to others. Although this form of healing was once very prevalent among Mexican American families, **curanderismo** is an art that for a period of time all but disappeared. But with today's re-emergence of natural and herbal remedies, there is a renewed interest in *curanderismo*.

Changes have also occurred in formalized religion. Since the beginning of this century, Protestant sectors have been far more active at proselytizing to Hispanics, particularly Puerto Rican Americans and Mexican Americans. The Protestant congregation has been much more seriously involved than the Catholic Church in social-action projects that support these sectors of the population. These efforts have paid off, as reflected by the substantial numbers of Puerto Rican Americans and Mexican Americans who have converted from Catholicism.

A Mexican presence is definitely maintained by individuals of Mexican origin in the United States, and cultural values have influenced their experience. Uncertainty remains, however, about how these cultural values will be influenced over the course of the next decade, as Mexican immigration to the United States increases.

The Immigration Experience

Mexican Americans are distinguished from other Hispanics by their appearance long before other Hispanics in North America. Although large numbers of Mexicans arrived in the United States after World War II, the immigration experiences of Mexicans have ranged from those who were original settlers in the Southwest to those who have migrated and produced subsequent generations of U.S.-born individuals. In spite of the extended history of legal immigration to the United States, entry has often been a result of conquest and subordination (Bean & Tienda, 1988).

Historically, the United States has welcomed Mexicans when there has been a need for cheap labor. Similarly, Mexicans have often fled their country during periods of unrest. Thus, the influx of many Mexicans to this country can be traced to periods of economic prosperity in the United States, as well as to civil and economic disturbances in Mexico. The period of the early 1900s best reflects this interrelatedness, especially during the Mexican Revolution of 1910 when the United States was experiencing great development and prosperity. Because of the United States' need for cheap labor, the estimated 1 million Mexicans who fled Mexico were able to obtain employment in agricultural, industrial, and railroad-related fields.

The Mexican Revolution, however, had an impact on how Mexican immigrants were viewed by Americans. Americans resented and feared the revolution. Many U.S. border towns were subject to raids by Mexicans attempting to secure supplies. Thus, Mexicans were perceived as undisciplined and violent, and many Americans could not comprehend the brutalities of war. By the end of the revolution in the 1920s, Anglo-American opinion of Mexicans was lower than before the revolution. Unfortunately, many of these emotions were taken out on Mexicans living in the United States.

During the 1920s, economic expansion in the United States continued. Many of the immigrants who came were from peasant or agricultural villages in Mexico, and their labor was increasingly used in urban manufacturing sites. The majority who came to the cities were seeking work and intended to return to their homeland, as were most of the Mexicans migrating during this period.

The 1930s were particularly important for Mexican Americans. During this period, the United States was grappling with the Great Depression. As jobs became scarce and the struggle for resources increased, the U.S. government halted immigration from Mexico. It also engaged in massive deportations of **illegal aliens**—Mexicans or anyone who appeared to be "illegal Mexican." Without an influx of Mexicans and Mexican culture to the United States, the stage was set for a cultural shift that would set the course of Mexican American adaptation. Thus, a generation of people of Mexican origin was greatly influenced by Anglo culture. This trend continued well into the 1940s. During World War II, many Mexican Americans responded enthusiastically to the U.S. wartime effort and volunteered for service in the various branches of the armed forces, thereby seeking to become part of American society.

In spite of the assimilation of many Mexican Americans, Mexican culture and influence did not subside entirely. During the 1940s, primarily because of the *Bracero* Program, immigration and influence from Mexico were revived. During this time, the U.S. government sent labor agents to Mexico to recruit workers to meet the needs prompted by wartime. The *braceros*, or manual laborers, inspired other Mexicans to migrate to the United States. Many worked in agriculture and railroad camps until the program subsided in 1965.

The postwar period of the 1950s was again a time of turmoil for people of Mexican origin. Many had assimilated and were participating in activities that contributed to American society, yet the United States once again experienced a recession and engaged in additional deportation of illegal aliens. The basis of these deportations was that the U.S. government could not withstand the additional strain on federal sources of support to illegal aliens, and that funds should be prioritized for American citizens (Acosta-Belen, 1988).

Adaptation, and the degree of difficulty experienced by Mexican immigrants to the United States, varied and often depended on their economic condition when they crossed the border. Many Mexican men were forced to seek work away from their wives and children because of meager resources. They could usually obtain employment in mining camps and railroad gangs, work that resulted in long periods of living apart from the family. This was also true of migrant workers, who were primarily male. Until the incorporation of the family system in migrant labor, men often resided apart from their wives and children during the course of seasonal work.

The processes of migration and settlement are difficult, yet the family provided social mechanisms that eased the transition. Mexican-origin families adapted by using models and cultural resources available to them, which often reinforced strongly supportive extended kinship structures. This was a change from the family form common in the early nineteenth century. Prior to that time, Mexican-origin families had been strongly gendered, with men acting as heads of the household and making the important decisions. However, as men were able to obtain only minimal employment and were forced to leave their families for periods of time, the role of women in the family was altered. Many women were forced into the labor force, and domestic and child-care responsibilities they had traditionally provided were now taken over by extended kin. In addition, sharing the resources of time, assistance, and money became imperative to the survival of the family.

Mexican-origin immigrants have surely prospered from the immigration experience; however, the United States has also prospered from the immigration of Mexicans. Mexican-origin immigrants and Mexican Americans have often been portrayed as uneducated, unskilled, or unmotivated. However, Buriel and Vasques (1984) contend that the Mexican immigrant is often an individual who tends to be more educated and more motivated than those who choose not to migrate; often, then, the immigrant represents a loss to Mexico and a gain for the United States. This is a perspective that has not received much recognition because it does not support the belief that the self-directed choices of Mexican immigrants have contributed to their becoming prime candidates for welfare and other entitlement programs. Issues related to poverty and deprivation are often viewed as being related to the Mexican culture. If responsibility for these problems can be attributed to the inadequacies of the Mexican-origin immigrant, such an explanation absolves mainstream America of any responsibility for either creating or addressing them.

This negative perspective has reinforced the thrust toward assimilating individuals of Mexican origin (Gonzales, 1980). Unfortunately, assimilation can also undermine their extended support system, including the family. Families are encouraged—and often forced—to deviate from patterns of support that have ensured their mutual dependency and survival. Furthermore, many feel that such traits are undesirable.

Much of this story has been omitted from historical documentation, and the hostile realities many Mexican immigrants and people of Mexican origin have encountered are not even acknowledged, much less understood. The misconceptions that have permeated the literature have led to unfair negative sentiment and a lack of compassion toward people of Mexican origin in the United States. Unless we make an effort to understand this historical perspective, prejudice and hostility will continue.

For many Mexicans and Mexican Americans, the immigration experience has resulted in an assault on their culture and family lives. Being conquered and exploited, while also facing discrimination, has led to the maintenance of many homeland survival strategies and the development of new adaptive measures (Klor de Alva, 1988).

Traditional and Emerging Family Systems

The Hispanic family is organized around a group of primary institutions that are common to all Hispanic groups in the United States, but the concept of family is expressed in many different ways. Despite the literature and the perpetuation of stereotypes, variations among the Hispanic subgroups are substantial (Klor de Alva, 1988). Individuals of Mexican origin tend to reflect more traditional beliefs and behaviors.

Household Size and Composition

The concept of family refers to more than just the nuclear family. While it often consists of a household of husband, wife, and children, people of Mexican origin are more likely to live in an extended family context, which includes parents, grandparents, brothers and sisters, cousins, and other blood relatives—commonly referred to as *la familia*, the greater family. Although this type of extended familial network has been a mainstay of the Mexican-origin family, it is in a process of change that may be related to migration patterns. In the past, Mexican immigrants migrated toward rural settings; however, there has been a notable change from rural concentration toward urban migration. Approximately 88% of Mexican immigrants to the United States are now migrating to urban areas. The impact of this relatively new phenomenon remains unclear, particularly because of **patriarchy** and **matriarchy** among Mexican-origin families. Undoubtedly there will be an impact on family dynamics, as well as changes in generational, residential, employment, and socioeconomic status patterns (Baca-Zinn, 1994c).

The average household size of Mexican American families tends to be large: 4.1 individuals, compared to 3.8 for all Hispanics and 3.1 for non-Hispanics (U.S. Bureau of the Census, 1991). High birth rates characterize this population; on average, they are about 60% higher than in the rest of the U.S. population. Although fertility rates for women of Mexican origin have declined by 6% for 2 consecutive years, the total birth rate for the same group continues to be substantially higher than that for other ethnic groups. The birth rate for women of Mexican origin between ages 15 and 44 is 111.8 births per 1000 women (Centers for Disease Control and Prevention, 1995).

This pattern of high fertility has often been said to relate to socioeconomic status, low levels of education, a strong religious affiliation with Catholicism, and a strong belief in consanguineal relationships. Because of the high birth rate, more families of Mexican origin have children living at home (52%) than do other U.S. families (41%) (Davis, Haub, & Willette, 1988).

The Socialization of Children

The Mexican-origin home is usually child-centered when children are young, yet the role of children is based on the belief that they should "be seen and not heard." Although both parents tend to be permissive, boys and girls are raised very differently in Mexican American families. Boys are granted far more liberty, and loud, aggressive behavior is generally tolerated. The male child is often overindulged and accorded greater status than the female. Young girls are expected to be demure and feminine, and girls are usually taught feminine roles, just as boys are taught masculine roles. Playmates are often segregated by gender, rather than by age, particularly as they grow older.

Adolescence marks differences in behavior patterns between boys and girls (Locke, 1992). The adolescent male is given much more freedom, and his decisions and actions are seldom questioned. His activities are seldom restricted and are not closely monitored. He is free to date and pursue intimate relationships, and he is expected to take on the role of the protector for his sisters.

Activities for girls are often restricted and closely monitored. They are expected to remain much closer to home. Regardless of age, but particularly during adolescence, girls are expected to be subservient to their older brothers. At this stage, a strong relationship with her mother is encouraged and is viewed as a means of preparing a girl for the role of wife and mother (Mirande, 1985). In families of Mexican origin, the *quinceanera*, or fifteenth birthday, marks the coming of age of a young girl. The *quinceanera* is celebrated by a mass or prayer service with a sermon, reminding the young girl of her future responsibilities.

Assimilation and acculturation have had an impact on socialization patterns. Whereas adolescent males still maintain greater degrees of independence, many adolescent females have challenged traditional gender roles and are exerting greater autonomy. However, the servile attitude of females remains present in many Mexican-origin families and is still encouraged and expected, regardless of the level of acculturation and assimilation.

As Mexican American children make the transition to adolescence, just like all teenagers, they may encounter difficulties with issues related to autonomy. Adolescence is a period during which individuals are attempting to assert their independence, and for many Mexican-origin adolescents, this is compounded by conflicts that arise between first and second generations.

When demands and desires accumulate and are in conflict with traditional expectations, teenagers have difficulty dealing with the competing influences in their lives. Adolescence is particularly problematic for children who are raised in homes with traditional cultural values. They often encounter a different set of values at school than at home. External expectations may be in direct opposition to traditional values, which reinforce that assimilation should be avoided altogether and that *la cultura* (the culture) should be maintained (Klor de Alva, 1988).

Skin tone and color can also affect the socialization process of a child or adolescent of Mexican origin. Montalvo (1992) reports a distinct difference between the experiences of light-skinned and dark-skinned individuals. Many of the light-skinned Mexican Americans he interviewed stated that they seldom considered the color of their skin or that of their peers. Furthermore, they did not feel that they were treated adversely because of their skin tone. They did, however, say that few, if any, of their dates or other Hispanic friends were dark-skinned. In contrast, most of the darker-skinned individuals of Mexican origin in Montalvo's research reported being acutely aware of their dark skin color and the role it played in their lives. They reported being treated adversely and felt it was a direct correlation to their dark skin tone. Many of their friends and dates were also darker-skinned and seldom interacted with their lighter-skinned peers.

Montalvo's research appears to support the view that assimilation pressures may cause Hispanic youths of light and moderate skin tone to minimize contact with their darker, more visibly ethnic peers. The response from darker-skinned peers is similar. Hispanic adolescents will often chide each other about acculturation and assimilation and will label each other with names such as "*piñon*" or "*biscochito*." These terms generally refer to the notion that someone is Mexican (or brown) on the outside and White on the inside because he or she embraces values and behaviors of the majority culture.

Intimate Relationships

Dating among Mexicans appears to be far less casual than it is in other Hispanic subgroups. Both old and young expect dating to precede marriage. Dating among individuals of Mexican origin also appears to be far less casual than dating among either European Americans or other Hispanics. Dating often involves meeting the family as well as interacting in social gatherings where there is an opportunity to converse with the person who is viewed as a potential family member. Interethnic dating is a critical indicator of the extent of assimilation and is less common among working-class Mexicans than among those in the middle class who do not reside in Hispanic neighborhoods.

Marriage is expected and is the norm for individuals of Mexican origin. They are more likely to be married than their counterparts in the general population, and they often marry younger than other Hispanics and non-Hispanics. The average marrying age for men is 22.8 years, and for women, 20.9 years. **Endogamy**, or marriage within the same ethnic group, is the norm. Thus, rates of **exogamy**, or **out-marriage**, in which Mexicans marry non-Mexicans, are low, although this pattern does vary and is often influenced by levels of assimilation. Currently, the percentage of women not married has increased modestly among Mexican-origin populations (Kane, 1993).

In traditional Mexican culture, the practice of using an intermediary to ask for a woman's hand in marriage was common. The intermediary presented the young man's marriage proposal to the young woman's parents, especially the father. When parents were considering the worthiness of the marriage partner for their daughter, greater emphasis was placed on the young man's moral character than on his economic status (Williams, 1990). Today, the practice of using intermediaries for marriage proposals has all but disappeared. Couples still seek permission to marry from the woman's family, but it is now the young man who ventures alone to inform the young woman's parents of the couple's desire to marry.

After a brief engagement, the wedding date is set. Couples are expected to marry in the church (generally Catholic) because a church ceremony is considered an essential foundation for marriage. Those who marry in the church typically have *padrinos* (advisors) who are the main sponsors of the bride and groom. *Padrinos* are chosen from the groom's or bride's family. It is expected that the *padrinos* will have been married in the Catholic Church, and that they will serve as advisors both before the wedding and after the ceremony. If the couple experiences marital difficulties, they contact the *padrinos*.

The actual marriage ceremony is often marked by the use of traditional religious symbols. These may include *arras*, 13 coins blessed by the priest during the ceremony, symbolizing that the husband will be the financial provider; *lazo*, a rosary placed around the bride and groom at a certain point during the ceremony, symbolizing the union of the two people into one; and *flores a La Virgin*, a bouquet of flowers placed at the Blessed Virgin Mother's feet in gratitude for protecting the young woman.

Weddings are generally small, although a few are large (over 300 people). The wedding ceremony usually has a generalized religious meaning, and festivities include a reception hosted at local community facilities with food, drink, and music. During the course of the reception or the dance is a period known as the *integrada*, or introduction. At this time the bride and groom kneel, and a song depicting significant people and events in their lives and the lives of their family is orchestrated. The *integrada* also marks the blessing of the couple by the parents of both the bride and the groom.

The relationship between husband and wife in Mexican-origin families has been rooted in stereotypes and misconceptions. Earlier writings were quite erroneous in stressing a lack of egalitarian behaviors between husbands and wives (Andrade, 1982; Baca-Zinn, 1994d; Chilman, 1993; Mirande, 1985). The stereotype of a passive female being subservient to a dominant male has permeated the literature. More recent studies, however, have shown egalitarian family patterns in the behavior of Mexican-origin families, with both wife and husband actively involved in household responsibilities, child rearing, and decision making.

Rebellion against the native culture is often expressed through sexual behavior. While sexual contact may be part of the process of selecting a mate, all Hispanic subgroups prohibit premarital sex, although men are granted more sexual freedom than women. In spite of cultural expectations, abstinence is often disregarded in practice. Furthermore, because sexuality is seldom acknowledged, conflicting cultural expectations create ambiguous situations that are particularly difficult for women. As a result, young Mexican-origin women may consent to various forms of sexual activity, such as oral and anal sex, avoiding vaginal penetration and thereby allowing them to maintain their virginal state.

Sexual activity prior to marriage, although prohibited, is common. High rates of pregnancy in the Mexican-origin teen population indicate that the onset of sexual activity comes at a relatively early age. Pregnancy among teenagers appears to be related to a denial that premarital sex is a reality: If an individual is not having sex, then there is not a need for contraception. The limited use of contraceptives may also be related to the teachings of the Catholic Church, which strongly forbids their use. Some evidence suggests, however, that individuals of Mexican origin are increasingly approving of and using contraceptives when they are available (Baca-Zinn, 1994c).

Perhaps the ultimate rebellion against native culture is the acknowledgment of homosexuality, when goes against two moral prohibitions: sexuality in general and homosexuality in particular. Homosexuality is viewed as somehow rendering the individual faulty, damaged, and unacceptable. Admitting homosexuality is equally unacceptable for males and females, and it is considered the ultimate violation of the family. Homosexuality is perceived to be extremely deviant—deviant being whatever is condemned by the community (Anzaldua, 1987).

Work Relationships and the Family

The income levels of Hispanic men and women in the early 1990s were lower than those of either African Americans or European Americans, and the situation is no different even in dual-earner families. The poverty rates for married Hispanics are triple those for European Americans. Poverty is a consideration for a majority of Hispanics, although among subgroups there are distinct differences. For example, family income is highest in Cuban American families and lowest in Mexican American families (Kane, 1993). A contributing factor may be the level of education: Cuban Americans are the most highly educated subgroup of Hispanics, while Mexican Americans attain the lowest level of education.

Another contributing factor can be traced back to the work history of people of Mexican origin. Many have tended to work in the economic sectors most vulnerable to cyclical employment, such as migrant work. A **migrant worker** is a person who is employed at a job temporarily or seasonally. Although not all migrant workers are farm workers, a large majority of migrant work does involve farm labor. Many of these seasonal farm workers experience long periods of unemployment and are among the lowest paid and least protected workers in the United States. Working conditions are often grueling, and living quarters are crowded and substandard. In spite of government efforts directed at alleviating the needs of migrant workers, they continue to suffer high rates of illness, which may be related to a lack of health benefits and poor working conditions. Moreover, low levels of education concide with migration patterns and the accompanying lack of consistent educational programs. Even though a large number of migrant workers eventually settle permanently once they have obtained steady employment, they often continue in employment sectors where income and benefits are minimal. Mexican Americans continue to remain highly overrepresented in manufacturing, operator, and service jobs.

Perhaps the greatest changes related to employment are the changes among women of Mexican origin. Recently we have seen a departure from traditional rates of labor-force participation for women of Mexican origin. There are currently 3.6 million Hispanic women in the work force, and of these, 58.5% are of Mexican origin (Kane, 1993). This change is important, considering that this is a segment of the population that has historically had the lowest rates of labor-force participation. The entrance of women into the work force has initiated major changes in gender roles and division of labor. Men are having to assume greater domestic responsibility, and extended family networks and external support systems are being utilized to a greater degree. This increase is creating far-reaching changes in family life, and its implications have yet to be clearly identified.

The greater labor-force participation of women of Mexican origin coincides with an increase in single heads of households. In spite of the increase in employment outside the home, poverty rates are increasing for these families. Historically, the percentage of female-headed Mexican American households was minimal, but the percentage is growing.

Life-Cycle Transitions

Prior to the 1970s, it was customary to describe Mexican-origin families as extremely warm and supportive of the individual. Recent literature on the family, however, criticizes the perpetuation of the stereotype that the family unit is cohesive, strong, and capable of fending off all external threats to the individual. Evidence suggests that extended family patterns are being broken down by urbanization, and that Mexican American families are beginning to adopt the middle-class American custom of not expecting family members to support their relatives (Newton, 1980). Although roles and values have changed, the debate continues as to whether traditional supports have been irrevocably eroded.

As stated earlier, marriage is the norm for individuals of Mexican origin. In this population, 57.7% are married, compared to 51.1% of Puerto Ricans. Divorce rates are low for all Hispanic subgroups and are particularly low for Mexican Americans at 6%, compared to Puerto Ricans (8.9%) and Cuban Americans (8.3%) (Reddy, 1993). However, the increase in labor-force participation for women of Mexican origin may affect this pattern. As Chilman (1993) notes, women's power in relationships within and outside the family tends to increase when they are employed outside the home. This invariably affects the family and contributes to the growing proportion of Mexican-origin families headed by women.

Although the family is considered a particularly important institution and a source of support, it can also be a source of stress and conflict. Many Mexican Americans believe that the individual should sacrifice everything for the family.

But this is an ideal, virtually impossible to fulfill. Competing demands in the larger society create enormous stress for these families. Recent data point to the erosion of familialism in the Mexican-origin network (Mindel, 1980). In areas where neighborhood, friends, and churches provide support services, the function of the family is shifting, and other institutions are increasingly assuming greater roles (Becerra & Shaw, 1984; Beckette & Dungee-Anderson, 1991; Torres-Gil, 1976).

The increasing size of the Hispanic elderly population creates a special concern. Indications are that Hispanics comprise the fastest-growing segment of the elderly population, and this growth will continue into the year 2050 (Gallegos, 1991). This is most troublesome for families of Mexican origin because, once again, early studies have helped proliferate the stereotype that the family is capable of fending off external threats to the older adult, that the family can and does meet all the needs of its elderly members. Although gerontologists agree that family relationships are significant to the elderly, they tend to disagree about the extent of family support for ethnic elderly people.

Furthermore, many programs and services have failed to recognize that families cannot meet the demands and expectations of the elderly of Mexican origin, and that families struggle with trying to fulfill an unrealistic ideal. Mexican American elderly, however, are aware of this inability and the impact of multiple strains on their family. To compensate, they strive for self-reliance in order to minimize the burden (Sanchez, 1994).

Family Strengths and Challenges

The extended family system has been a mainstay in many Mexican-origin families, and supportive institutions of *la familia*—including *parentesco*, the concept of family, *compadrazgo*, godparents, and *confianza*, trust—have helped set the standard for families. These ideologies reinforce the view that family is the central and most important institution in life. Although these concepts influence actual behavior, their ideals can never be fully realized; however, they provide a basis that helps establish norms and expectations (Kane, 1993).

Mexican-origin families have an extended family structure that serves as a vital link between family and community in Mexican American society. While it is a very strong institution, it varies from one generation to the next. **Compadrazgo**, or godparents, who have a moral obligation to act as guardian, provide financial assistance in times of need, and substitute as parents in the event of death. The *compadrazgo* relationship is formed usually through baptism and confirmation ceremonies in the church. The parental relationship is maintained throughout life and extends beyond the child. Godparents often refer to each other as *comadre* (co-mother) or *compadre* (co-father) and are expected to maintain a reciprocal relationship of support and mutual assistance.

Parentesco is a kinship concept that extends family sentiment to kin and nonkin, ensuring that there is an automatic family network. This concept often helps build networks of support and reciprocity and also helps establish a sense of community support among individuals who share regional or geographic origins.

Confianza, commonly referred to as trust, is essential to the relationship between *compadrazgo* and *parentesco*. Yet it means more than trust and includes the notions of respect and intimacy. It builds relationships and provides the foundation for reciprocity. *Confianza* is seen as an institution that has facilitated adaptation after immigration.

Much of what the culture condemns is related to kinship relationships. The family is perceived as more important than the individual. Selfishness is condemned, and its absence is considered a virtue. The strength of the family in providing security to its members is sometimes expressed through the sharing of material things with other relatives, even when there is precious little to meet one's own immediate needs (Locke, 1992). The concept that one should sacrifice everything for family has its costs, however.

In traditional Mexican life, a set of family, religious, and community obligations was significant. Women had certain legal and property rights that acknowledged the importance of their work, their families of origin, and their children. However, the imposition of American law and custom ignored and ultimately undermined many aspects of the extended family in Mexican culture. Because of economic changes that occurred in the family as a result of these laws, many Mexican American women were forced to participate in the economic support of their families by working outside the home. The preservation of traditional customs, such as language, celebrations, and healing practices, became an important element in maintaining and supporting familial ties (Thornton-Dill, 1994).

The culture and identity of Mexican Americans will continue to change as they are affected by inevitable generational fusion with Anglo society and the influence of immigrants. The United States will continue to receive immigrants of Mexican origin, and their numbers are likely to increase. Current anti-immigration legislation and the growing scarcity of resources in the United States will undoubtedly have an impact on how we view immigration. Mexican-origin families are already feeling the burden of these sentiments, particularly in California. California's Proposition 187 has been hailed as a resolution for dealing with the enormous amount of federal resources spent on illegal aliens, yet only about 33% of individuals of Mexican origin in California were born in Mexico, while 67% were born in the United States (Rochin & Rivera, 1995).

Efforts directed at forced assimilation are being met with resistance by many people categorized as Hispanic. People of Mexican origin have responded by registering to vote in greater numbers. Undoubtedly this resistance will increase, will be viewed as anti-American, and will contribute to anti-immigrant sentiments. Efforts will have to be directed toward understanding the challenges, problems, and circumstances that immigration fosters. Instead of fighting for scare resources, people should make an effort to understand how immigration policies affect everyone.

Changes in ethnic and religious group identification, as well as larger demographic changes, have all been associated with changes in family structure and family norms (Goldscheider, 1989). Families have been affected by the participation of women in the work force, patterns of marriage and divorce, and the increase in female-headed households. This is particularly true in families of Mexican origin. The unprecedented increase of Mexican American women working outside the home, as well as increases in poverty, will have serious consequences for families (Baca-Zinn, 1994b). The strains caused by issues such as the affordability of child care and elder care will prompt a re-examination of the Mexican-origin family's ability to provide support. At the same time, the substantial increase of elderly in this population, coupled with the shortage of quality nursing care and home care, will undoubtedly create challenges for these families that are difficult to predict. The rising costs of housing, energy, food, transportation, and health care will reinforce the severity of many of these issues.

This is a particularly interesting and challenging time for families of Mexican origin—and for family study in general. As these families assert their rights as U.S. citizens, we will move away from the belief that the family is capable of providing individual members with all forms of support. At the same time, the Mexican American family has much to teach us, particularly how, in spite of historical oppression and severely constrained options, family life can be maintained. Perhaps if we build on these family strengths and provide additional sources of community and societal support, we will develop family systems capable of dealing with the sources of external stress in a more effective fashion.

Misconceptions and Stereotypes

The assumption that all Mexican-origin families function as extended family households is a notion that continues in the literature. In reality, the nuclear family household is preferred to the extended family household. Extended family households are often rooted in economic need and are not a characteristic of the family's desire to remain connected and isolated from the larger society. Although the family is an important institution for individuals of Mexican origin, it can be a source of conflict as well as support. These families are not immune from external stressors and cannot always withstand threats to family stability.

Another assumption that has been a mainstay in our understanding of Mexican American families is the stereotype of the ideal family as a patriarchy that revolves around a strong male figure. This stereotype is related to the concept of Mexican masculinity, or **machismo**. In American culture, the concept of *machismo* is based on the belief that the male is virile, aggressive, and accountable only to himself. It has been referred to as a male's dominance over women in both a physical and a psychological sense. Contrary to this belief, *machismo* is not necessarily a negative trait. Although degrees of authoritarianism exist in many families of Mexican origin, women often have the authority and contribute to family decision making. Baca-Zinn (1982) contends that *machismo* is a primary concept that has been used to explain family structure in Mexican-origin families and that it is based on exaggerated masculinity used to compensate for the male's cultural inferiority. *Machismo* has thus become a positive coping strategy and maintains positive characteristics that contribute to the structure of the family. Mirande (1985) identifies the positive aspects of *machismo* as bravery, courage, self-defense, responsibility, respect, altruism, pride, protection, steadfastness, individualism, androgyny, and honor. Subsequent studies have reinforced these attributes of *machismo*, supporting the idea that it is a positive rather than a negative trait (Baca-Zinn, 1994a).

Finally, Hispanics and individuals of Mexican origin, although resistant to forced assimilation, are not averse to working hard and to learning the English language. For many, all that is needed is a pathway to change. This is a difficult process that will entail building an agenda to alleviate poverty and increase educational opportunities that will ultimately affect productivity, income, and health. With such an agenda, we can then foster and strengthen the solid support systems that for many families of Mexican origin have ensured their existence in the United States.

Personal Interview

Carmen is a 65-year-old woman who describes herself as "a dinosaur—a dying breed," which is taken to mean a traditional Mexican-origin female. In her assessment, there aren't many people like her left. Currently retired, she lives in California. Although she spent many of her formative years in Mexico as a result of laws regarding dual citizenship prior to the 1940s, Carmen is a U.S. citizen. Her father was born in the United States, but his family were original settlers in Mexico who owned property on both sides of the border. Women in Carmen's family had children in both countries, resulting in dual citizenship.

In describing her immigration experience, she clarifies that because she was a U.S. citizen, she was not considered an immigrant. However, she describes what she terms "family migration."

Carmen: My family was forced to migrate to the United States during the early 1940s. This, of course, was related to World War II, and because my father was a U.S. citizen, he was no longer allowed to renew permission to reside in Mexico. He would have been considered an absconder from the draft. Since my mother and three of my siblings were Mexican and three of us were U.S. citizens, the decision was made to cross the border as a family. We crossed over to Laredo, Texas. I was about 11 years old.

My migration experience was very different because, at the time, Laredo was 100% Mexican, so there was no oppression. The greatest change that occurred as a result of migration was related to resources. When we migrated, my father, who was once a property owner in Mexico, was now a property worker in the United States. Although at one time he had also owned land in the U.S., when taxation was imposed, he lost the land because he didn't understand the complex system.

What was the subsequent change in status like?

Carmen: We were prominent settlers in Mexico, as reflected by our house. Our house was situated in the plaza. We were viewed as wealthy, in terms of land ownership. When we moved to the U.S., all that changed. We now lived like everyone else.

In Mexico, children received formal education up until the sixth grade; if they wanted to continue schooling, they would have to leave their families and would also have to pay for it.

When you came to the United States, you had completed the fourth grade, and, although formal education was now available, your social education was more important. Why?

Carmen: Although I started attending school when we got to the U.S., I was soon withdrawn because my father would say that my mother needed my help in the home. Many children were also taken out of school to harvest the fields, since the war meant that there were only old men and children to complete the work. My experience was common to all other families in the area so I didn't feel deprived.

When you were growing up, what were the differences in how male and female children were treated?

Carmen: It was a feudal-like society, with the eldest son inheriting everything. Boys were given more freedom from chores and restrictions and were allowed to roam without permission. Girls, on the other hand, were expected to stay home and help their mother. Children were often the center of family life and were not left with babysitters, but they were not included in adult issues. Socializing was also very formal. Entertainment was family-based and enabled boys and girls to socialize and identify potential mates. If there was an attraction, the boy would have to request permission to visit the girl at her house. These visits would occur under the supervision of the parents, and physical contact, in any form, was prohibited. We weren't allowed to hug and kiss, and it was instilled in us that there was only one proper way to do things—when you are married. There was certainly no sex. If someone had sex prior to marriage, the family was dishonored. It was a very small community, and you couldn't afford to make social mistakes.

Describe your engagement and wedding.

Carmen: There was no formal engagement. The groom selects a committee of elders from the community (three or four men) who advise the family that they will be coming to the house to ask for the daughter's hand in marriage. The parents don't respond immediately, giving about one month before agreeing. They don't want to appear too presumptuous. About six weeks after my hand was sought in marriage, my family agreed and we began the formal planning. We were married during the high mass and had a *lazo* of dried flowers, *arras*, and I paid homage to the Blessed Virgin.

You were married for 23 years, and then divorced. What was that like?

Carmen: The divorce was not accepted very well in my family. When my family of origin found out about the separation and subsequent divorce, I was advised that the family had gotten together and determined that I had shamed the family. I was therefore disowned. I was told that I was the first divorcee in 200 years of history in the family and that it was unacceptable. I think geographical distance contributed to my inability to explain the reasons behind the divorce. They didn't understand that my husband left me. In their minds, he left for a good reason. Coming from Mexico, I only had a fourth-grade education. That wasn't because I wasn't smart; I always had a desire to learn. So after moving to the Midwest and living there for a long time, I decided to return to school and complete my GED. I didn't know English, but as I learned the lessons, I learned the language. I completed my GED and decided to take classes at the community college. It was during my sec-

ond quarter of classes that he left. It was never clear why he left because we really didn't have conflict. It may have been related to his inability to reconcile my gaining an education.

Did you regret the divorce?

Carmen: It was quite a trade-off. I lost my family, friends, marriage, and the church. I have no regrets, just moments of doubt. They don't include whether I should have done it; rather, I question whether I could have done it differently. Perhaps I could have had a marriage and a career, yet I know I would have needed his cooperation to do this. It was something I never had. His basic statement to me was, "If I can't stop you, I won't help you." Personally, I prefer to be married than divorced, but I would not have foregone going to school for the sake of maintaining the marriage.

What did you do after the divorce?

Carmen: I completed my GED and went on to earn a bachelor's degree and a master's in social work. When I entered the work force, my youngest child was 10 years old. I managed with the support of my two older children. Although times were difficult, I managed to support my family. As a single woman I have been better educated and financially stable. I have augmented beyond expectations because I had no one to tell me that I shouldn't and I couldn't.

What are your expectations for your children? Are they different from those held by a traditional family of Mexican origin?

Carmen: My quest for my children is that they have independence and be self-sufficient. Two have completed college, all are independent, and all are earning their own living. I don't expect my children to take care of me. I worked 80 hours a week to ensure that I could take care of myself in my old age. I feel my children need to follow the rules of the dominant culture because that is where they were raised. There was a lack of support to carry out any other value system, so that worked against the maintenance of the traditional family system. Like I said before, I am like a dinosaur, a dying breed.

Questions for Discussion

1. How does the immigration experience for Mexican American individuals differ from that of other Hispanic subgroups? What impact does this have on the family and the individual?

2. What are some of the stereotypes about Mexican and Mexican American families? What reactions have these provoked? Do these reactions create or dispel difficulties for Mexican American families?

3. What generation gaps exist in Mexican-origin families, and what factors perpetuate these gaps?

4. What are some of the specific political issues the majority culture will have to address regarding individuals of Mexican origin? Why?

5. Should Mexican Americans be forced to learn English? Why or why not?

6. Consider the interview in this chapter. Are there similarities to your life? What are the similarities to other interviews in this book?

7. What influence does religion have in the family life of Mexican Americans? How does it compare to the influence of religion in your family?

8. What purpose does religion serve in family life? What are the similarities between American Indian spirituality and Catholicism?

Suggested Resources

Commission Fermenil Mexicana Nacional, Inc.
(National Mexican Women's Commission)
379 South Loma Drive
Los Angeles, CA 90017
(213) 484-1515

Hispanic Association of Colleges and Universities
411 SW 24th Street
San Antonio, TX 78207
(512) 433-1501

Mexican American Legal Defense and Education Fund
634 South Spring Street
Los Angeles, CA 90014
(213) 625-2512

National Council of La Raza
810 First Street, NE, No. 300
Washington, DC 20002
(202) 289-1380

National Hispanic Council on Aging
2713 Ontario Road, NW
Washington, DC 20009
(202) 745-2521

Readings

Augenbraum, H., Stavans, I. (Eds.). (1993). *Growing up Latino: Memoirs and stories*. Boston: Houghton Mifflin.

Gonzales, R. (Ed.). (1994). *Currents from the dancing river: Contemporary Latino fiction, non-fiction, and poetry*. Orlando, FL: Harcourt Brace.

Herrera-Sobek, M. (1985). *Beyond stereotypes: The critical analysis of Chicana literature*. Binghamton, NY: Bilingual Review Press.

Simmen, E. (Ed.). (1992). *New voices in literature: The Mexican-American experience in short fiction*. New York: Mentor.

Sotomayor, M. (Ed.). (1991). *Empowering Hispanic families: A critical issue for the 90's*. Milwaukee, WI: Family Service America.

Videos

Films Four International (Producers), & Andrews, A. (Director). (1994). *La vida loco*. (Available from FACETS Media, 1517 W. Fullerton Avenue, Chicago, IL 60614)

New Mexico Public Television (Producer). (1993). *The Latino family*. (Available from Films for the Humanities, P.O. Box 2053, Princeton, NJ 08543)

Thomas-Newcommer, A. (Producer), & Nava, G. (Director). (1995). *Mi familia*. (Available from New Line Home Video, 116 N. Robertson Boulevard, Los Angeles, CA 90048)

References

Acosta-Belen, E. (1988). From settlers to newcomers: The Hispanic legacy in the United States. In E. Acosta-Belen and B. Sjostorm (Eds.), *The Hispanic experience in the United States: Contemporary issues and perspectives* (pp. 81–86). New York: Praeger.

Alvirez, D., & Bean, F. (1976). The Mexican-American family. In C. Mindel and R. Habenstein (Eds.), *Ethnic families in America* (pp. 141–159). New York: Elsevier.

Andrade, S. (1982). Social science stereotypes of the Mexican American woman: Policy implications for research. *Hispanic Journal of Behavioral Science, 4,* 223–243.

Anzaldua, G. (1987). *Borderlands, la frontera: The new mestiza.* San Francisco: Spinsters / Aunt Lute.

Baca-Zinn, M. (1982). Chicano men and masculinity. *Journal of Ethnic Studies, 10,* 19–31.

Baca-Zinn, M. (1994a). Adaptation and continuity in Mexican-origin families. In R. Taylor (Ed.), *Minority families in the United States: A multicultural perspective* (pp. 64–81). Englewood Cliffs, NJ: Prentice-Hall.

Baca-Zinn, M. (1994b). Difference and domination. In M. Baca-Zinn and B. Thornton-Dill (Eds.), *Women of color in U.S. society* (pp. 3–12). Philadelphia: Temple University Press.

Baca-Zinn, M. (1994c). Feminist rethinking from racial-ethnic families. In M. Baca-Zinn and B. Thornton-Dill (Eds.), *Women of color in U.S. society* (pp. 303–314). Philadelphia: Temple University Press.

Baca-Zinn, M. (1994d). Mexican heritage families in the United States. In F. Padilla (Ed.), *Handbook of Hispanic cultures in the United States: Sociology* (pp. 165–166). Houston, TX: Arte Publico Press.

Bean, F., & Tienda, M. (1988). The Hispanic population of the United States. New York: Russell Sage Foundation.

Becerra, R. M., & Shaw, D. (1984). *The Hispanic elderly: A reference guide.* Baltimore, MD: University Press of America.

Beckette, J., & Dungee-Anderson, D. (1991). Alzheimer's disease in African American and White families: A clinical analysis. *Smith College Studies in Social Work, 62,* 155–168.

Buriel, R., & Vasques, R. (1984). Stereotypes of Mexican descent persons: Attitudes of three generations of Mexican Americans and Anglo-American adolescents. *Journal of Cross-Cultural Psychology, 13,* 59–70.

Centers for Disease Control and Prevention. (1995). *Monthly vital statistics report: Final data.* Washington, DC: U.S. Department of Health and Human Services.

Chilman, C. (1993). Hispanic families in the United States: Research perspectives. In H. McAdoo (Ed.), *Family ethnicity: Strength in diversity* (pp. 141–163). Newbury Park, CA: Sage.

Davis, C., Haub, C., & Willette, J. (1988). U.S. Hispanics: Changing the face of America. In E. Acosta-Belen and B. Sjostrom (Eds.), *The Hispanic experience in the United States: Contemporary issues and perspectives* (pp. 3–55). New York: Praeger.

Gallegos, J. (1991). Culturally relevant services for Hispanic elderly. In M. Sotomayor (Ed.), *Empowering Hispanic families: A critical issue for the 90's* (pp. 176–178). Milwaukee, WI: Family Service America.

Goldscheider, M. (1989). Family structure and conflict: Nest leaving expectations of young adults and their parents. *Journal of Marriage and the Family, 2,* 87–97.

Gonzales, S. (1980). La Chicana: An overview. In *Conference on the educational and occupational needs of Hispanic women*. Washington, DC: U.S. Department of Education.

Hayes-Bautista, H. (1989). *Latino adolescents, families, work and the economy: Building upon strength or creating a weakness?* Paper prepared for Carnegie Commission on Adolescent Development, Washington, DC.

Hoppe, S., & Heller, P. (1975). Alienation, familism, and the utilization of services by Mexican Americans. *Journal of Health and Social Behavior, 16,* 304–314.

Kane, N. (Ed.). (1993). *The Hispanic American almanac: A reference work on Hispanics in the United States*. Detroit, MI: Gale Research.

Klor de Alva, J. (1988). Telling Hispanics apart: Latino sociocultural diversity. In E. Acosta-Belen and B. Sjostrom (Eds.), *The Hispanic experience in the United States: Contemporary issues and perspectives* (pp. 107–136). New York: Praeger.

Locke, D. (1992). *Increasing multicultural understanding*. Newbury Park, CA: Sage.

Macklin, B. J. (1976). *Structural stability and cultural change in the Mexican American community*. New York: Arno Press.

Mindel, C. (1980). Extended familism among urban Mexican Americans, Anglos, and Blacks. *Hispanic Journal of Behavioral Sciences, 2,* 21–34.

Mirande, A. (1985). *The Chicano experience: An alternative perspective*. South Bend, IN: Notre Dame Press.

Montalvo, F. (1992). Phenotyping, acculturation, and biracial assimilation of Mexican Americans. In M. Sotomayor (Ed.), *Empowering Hispanic families: A critical issue for the 90's* (pp. 100–102). Milwaukee, WI: Family Service America.

Newton, F. C. (1980). Issues in research and service delivery among Mexican

American elderly: A concise statement with recommendation. *The Gerontologist* 20(2), 208–213.

Ortiz, V. (1994). Women of color: A demographic overview. In M. Baca-Zinn and B. Thornton-Dill (Eds.), *Women of color in U.S. society* (p. 15). Philadelphia: Temple University Press.

Ramirez, O., & Arce, C. (1980). The contemporary Chicano family: An empirically based review. In A. Baron, Jr. (Ed.), *Explorations in Chicano psychology* (pp. 8–11). New York: Praeger.

Reddy, M. A. (Ed.). (1993). *Statistical record of Hispanic America*. Detroit, MI: Gale Research.

Rochin, R., & Rivera, J. (1995). Focus on Latinos. In *Western Wire: Western Rural Development Center, Fall 1995*. Eugene: Oregon State University.

Sanchez, Y. (1994). *Perceptions of financial exploitation in Mexican American families*. Unpublished doctoral dissertation, Michigan State University, Lansing.

Thornton-Dill, B. (1994). Fictive kin, paper sons, and *compadrazgo*: Women of color and the struggle for family survival. In M. Baca-Zinn and B. Thornton-Dill (Eds.), *Women of color in U.S. society* (p. 163). Philadelphia: Temple University Press.

Torres-Gil, F. (1976). The political behavior of Mexican American elderly. *The Gerontologist, 17*(5), 392–399.

U.S. Bureau of the Census. (1991). *Statistical abstract of the United States* (11th ed.). Washington, DC: U.S. Government Printing Office.

Williams, N. (1990). *The Mexican-American family: Tradition and change*. New York: General Hall.

Wells, M. J. (1976). Emigrants from the migrant stream: Environment and incentives in relocation. *Aztlan, 7*(2), 271–295.

James D. Lambert
Gordon C. Thomasson

5

Mormon American Families

An Overview of History and Cultural Background

To understand Mormon American families, we must transcend powerful stereotypes. "Mormon" is another name for a member of the Church of Jesus Christ of Latter-Day Saints. As O'Dea (1966) explains: "The Mormon Church did not become either a denomination or an established sect . . . they became a people. The result is a specifically religious organization . . . with its own history, its own traditions, . . . even its native territory or homeland" (p. 70).

Mormon Americans as a group are a special case within the spectrum of multicultural American family patterns. Beginning with the earliest Mormon missionary efforts in Canada in the 1830s, religious converts from all over the world have migrated to the United States and have been socialized into the Mormon community. Thus, in considering Mormon American families, we often must take into account a double- or multiple-origin pattern and the existence of cultural subgroups. It is almost as accurate to speak, for example, of Mormon Icelandic Americans, Mormon Japanese Americans, Mormon Ghanaian Americans, Mormon Bolivian Americans, or Mormon Polynesian Americans, as it is to speak of Mormon Americans. But while each subgroup reflects certain unique ethnic, linguistic, and national origins (currently the Mormon Church is found in more than 150 countries), all share certain distinctively Mormon patterns as well. As a result, intermarriage between various subgroups but within the larger Mormon community are common. Mormonism, then, is both a distinctive ethnic group tending toward homogeneity and a functioning multicultural society.

The story of Mormonism began in the 1820s, with a series of revelations

The first author gratefully acknowledges that the completion of this chapter was made possible by the immeasurable support and encouragement of Nadine Marks.

from God and visitations of angelic beings to Joseph Smith, Jr. (Allen & Leonard, 1993; Arrington & Bitton, 1992; Bushman, 1984; Roberts, 1965). These led to Smith's translation and publication of *The Book of Mormon* in 1829–1830. This scripture, along with the Holy Bible and later revelations, laid a foundation for the church that was organized to implement and spread the gospel in 1830.

The Mormon religion is not a static tradition. It is based on a belief in the reality of history and, consequently, the virtue and necessity of a *continuing revelation* of God's will to the community of believers as well as individuals. As a revealed religion, it affirms the need for divine intervention in history and in the present day, rather than an exclusive reliance on finite reason. Ultimate truth is understood to come from God to humans. Such truth is then articulated as doctrine by those called of God and accepted by the community through common consent.

Continuing revelation, additional scriptures, and questions of divine authority were controversial enough to generate persecutions. By mid-1833, the generally northern/Yankee anti-slavery sentiments of most early converts to Mormonism also led to open persecution by pro-slavery populations in Missouri. Moreover, there were fears among the pro-slavery community in Independence, Missouri, that the Mormon population could grow to the point of outvoting them or becoming a deciding swing vote. (Persecuted minorities, in fact, often resort to block voting to protect themselves.) But the persecutions that were inflicted on early Mormon Americans are still remembered as some of the most criminal events in American history. Nowhere was the attack on the Mormon minority more succinctly summarized than in the 1838 extermination order of Missouri Governor Lilburn Boggs: "The Mormons must be treated as enemies and must be exterminated or driven from the state, if necessary, for the public good" (quoted in Furniss, 1960, p. 1). Like prejudice against other ethnic groups, anti-Mormonism has persisted up into the present day. From the Missouri persecutions by pro-slavery mobs in the early 1830s onward, Mormon Americans as a people have been opposed by the majority culture because of their social, political, and economic beliefs.

When the Republican Party was founded in 1854, it consisted of a coalition of anti-slavery forces and, among others, long-time anti-Mormons. The anti-Mormons did not have an issue that gave them national credibility until 1852, when the practice of **polygyny**, having more than one wife at the same time, among Mormon Americans became public knowledge. This is sometimes referred to as **polygamy**, the practice of having more than one husband or wife at the same time, but technically the Mormon practice was polygyny because wives were not allowed to have more than one husband. The anti-Mormon agenda now had a kind of legitimacy, so from the 1856 presidential election onward, the Republican Party platform was a commitment to eliminate the "twin relics of barbarism"—slavery and polygamy.

If socially "deviant" (non-European) marriage practices were really a concern to Republicans, they did not have to look to Mormons for a "cause." The Oneida (New York) Perfectionists, following John Henry Noyes, practiced a pattern of "complex marriage," in which each adult man was married to every adult woman, and vice versa. This practice persisted from 1847 to 1879. But although widely known, the Perfectionists never were the objects of national persecutions. Adultery was never the focus of a national crusade either. Mormon Americans were quick to publicize each case in which federal officials, ranging from President Grover Cleveland to the carpetbag judges sent to govern Utah, were fathering illegitimate children. Mormon Americans also pointed out the commonplaceness of abortion and infanticide in non-Mormon society at that time. But like complex marriage, all this was beside the point. Marriage and sexuality were not really the issues.

By 1890, in *Davis* v. *Beason*, even the U.S. Constitution (art. 6, sec. 3), which guarantees that "no religious test shall ever be required as a Qualification to any Office or Public Trust under the United States," was found not to apply to Mormon Americans. Whether or not a man was, or ever intended to be, a polygamist, mere membership in the Mormon Church was sufficient cause to deny him the right to vote in any election, serve on a jury, be executor for a relative's estate, or hold any public office. Federal judges denied immigrants citizenship because, as Judge T. J. Anderson ruled:

> The teachings, practices, and aims of the Mormon Church are antagonistic to the government of the United States, utterly subversive of good morals and well-being of society, and . . . its members are animated by a feeling of hostility towards the government and its laws and therefore, an alien who is a member of said church is not a fit person to become a citizen of the United States. (quoted in Larson, 1971, p. 250)

Migration and Immigration

After the assassination of Joseph Smith in 1844, political and mob pressure for the removal of Mormon populations continued to increase. Finally, to avert violence, evacuations began in the winter of 1846, and the refugees migrated out of the United States into Mexican territory, which later became the state of Utah. This migration occurred within a very different frame of reference than other westward migrations in U.S. history. The Mormon Americans did not move as individual families who happened to migrate together in wagon trains across the continent, like those going to California or Oregon. They consciously and explicitly united and organized their families as "Camps of Israel" (*Doctrine and Covenants*, 1981, Sec. 136). Mormon ancestors who migrated before the completion of the transcontinental railroad in 1869 are still remembered today as much for the immigrant company in which they traveled as by their family. Their fastest means of travel was by walking and pulling their goods in handcarts.

Having been driven from their homes and the cities they had built numerous times, the Mormon Americans were highly sensitive to the fact that Native American peoples had legitimate claim to the lands they occupied. Therefore, unlike other westward migrants, the Mormon Americans negotiated the purchase of lands and followed a formal policy that it was better "to feed the Indians than to fight them." Missionaries were called to teach modern farming methods, and intermarriage was even advocated in various situations.

A substantial proportion of nineteenth-century Mormon American immigrants were more like seventeenth-century immigrants to America, in that one of the motivations for emigration was to escape religious persecution. Economic improvement was also a factor, as countless converts sought to escape the working-class poverty brought by the Industrial Revolution. Many such converts embraced the semiurban communal agricultural lifestyle advocated by Joseph Smith and his successor, Brigham Young (Arrington, Fox, & May, 1976; Hayden, 1976). There is evidence not only of the success of that model but also of the persistence of its value system into the present (Maass & Anderson, 1978).

Chain migration was common to later American and Mormon experiences, in which previous migrants facilitated the migration and settlement of subsequent individuals and family members through remittances. As more converts left an area of origin (such as Europe), the desire of those remaining to emigrate increased proportionally. The Mormon Church as a whole created a characteristically cooperative mechanism for sponsoring immigration: the Perpetual Emigrating Fund (a revolving credit program). This was a reflection of both Mormon cooperative economics and the concept of larger familial obligations within the community of Latter-Day Saints.

Church growth was subsequently enhanced by strong leadership, a more stable population base in local congregations, and a corresponding increase in the availability of preferred marriage partners (other Mormons). Temples were constructed outside the intermountain region of Idaho, Utah, and Arizona. As more temples were built, one of the major incentives for migration became less compelling. Migration declined to the old core area of what geographers call the Mormon region. By the 1960s, a planned increase in local leadership and in the missionary program began a period of rapid growth in conversions that continues today. Many areas of the world that for generations only exported individual converts and families to the United States are now populated by multigeneration families of Mormons. The Mormon American population has grown from zero in 1820 to more than 4.5 million in the United States in 1995, and its worldwide membership exceeds 9 million (Heaton, 1992; Watson, 1995).

Traditional and Emerging Family Systems

Understanding Mormon Americans and their families requires some grasp of their most important doctrines or revealed teachings. Perhaps the most important belief Mormons have concerning families, both nuclear and extended, is that they are eternal (Campbell & Campbell, 1988). Marriage and family are not thought of as social institutions existing "till death do us part." Mormon couples who marry in church temples are "sealed together" or "married for time and all eternity." Heaven, for Mormons, is an eternally bonded or sealed extended family that includes all of the human family who accept union with the heavenly family.

From childhood or conversion, Mormons are taught that perfecting individuals within the context of the family, known as **eternal progression**, is the highest goal, and that "no other success can compensate for failure in the home" (McKay, 1964, p. 445). It is in the context of these tenets that any discussion of Mormon American families must occur.

Household Size and Composition

Heaton (1988) suggests that the most distinctive demographic characteristic of the Mormon family is the high rate of fertility. Compared to the general population, Mormon Americans are more likely to have larger families and to express a larger ideal family size (Bahr, 1992; Heaton, Goodman, & Holman, 1994; Mosher, William, & Johnson, 1992). Historically, Mormon American birth rates have remained close to twice the national average (Heaton, 1986; May, 1980); more recently, they have decreased significantly, although they continue to remain above national levels (currently 23 births per 1000 people, compared to 16 births per 1000) (Heaton, 1988, 1992).

It has been suggested that the same social forces that have negatively affected birth rates in the general population—namely, urbanization and industrialization—have influenced fertility rates in the Mormon subculture as well (Bean, Mineau, & Anderton, 1983; Campbell & Campbell, 1988). However, socioeconomic variables commonly associated with lower birth rates in national populations, such as higher family income and educational attainment, do not result in overall lower fertility for Mormons (Heaton, 1986; Thomas, 1983).

Heaton and Calkins (1983) suggest that pro-family attitudes, rather than anti-contraception beliefs, are the reason for the persistence of higher-than-average Mormon fertility rates. In fact, several studies reveal that, though they may delay use until after the birth of their first child, Mormon American couples use contraceptives with the same frequency as other Americans (Bush, 1976; Heaton & Calkins, 1983; Thomas, 1992).

Fertility has been related to **religiosity**, in that family size is greater for Mormons who are actively involved in their religion (Bean et al., 1983; Heaton, 1986; Thornton, 1979). One reason is that socioeconomic variables have a different effect on members with higher levels of religious participation than on those who are less active. In short, Mormon teachings regarding family relationships appear to sustain high fertility patterns among the more active members (Bean et al., 1983; Heaton, 1986, 1988; Mauss, 1994).

Parenthood, like marriage, is a critical component of spiritual development. Thus, bringing children into the world is seen as both a joy and a responsibility. Mormons are taught that worthy parents and children will continue to associate as a family in the next life.

The extended kinship network goes beyond those family members who are currently living. Members of the Mormon Church extend and unify their family ties by identifying ancestors who did not have the opportunity to hear the gospel and arranging for ordinances essential to their eternal salvation, such as baptism and marriage, to be performed by proxy in the temple (Wagner, 1977). Mormons believe that their deceased ancestors still have the ability to accept or reject these ordinances (May, 1980). To assist in this work, the Mormon Church has developed one of the most extensive family history, or **genealogy**, libraries in the world. Mormons who participate in these activities are particularly aware of the names and histories of their ancestors, which may benefit their sense of identity and heritage (Jacobsen, Kunz, & Conlin, 1989).

The Socialization of Children

As with other religious and cultural groups, the Mormon Church encourages commitment from its young people. Mormon youths are viewed as the future leaders of the church. Thus, the intergenerational transmission of beliefs and values is seen as important to both the growth and the success of the church. Mormon doctrine states that children are the spirit sons and daughters of heavenly parents, and that God holds parents responsible for their stewardship in raising them in righteousness (Benson, 1992). Parents are taught that "the most important of the Lord's work [you] will ever do will be within the walls of your own homes" (Lee, 1973, p. 7). With the support of the church, parents are to teach their children during the formative years, when they develop habits and attitudes that last a lifetime (Wirthlin, 1991).

As in most cultures, transmitting values in Mormon American families is challenging in the contemporary world. Mormon youths, often in the face of social pressures to the contrary, are expected to abstain from smoking, drinking, and drug use; avoid all forms of premarital sexual behavior; contribute 10% of their income to the church; spend 2 years in missionary work; and marry in the temple. Church leaders continue to stress that children learn these values and behaviors most effectively in the home.

Interestingly, the Mormon Church's emphasis on the family does not translate into more frequent individual contact with their children (Wilkinson & Tanner, 1980). In fact, because of the demands of larger family size, Mormon American parents may actually have less-frequent individual contact in such activities as helping with homework and having private talks (Heaton et al., 1994). However, research has shown that Mormon Americans may be more effective than some populations in socializing certain values and behavior, particularly those related to sexual activity and substance use (Bahr, 1994; Christensen, 1976; Smith, 1976). One reason for this may be that, while they may spend less time individually with each child, Mormon Americans spend more time in activities that include the entire family (Wilkinson & Tanner, 1980). Research also suggests that the degree to which Mormon American families participate in activities such as family prayer, scripture study, and Family Home Evening has a particularly important influence on the transmission of values (Cornwall, 1988; Stott, 1988). Finally, Wilkinson and Tanner (1980) suggest that the pro-family messages Mormon American parents receive from the church influence their attitudes and behavior, often resulting in contact that is positive and affectionate.

Cornwall (1988) examined the socialization process and concluded that Mormon American parents direct their children into church programs that influence peer associations. This integration into the church network usually reinforces the religious values being learned at home. Furthermore, participation in church activities allows young people to interact with adult advisors who can act as mentors or role models. The socializing influence of an informal mentor may be particularly important during the adolescent years, when family influence tends to weaken.

The socialization of children in the Mormon Church can be characterized by several age-graded **rites of passage**. At age 8, Mormon children reach the age of accountability and become eligible for baptism. This rite of passage usually signifies the first of many interviews with their bishop, or congregational leader. This interview enables the bishop to assess whether or not the child has learned to distinguish good from evil and understands the significance of baptism. Up to this point, children are seen as not accountable for "sins of any kind" (Kimball, 1982, p. 111).

The next significant rite of passage for Mormon children occurs at age 12. Transition from childhood to adolescence is marked by leaving the gender-undifferentiated classes of Primary and entering the gender-segregated Young Women's and Young Men's programs (Sunday school remains unsegregated). Besides attending classes on Sunday, youths in these organizations usually meet once a week, under the supervision of an adult advisor, for a variety of social and cultural activities, such as service projects, scout camps, and homemaking demonstrations (Ludlow, 1992). Occasionally, joint activities bring the young men and women together to help them develop appropriate social relationships (Miller & Goddard, 1992). These are structured and well-supervised social and religious activities, such as dances and "firesides." Age 12 is also a pivotal age for young men because they typically are ordained in the Aaronic (preparatory) priesthood and have the opportunity for service and leadership experiences.

Perhaps the most crucial rite of passage into adulthood and spiritual maturity, particularly for Mormon males, is the missionary experience. When young men turn 19, they are expected to serve a full-time mission (Kimball, 1982). Young women have the opportunity upon turning 21. For many young men and women, serving for 18 months (women) or 2 years (men) becomes a "rite of passage from a culturally based religious identity to one that is spiritually based, or internalized" (Weed, 1992, p. 1509).

Young women and young men may advance to the next class in their respective organizations when they turn the required age, but advancement in the priesthood and missionary service are based on worthiness, or obedience to the laws of the church. For teenagers, perhaps the most relevant issue related to worthiness is morality. Thus, church leaders repeatedly stress the importance of obedience to the "law of chastity."

Intimate Relationships

The law of chastity forbids all sexual relationships outside of marriage. Church members are taught that procreative powers are from God, and that immorality "tampers with this life-beginning process and brings complications into the lives of all involved" (Ludlow, 1992, p. 389).

Mormons are taught that "chastity should be the dominant virtue among young people" (McKay, 1953, p. 458). Parents have the obligation to help their children understand the need to control their sexual desires, and they are encouraged to discuss issues of sexuality openly with their children. Mormon youths are also taught that they should not participate in sexual activities that often precede sexual intercourse (Kimball, 1982). Furthermore, Mormon leaders teach that masturbation should be avoided and pornography rejected, and that the law of chastity also applies to immodest dress, vulgar speech, and immoral thoughts. Mormon scriptures counsel: "See that ye bridle all your passions that ye may be filled with love" (*Book of Mormon*, 1981, Alma 38:12).

In view of the conservative nature of the Mormon Church's teachings on sexuality, it is not surprising that Mormon American youths often face incongruity as they socialize with non-Mormon peers. An interesting contrast emerges when considering the rites of passage that signify a "coming of age" for males in the general American culture as opposed to the Mormon culture. For example, masturbation is considered by many outside the church to be a sign of movement from childhood to adulthood, while sexual performance is one of the "tests by which American men learn and prove their masculinity" (Knowlton, 1992, p. 26). Mormon males, of course, find these rites of passage in opposition to church doctrine (Kimball, 1982). They are taught that "the time of youth and early manhood is the proper time to gain mastery over bodily appetites and passions" (Jessee, 1974, p. 130). Thus, while the issue of sexuality is an important rite of passage within the Mormon culture, it is through restrained and controlled sexuality that a "coming of age" is exhibited (Knowlton, 1992). The result of this apparent paradox is that Mormon males must either meet the demands of their peers and suffer potential shame within the church, or conform to the church's strict moral code and risk ridicule from their peers.

For the most part, the Mormon Church has been successful in influencing appropriate sexual actions and attitudes of its members. Studies conducted over the last two decades show that Mormon Americans are less approving of teenagers having sex or cohabiting than non-Mormons (Christensen, 1976; Heaton et al., 1994; Smith, 1976). They are also less likely to have engaged in premarital sexual intercourse than members of other populations (Heaton, 1988).

With the emphasis that the Mormon Church places on premarital chastity, it is surprising that Utah, with its large Mormon population, has an apparently high incidence of teenage pregnancy. While this seems contradictory to claims of low premarital intercourse, Heaton (1988) points out that when teenage abortions are included in U.S. teen pregnancy estimates, the teen pregnancy rate for Mormons is actually relatively low (Chadwick, 1993). Overall, abortion rates in Utah are relatively low and reflect the family-oriented values of the Mormon American population.

Because unmarried teenagers are expected to abstain from premarital sex, they are told very little, if anything, about contraception. In fact, regarding formalized sex education, the Mormon Church takes the position that the teacher and course materials should in no way encourage sexual permissiveness and should advocate abstinence from sex before marriage. The church counsels parents to ensure that when such programs are taught, the family-oriented standards espoused by the church are acknowledged. Thus, while Mormon American teens are less likely to engage in premarital sex, they may also be less likely to use protection when they do have sexual intercourse.

Predictably, Mormon dating practices are somewhat conservative. For example, Mormon youths are not allowed to begin dating until the age of 16. This is considerably older than for most young people outside the church, where during the 1980s the average age dating began was 13 (Miller & Goddard, 1992). Much like contemporary courtship practices, dates are often informal and unsupervised. There is also no set pattern of progression in courtship, except that Mormons teach that steady dating and marriage-oriented courtship should be delayed, ideally until after a mission for young men and at least until the completion of high school for young women (Miller & Goddard, 1992).

Mormon couples who are seriously considering marriage usually follow some fairly common practices. The choice of a partner is usually discussed with the parents. It is also common for young couples planning to marry to seek the advice of their church leaders. Finally, and most importantly, Mormons are likely to pray for heavenly confirmation regarding their marriage decision (Kimball, 1982).

Despite the postponing effect of missions on dating activities, Mormon American men tend to marry over a year earlier than national averages, and Mormon American women marry at or slightly below the average age (Heaton et al., 1994). This tendency toward earlier marriage may be due in part to the consistent message from church leaders that it is wrong to delay marriage unnecessarily (Benson, 1988; Kimball, 1982). Thus, Mormons may be less likely than other Americans to postpone marriage to allow for education and career advancement. Another factor that may influence marital age is the fact that Mormon Americans are less likely to cohabit instead of getting married (Heaton et al., 1994).

When a couple marries, the Mormon Church teaches that neither the husband nor the wife is more important, and both share in the family responsibilities (Ludlow, 1992). However, Mormon families are traditionally patriarchal. The church teaches that the father's responsibility is to serve as the head of his home and family. His key roles are those of a leader, provider, and role model. He should lead the family through kindness and humility, not force or arrogance. As a provider, he should assume financial responsibility for the family's material needs, assisted by other family members as necessary.

Similarly, the main expectations of the wife in a Mormon American family are to be a mother, teacher, and role model. David O. McKay, a former president of the Mormon Church, taught that "motherhood is a woman's noblest calling" and that bringing spirit children into the world is a sacred partnership with God (McKay, 1962, p. 54). He also taught that "motherhood is the greatest potential influence either for good or ill in human life" (McKay, 1953, p. 452). Church members are also taught that the key word in parenting is partnership, and that both husband and wife have important, complementary roles in the family.

Work and Family Relationships

The Mormon Church has been somewhat responsive and accommodating toward changing women's roles (Cornwall, 1994; Iannaccone & Miles, 1990). In recent years, church leaders have been less likely to discourage women's participation in the labor force (Cornwall, 1994). Overall, there has been an increased emphasis on the important contributions, above and beyond their traditional roles of wife and mother, that women make to society (Hinckley, 1989).

Despite these apparent changes, however, the leaders of the Mormon Church continue to emphasize that one of a woman's fundamental responsibilities is to bear and raise children (Benson, 1987; Elliot, 1991; Mauss, 1994; Nelson, 1989). Former church president Ezra Taft Benson said that "contrary to conventional wisdom, a mother's calling is in the home, not in the marketplace" (Benson, 1987, p. 3). Women who choose to work must often justify their decision, citing extenuating circumstances such as when her husband or the children's father is absent, disabled, unemployed, or underemployed (Heaton, 1988). And although women are increasingly being encouraged to pursue careers, they are advised to wait until after the children are raised, which can be a distinct disadvantage in the job market (Goodman & Heaton, 1986). Thus, Mormon leaders continue to promote the traditional roles of mother as homemaker and father as provider (Heaton et al., 1994).

Interestingly, it seems that these conservative attitudes do not necessarily translate into actual behaviors. Contemporary Mormon women are just as likely to be employed as their non-Mormon counterparts (Bahr, 1979; Heaton, 1992; Heaton et al., 1994; Mason, 1986). Moreover, when asked who actually performs certain tasks that are traditionally considered gendered, Mormon American couples score consistently high on measures of egalitarian role performance (Brinkerhoff & MacKie, 1984, 1988; Thomas, 1983, 1988). Thus, while "Mormons use a great deal of traditional patriarchal rhetoric, relationships between husbands and wives are in actual practice as egalitarian as in non-Mormon families" (Mauss, 1994, p. 135).

Several researchers have attempted to explain these apparently paradoxical attitudinal and behavioral patterns. One explanation is that Mormon Americans are being affected by the same social and economic forces as non-Mormons (Bahr, 1979). Given the increasing economic costs related to having and raising a child, the tendency among Mormon Americans to have larger families may make two incomes necessary. In fact, while the reported average household income of Mormon Americans is at or slightly above the national average, per-capita income is lower because of larger family size (Bahr, 1992; Heaton, 1992).

An alternative explanation is that Mormons emphasize education for both men and women (Campbell & Campbell, 1988; Corbett, 1990). The proportion of Mormon college-age women attending college is among the highest in the nation (Bahr, 1992; Heaton, 1992; May, 1980). Campbell and Campbell (1988) suggest that highly educated Mormon women are less likely to assume a submissive role in marriage. They may also be more employable. In a comparison across religions, Bahr (1992) found that Mormon American women are more likely to be employed as professionals and managers than women in most other populations.

Thomas (1988, 1992) suggests that the tendency for egalitarian role performance among Mormons, rather than being linked to larger societal influences, may be embedded within the teachings of the Mormon Church. He found that Mormon American couples who were married in the temple and who participate in activities such as family prayer, scripture study, and Family Home Evening are more likely to share in child-rearing duties and responsibilities (Thomas, 1988). Mormon fathers are often encouraged to be involved in the raising of their children (Hart, 1995; Pinegar, 1977; Sorenson, 1995; Thomas, 1988). They are also taught that patriarchy does not mean "unrighteous dominion" (*Doctrine and Covenants*, 1981, Sec. 121).

Ultimately, the juxtaposition of patriarchal doctrine and egalitarian practices may be related to the church's teachings on **free agency**, the sense of responsibility for personal choices, actions, and consequences. As with other difficult issues (such as contraception), the Mormon Church suggests that whether or not a mother seeks employment is ultimately a personal decision to be made between the individual and God. In response, employment for Mormon American wives has become justifiable under the conditions that the husband approves, the children are well cared for, and the couple has prayed and received approval from God (Iannaccone & Miles, 1990). Furthermore, when working is seen as a means of supplementing income or using talents, rather than as an intrusion upon the father's role as a provider, it is possible for wives to work without violating church doctrine (Heaton, 1988). In this way, the church's position on women has actually evolved such that the traditional ideal is reaffirmed even as new roles and behaviors are accommodated (Heaton, 1988; Iannaccone & Miles, 1990).

Life-Cycle Transitions

In keeping with the belief that the family unit is an eternal entity, the Mormon Church explicitly discourages divorce. Church members are taught that divorce is the result of selfishness and/or infidelity, and that relatively few divorces are justifiable (Kimball, 1982). Parents seeking divorce are reminded of the suffering that will be experienced by their innocent children. Nevertheless, church members are permitted to obtain divorces in both civil and temple marriages.

Traditionally, the Mormon Church's emphasis on family ties has led to lower rates of marital dissolution compared to the national population (Goodman & Heaton, 1986; Heaton, 1988). More recent trends, however, indicate that the divorce rate for Mormons is only slightly below the national average (Mauss, 1994). In fact, Mormons have slightly higher rates of divorce during the first 3 years of marriage, which may be attributable to the traditional Mormon preference for early marriage (Heaton et al., 1994). After the first 3 years, however, the Mormon divorce rate is slightly lower than that of other Americans (Heaton et al., 1994). If these trends continue, researchers project that about 33% of recent Mormon marriages will end in divorce or separation, compared to 50% nationally (Cherlin, 1992; Goodman & Heaton, 1986).

Once again it is important to distinguish differences within the Mormon population. For example, Mormon couples married in a civil ceremony are five or six times more likely to divorce than those with temple weddings (Goodman & Heaton, 1986). The latter group may also be more inclined to stay married for the benefit of their children. Further, divorce rates are negatively associated with regular church attendance and other indications of active membership, such as prayer and tithe paying (Heaton & Goodman, 1985). What is not clear is whether or not being less active in the church is the cause or the consequence of divorce—or both.

As in the general population, Mormons who divorce may experience economic and personal difficulties. The effects of divorce may be particularly acute for women who have embraced the traditional role of homemaker. They may not be prepared to support themselves and their children, a problem that can be compounded by a lack of child-care support. About one-third of female-headed Mormon households are living in poverty (Goodman & Heaton, 1986). Single-parent families may experience feelings of shame and isolation because of the church's strong orientation toward two-parent families. Children in single-parent households attend church less frequently than children in two-parent households, even when the custodial parent attends regularly (Goodman & Heaton, 1986).

Currently, single-parent families constitute a little over 5% of Mormon households (Heaton, 1992). Overall, it is estimated that about 33% of all Mormon children will spend some or all of their childhood in a single-parent family or stepfamily (Goodman & Heaton, 1986). Predictably, the majority of these children will be residing in households headed by their mothers.

One reason for the relatively low incidence of single-parent families in the Mormon population is the high rate of remarriage. In keeping with the emphasis on the importance of conjugal relationships, Mormons are more likely than members of the general population to remarry. Remarriage rates for divorced Mormons may be as high as 75% (Goodman & Heaton, 1986).

Family Strengths and Challenges

Citing research by sociologists and others (Cornwall, 1988; Dyer & Kunz, 1986; Swinton, 1987) that investigated the characteristics of strong Mormon American families, Ludlow (1992) summarized the results into ten family strengths:

1. **Active commitment to the gospel of Jesus Christ.** Families that are committed to living according to the gospel are more likely to participate in family-oriented activities, such as family prayer and Family Home Evening, which have been shown to be associated with positive relationships and outcomes (Cornwall, 1988).

2. **A positive home environment.** Perhaps the most popular motto among Mormons, often seen in framed stitchwork and on bumper stickers, is "Families are forever." This emphasis on the eternal nature of family relationships helps Mormon parents recognize that their responsibility goes beyond nourishing and clothing their children.

3. **Clear communication patterns.** Strong Mormon American families spend a good deal of time talking with each other. These conversations can be informal, such as when discussing problems, or more formal, as in Family Home Evenings.

4. **Affectionate interaction.** Verbal and physical expressions of love and affection are commonplace in strong Mormon American families.

5. **Strong marital relations.** When couples in the Dyer and Kunz study (1986) rated the happiness of their marriage, the average score was 8.5 on a 9-point scale. The emphasis within the church on eternal marriage helps couples work through their problems and develop a strong marital bond. The strength of their relationship becomes a model for the entire family.

6. **Firm but fair discipline.** Mormon American parents are inclined to establish and enforce family guidelines, with high expectations. General rules include treating family members with respect, letting parents know where you are going and when you'll be back, and being honest and dependable. Virtually all Mormon American parents say the most common form of discipline is through talking and reasoning; in one study, 45% said they had never spanked their children (Dyer & Kunz, 1986).

7. **Support of education.** In general, Mormon Americans place a high priority on reading, learning, and quality education. Many parents consider teaching to be one of their most important responsibilities, and thus their efforts are likely to support those of their children's teachers. To provide the time for this learning, strong Mormon American families watch less than half as much television as the national average and are more selective in their television viewing (Dyer & Kunz, 1986).

8. **A strong work ethic.** With the tendency toward larger families, it is important that all family members do their share of the work around the home. In one study, 77% of the parents said their children did some chores, while 60% indicated that they actually did them willingly (Dyer & Kunz, 1986). As a result of their learned work ethic, Mormons usually have a good reputation in their communities for hard work and honesty.

9. **Extended kin relationships.** The base of support in Mormon American families extends beyond the immediate family. In times of need, individuals can reach out to the family first for help and support, including the extended family. Furthermore, the emphasis on strengthening family ties and maintaining family history through activities such as reunions and genealogy helps younger family members develop a strong sense of identity.

10. **Unity during adversity.** Mormon American families tend to pull together during difficult times. The roots of solidarity and commitment Mormon American families exhibit during adversity may have been planted by the persecutions during the early years of the church.

It is important to note that the information above was gathered from Mormon American families that were considered by their peers to be highly successful. Obviously, not all Mormon families embody the strengths listed here, and even those that do experience varying degrees of success. However, research indicates that Mormon American families that are actively involved in their faith have a tendency toward exhibiting these strengths (Dyer & Kunz, 1986; Wilkinson & Tanner, 1980).

Mormon Americans, like other cultural or ethnic groups, face the threat of losing their youths to mass/popular culture. In secondary schools and colleges, Mormon programs encourage young people to continue to be active and committed to their religion and culture, and their values and norms. But inevitably, fraternization and peer pressure lead some youths to abandon their religious roots and culture. This path is sometimes linked to a desire to escape prejudice or persecution from outsiders. Cultural norms that discourage early dating, sexual activity, substance abuse, and participation in many popular forms of entertainment such as R-rated movies, for example, can become obstacles or points of rebellion. At the same time, religion and culture can provide an attractive counterculture—a means of interpreting and coping with the stresses of modern life and the alienation that sometimes accompanies it. Mormon Americans have available to them a clear alternative identity, if they do not wish to assimilate into the majority culture.

Equally challenging is the drastic decline in the economic viability of American family farms. Mormon American family farms and ranches, once a substantial part of the church population, are declining. Thus, the large family sizes that were possible, desired, and indeed economically advantageous in previous generations are increasingly difficult to support. Today, many Mormon children who inherit a rural livelihood must have employment in a city in order to survive financially. But urban two-parent families also find it hard to meet family needs on a single income.

The widespread transition from rural to urban life, and most recently to urban employment, has been accompanied by falling Mormon American birth rates. As a result, the traditionally large Mormon American families are experiencing severe strains. Urban Mormon Americans have, in fact, tended to have higher education levels throughout this century than members of the general population. As the cost of higher education increases, with its implications for the cost of raising children, Mormon patterns of courtship and mate selection are endangered. In the 1960s, the ideal was that every young Mormon American serving as a full-time missionary could achieve middle-class socioeconomic status. However, as the economy continues to erode, the ideal of every new Mormon American family having a foundation of missionary service and temple experience before marriage is becoming more difficult to attain.

The increasing rates of divorce and single parenthood among Mormon Americans place additional stress on grandparent families, who are considered to be the resource of first resort in the event of their children's economic distress, and on the church's welfare system as a backup. The materialism of the consumer society continues to clash with traditional Mormon social and economic ideals. Communitarian and self-sufficient economic models are attractive yet seemingly unattainable alternatives. The outward stresses are the same as in the general society, but the response to them is determined by very different cultural patterns.

Misconceptions and Stereotypes

Perhaps the most well-known and yet widely misunderstood and controversial aspect of the Mormon Church is polygamy (technically polygyny). However offensive or exotic the idea of one man being simultaneously married to more than one woman might seem today, as with any cultural difference, polygamy, or plural marriage, as it was known, should be considered in historical and cultural context.

Throughout history, the vast majority of Mormon American families have been monogamous. Scholars estimate that up to 1890, after which no new polygynous marriages were permitted to be performed in the United States, only 8–12% of Mormon men had more than one wife. Of these families, 70% were families with two wives, 21% consisted of three, and 9% involved four or more wives (May, 1980). Even at its height, polygamy involved only a minority of Mormon Americans, and records suggest that many of these may have been reluctant participants at best.

The stereotype that Mormon Americans are polygamists still persists. Despite the prohibition on new plural marriages that has been in place since 1890, prejudices that were created over 70 years ago still remain. While it is true that a tiny minority of people, some of whom were once members of the Mormon Church, do practice polygamy, one cannot be in a polygamous marriage and maintain membership in the Church of Jesus Christ of Latter-Day Saints.

It is important to note that polygamy was *not* at the root of nearly 70 years of anti-Mormon persecutions during the nineteenth century. Objections to polygamy were a means of mobilizing public opinion against the Mormon American minority. As one non-Mormon scholar notes:

> Protestant America is reluctant to believe that any other agent of
> history except the United States can carry forward God's purposes
> in the world. Any group . . . which claims truth and serves purposes
> not [the nation's] own is suspect of the ultimate sin, the sin of un-
> Americanism. When Mormons pretended that they were the heirs
> of ancient Israel, they were viewed as un-American. Could the Church
> of the Latter-Day Saints embody values not already in the nation? . . .
> Only the nation bears ultimate universal purposes and has continuing
> historic meaning. (Smylie, 1963, pp. 315–316)

In *The Book of Mormon*, sexual promiscuity is roundly condemned, and monogamy is generally affirmed: "For there shall not any man among you have save it be one wife; and concubines he shall have none" (*Book of Mormon*, 1981, Jacob 2:27). This corresponded with the cultural background of virtually all nineteenth-century Mormon Americans. Many who practiced polygamy had to be specifically given what they understood as a commandment from God to go against cultural norms and values. Since 1890, the Mormon Church has taken the position that there is no longer any authorization for polygamy.

Another common misunderstanding related to Mormons is that they are not Christians. This stereotype remains despite the church's emphasis on the teachings and Atonement of Christ and the fact that the full title of the church is the Church of Jesus Christ of Latter-Day Saints. This prejudice, however, is common throughout the history of Christianity. In the sixteenth century, Protestants and Catholics alike were denying each other legitimacy as Christians. Recently, M. F. Mannion, rector of the Roman Catholic cathedral in Salt Lake City, explained:

> Anti-Mormonism and anti-Catholicism are bred in the same stable. The very arguments used to show Mormons are not Christians are the very same arguments used in the early years of our century to show Catholics were not Christians. (quoted in Johnston, 1995, p. 73)

For Mormons, however, such rejections continue to persist today.

Personal Interview

Norman Mormon (not his real name) has been married for 7 years and has two children: a son, age 5, and a daughter, age 3. He is currently a doctoral student and research assistant at a large midwestern university.

What are some of the challenges of being a Mormon in American society?

Norman: There are additional pressures that result from church commitments. We want to be successful in our families and careers, be active in community service and sports, like everyone else. Yet in addition we are expected to perform regular church service, temple worship, genealogy, family history, and missionary work. While all of these things may not get done, at the same time they are always on our minds. Furthermore, there is some social and/or spiritual pressure to reserve Sunday only for family and church-related commitments. In addition to the time consideration, there also social implications to this. In a society in which Sunday has long been viewed as any other day for the most part, it is difficult to explain and be understood by em-

ployers and friends why there are certain things we would rather not do on Sunday. One last point involves the size of families. We are encouraged to have more than one or two children where possible, in a society in which this is much less common and is often considered careless rather than planned.

Do you feel that, in general, Mormons are understood by the dominant culture?

Norman: No. From the people I have talked to, they either know nothing about Mormons or still think we practice polygamy, can't dance, have fun, etc. Very few people know or understand our doctrine or practices.

Have you been a member of the church all your life, or did you convert?

Norman: My family has been in the church for many generations, but I have experienced my own very individual conversion. Before my conversion to Jesus Christ I was aimless, and happiness resulted from whatever pleasure I could obtain. Now happiness is much deeper. It comes from an inner peace, which is the result of knowing I am doing right and helping those around me to do the same. My conversion came when I was 15 years old. I was encouraged to read *The Book of Mormon* by my father, which I did. This led to my conversion. I knew after a prayerful reading of *The Book of Mormon* what kind of life I wanted to live.

Have you experienced discrimination on the basis of your religion?

Norman: Discrimination to me would imply that I was left out of something or rejected from something purely on the basis of religion. I do not recall anything like that. Certainly not recently. I have been ridiculed, but not seriously. On the other hand, I know of others who have.

What do you view as the principal teachings of the Mormon Church, and how have those teachings affected how you function daily?

Norman: If I had to pick one teaching, I would say it is that Jesus Christ is the Son of God and that he came into the world to redeem us from our fallen state, which is a consequence of our own sins. If we believe this, ask for his forgiveness and follow all his commandments, we will eventually become like him and be joint heirs in his kingdom in heaven. Trying to follow *all* God's commandments requires total commitment. It requires that we offer all that we have and are to building God's kingdom on earth. In this way, then, this teaching finds its way into almost every decision I make and everything I do.

Questions for Discussion

1. How does the combination of religious conversion and immigration become part of the Mormon American community differ from immigration in other American cultural or ethnic groups?

2. How has the persecution experienced by early Mormon families influenced the nature of the contemporary Mormon American family? Compare this to the influence of early experiences of persecution on contemporary American Indian and African American families. How are they similar and different?

3. What potential influence does the Mormon concept of the eternal family have on husband-wife relationships, as well as on parent-child relationships?

4. What role does free agency play in the ability within the Mormon culture to reaffirm traditional ideals, even as new roles and behaviors are accommodated?

5. What are some of the strengths of active Mormon American families that are also found in American Indian and African American families? How do these strengths compare to your own family's strengths?

6. What are some common misconceptions about Mormon American ethnicity and families? How do they compare to those about American Indian and African American families? How do they compare to misconceptions about your own family?

Suggested Resources

Readings

Ludlow, D. H. (Ed.). (1992). *Encyclopedia of Mormonism: The history, scripture, doctrine, and procedure of the Church of Jesus Christ of Latter-Day Saints.* New York: Macmillan.

Electronic Database on CD-ROM

LDS collectors library. (1995). Provo, UT: Infobases. Contains *The Book of Mormon: Another Testament of Jesus Christ, The Doctrine and Covenants of the Church of Jesus Christ of Latter-Day Saints, The Pearl of Great Price*, and some 800 other primary and secondary sources for the study of Mormonism, including the *Encyclopedia of Mormonism.*

Videos

The Church of Jesus Christ of Latter-Day Saints (Producer) (1987). *How rare a possession: The Book of Mormon.* (Available from Salt Lake Distribution Center, 1999 West 1700 South, Salt Lake City, UT 84104)

The Church of Jesus Christ of Latter-Day Saints (Producer). (1988). *Together forever.* (Available from Bonneville Media Communications, Salt Lake City, UT 84112)

Gold, H. (Editor), & Bloom, A. (Director). (1996). *The Mormons.* In D. Hewitt (Executive Producer), *60 minutes.* (Available from Columbia Broadcasting System, 51 West 52nd Street, New York, NY 10019)

May, D. (Producer). (1989). *A people's history.* (Available from University of Utah, 101 University Services Building, Salt Lake City, UT 84112)

References

Allen, J. B., & Leonard, G. M. (1993). *The story of the Latter-Day Saints.* (2nd ed.) Salt Lake City, UT: Desert Books.

Arrington, L. J., & Bitton, D. (1992). *The Mormon experience: A history of the Latter-Day Saints.* (2nd ed.) New York: Knopf.

Arrington, L. J., Fox, F. Y., & May, D. L. (1976). *Building the city of God: Community and cooperation among the Mormons.* Salt Lake City, UT: Desert Books.

Bahr, H. M. (1979). The declining distinctiveness of Utah's working women. *BYU Studies, 19*, 525–543.

Bahr, H. M. (1992). Social characteristics. In D. Ludlow (Ed.), *Encyclopedia of Mormonism* (Vol. 4, pp. 1371–1378). New York: Macmillan.

Bahr, H. M. (1994). Religion and adolescent drug use: A comparison of Mormons and other religions. In M. Cornwall, T. B. Heaton, & L. A. Young (Eds.), *Contemporary Mormonism: Social science perspectives* (pp. 118–137). Urbana: University of Illinois Press.

Bean, L. L., Mineau, G., & Anderton, D. (1983). Residence and religious effect on declining family size: An historical analysis of the Utah population. *Review of Religious Research, 25*, 91–101.

Benson, E. T. (1987). *To the mothers of Zion* [Pamphlet]. Salt Lake City, UT: Church of Jesus Christ of Latter-Day Saints.

Benson, E. T. (1988, May). To the single adult brethren of the church. *Ensign, 18*, 51–53.

Benson, E. T. (1992, July). Salvation: A family affair. *Ensign, 22*, 2–5.

Book of Mormon: Another testament of Jesus Christ. (1981). Salt Lake City, UT: Church of Jesus Christ of Latter-Day Saints. (Original work published 1830)

Brinkerhoff, M. B., & MacKie, M. (1984). Religious denomination's impact on gender attitudes: Some methodological implications. *Review of Religious Research, 25*, 365–378.

Brinkerhoff, M. B., & MacKie, M. (1988). Religious sources of gender traditionalism. In D. Thomas (Ed.), *The religion and family connection: Social science perspectives* (pp. 230–257). Provo, UT: Religious Studies Center.

Bush, L. E. (1976). Birth control among Mormons: Introduction to an insistent question. *Dialogue: A Journal of Mormon Thought, 10*, 12–44.

Bushman, R. L. (1984). *Joseph Smith and the beginnings of Mormonism*. Urbana: University of Illinois Press.

Campbell, B. L., & Campbell, E. E. (1988). The Mormon family. In C. H. Mindel, R. W. Habenstein, & R. Wright (Eds.), *Ethnic families in America* (pp. 325–366). New York: Elsevier.

Chadwick, B. A., & Garrett, H. D. (1993). Religion, employment, and family roles: The Latter-Day Saint women's experience. Poster presented at the annual meeting of the National Council on Family Relations, Baltimore, MD.

Cherlin, A. J. (1992). *Marriage, divorce, remarriage* (2nd ed.). Cambridge, MA: Harvard University Press.

Christensen, H. T. (1976). Mormon sexuality in cross-cultural perspective. *Dialogue: A Journal of Mormon Thought, 10*(2), 62–75.

Corbett, J. M. (1990). *Religion in America*. Englewood Cliffs, NJ: Prentice-Hall.

Cornwall, M. (1988). The influence of three agents of religious socialization:

Family, church, and peers. In D. Thomas (Ed.), *The religion and family connection: Social science perspectives* (pp. 207–231). Provo, UT: Religious Studies Center.

Cornwall, M. (1994). The institutional role of Mormon women. In M. Cornwall, T. B. Heaton, & L. A. Young (Eds.), *Contemporary Mormonism: Social science perspectives* (pp. 239–264). Urbana: University of Illinois Press.

Doctrine and covenants of the Church of Jesus Christ of Latter-Day Saints (1981). Salt Lake City, UT: Church of Jesus Christ of Latter-Day Saints. (Original work published 1847)

Dyer, W. G., & Kunz, P. R. (1986). *Effective Mormon families: How they see themselves.* Salt Lake City, UT: Desert Books.

Elliot, D. W. (1991). Women, the Mormon family, and class mobility: Nineteenth-century Victorian ideology in a twentieth-century church. *Sunstone, 15*(6), 19–26.

Furniss, N. F. (1960). *The Mormon conflict: 1850–1859.* New Haven, CT: Yale University Press.

Goodman, K. L., & Heaton, T. B. (1986). LDS church members in the U.S. and Canada: A demographic profile. *AMCAP Journal, 12,* 88–107.

Hart, J. L. (1995, December 2). A father's greatest gift to his children is to love and care for their mother. *Church News, 66,* 6–7.

Hayden, D. (1976). *Seven American utopias: The architecture of communitarian socialism, 1790–1975.* Cambridge, MA: MIT Press.

Heaton, T. B. (1986). How does religion influence fertility? The case of the Mormons. *Journal for the Scientific Study of Religion, 25,* 245–258.

Heaton, T. B. (1988). Four c's of the Mormon family: Chastity, conjugality, children, and chauvinism. In D. Thomas (Ed.), *The religion and family connection: Social science perspectives* (pp. 107–124). Provo, UT: Religious Studies Center.

Heaton, T. B. (1992). Vital statistics. In D. Ludlow (Ed.), *Encyclopedia of Mormonism* (Vol. 4, pp. 1518–1537). New York: Macmillan.

Heaton, T. B., & Calkins, S. (1983). Family size and contraceptive use among Mormons: 1965–1975. *Review of Religious Research, 25,* 102–113.

Heaton, T. B., & Goodman, K. L. (1985). Religion and family formation. *Review of Religious Research, 26,* 343–359.

Heaton, T. B., Goodman, K. L., & Holman, T. B. (1994). In search of a peculiar people: Are Mormon families really different? In M. Cornwall, T. B. Heaton, & L. A. Young (Eds.), *Contemporary Mormonism: Social science perspectives* (pp. 87–117). Urbana: University of Illinois Press.

Hinckley, G. B. (1989, November). Rise to the stature of the divine within you. *Ensign, 19,* 94–98.

Iannaccone, L. R., & Miles, C. A. (1990). Dealing with social change: The

Mormon Church's response to change in women's roles. *Social Forces, 68,* 1231–1250.

Jacobsen, C. K., Kunz, P. R., & Conlin, M. W. (1989). Extending family ties: Genealogical researchers. In S. Bahr & E. Peterson (Eds.), *Aging and the family.* Lexington, MA: Lexington Books.

Jessee, D. C. (1974). *Letters of Brigham Young to his sons.* Salt Lake City, UT: Desert Books.

Johnston, J. (1995). Mormon Catholic roundtable: Talking together about our common ground. *This People, 73,* 68–70.

Kimball, E. L. (Ed.). (1982). *The teachings of Spencer W. Kimball.* Salt Lake City, UT: Bookcraft.

Knowlton, D. (1992). On Mormon masculinity. *Sunstone, 16*(2), 19–31.

Larson, G. O. (1971). *The "Americanization" of Utah for statehood.* San Marino CA: Huntington Library.

Lee, H. B. (1973). *Strengthening the home* [Pamphlet]. Salt Lake City, UT: Church of Jesus Christ of Latter-Day Saints.

Ludlow, V. L. (1992). *Principles and practices of the restored gospel.* Salt Lake City, UT: Desert Books.

Maass, A., & Anderson, R. L. (1978). *And the desert shall rejoice: Conflict, growth, and justice in arid environments.* Cambridge, MA: MIT Press.

Mason, J. (1986). Family economics. In T. K. Martin, T. B. Heaton, & S. J. Bahr (Eds.), *Utah in demographic perspective* (pp. 91–110). Salt Lake City, UT: Signature Books.

Mauss, A. L. (1994). *The angel and the beehive: The Mormon struggle with assimilation.* Urbana: University of Illinois Press.

May, D. L. (1980). Mormons. In S. Thernstrom (Ed.), *Harvard encyclopedia of American ethnic groups* (pp. 720–731). London: Belknap Press of Harvard University.

McKay, D. O. (1953). *Gospel ideals.* Salt Lake City, UT: The Improvement Era.

McKay, D. O. (1962). *Treasures of life.* Salt Lake City, UT: Desert Books.

McKay, D. O. (1964, June). What a person does practically believe determines his character. *The Improvement Era, 67,* 444–445, 520, 522.

Miller, B., & Goddard, H. W. (1992). Dating and courtship. In D. Ludlow (Ed.), *Encyclopedia of Mormonism* (Vol. 2, pp. 357–359). New York: Macmillan.

Mosher, W. D., William, L. B., & Johnson, D. P. (1992). Religion and fertility in the United States: New patterns. *Demography, 29,* 199–214.

Nelson, R. M. (1989, November). Women of infinite worth. *Ensign, 19,* 20–22.

O'Dea, T. F. (1966). *The sociology of religion.* Englewood Cliffs, NJ: Prentice-Hall.

Pinegar, E. J. (1977). *Fatherhood.* Salt Lake City, UT: Desert Books.

Roberts, B. H. (1965). *A comprehensive history of the Church of Jesus Christ of Latter-Day Saints* (Vols. 1–6). Provo, UT: Brigham Young University Press.

Smith, W. E. (1976). Mormon sex standards on college campuses, or deal us out of the sexual revolution! *Dialogue: A Journal of Mormon Thought, 10*(3), 76–81.

Smylie, J. E. (1963, October). Editorial. *Theology Today, 20,* 315–316.

Sorenson, K. C. (1995, February). A latter-day father's guidebook. *Ensign, 25,* 14–17.

Stott, G. N. (1988). Familial influence on religious involvement. In D. Thomas (Ed.), *The religion and family connection: Social science perspectives* (pp. 258–271). Provo, UT: Religious Studies Center.

Swinton, H. (1987, February/March). The truth behind the ideal family. *This People, 20,* 26.

Thomas, D. L. (1983). Family in the Mormon experience. In W. V. D'Antonio & J. Aldous (Eds.), *Families and religions: Conflict and change in modern society* (pp. 267–288). Beverly Hills, CA: Sage.

Thomas, D. L. (1988). Future prospects for religion and family studies: The Mormon case. In D. Thomas (Ed.), *The religion and family connection: Social science perspectives* (pp. 357–382). Provo, UT: Religious Studies Center.

Thomas, D. L. (1992). Family life. In D. Ludlow (Ed.), *Encyclopedia of Mormonism* (Vol. 2) (pp. 1507–1509). New York: Macmillan.

Thornton, A. (1979). Religion and fertility: The case of Mormonism. *Journal of Marriage and the Family, 41,* 131–142.

Wagner, G. E. (1977). *Consecration and stewardship: A socially efficient system of justice.* Unpublished doctoral dissertation, Cornell University, Ithaca, NY.

Watson, F. M. (1995, May). Statistical report 1994. *Ensign, 25,* 22.

Weed, S. E. (1992). Transmission of values. In D. Ludlow (Ed.), *Encyclopedia of Mormonism* (Vol. 4) (pp. 1507–1509). New York: Macmillan.

Wilkinson, M. L., & Tanner, W. C. (1980). The influence of family size, interaction, and religiosity on family affection in a Mormon sample. *Journal of Marriage and the Family, 42,* 297–304.

Wirthlin, J. B. (1991, November). Fruits of the restored Gospel of Jesus Christ. *Ensign, 21,* 15–17.

Masako Ishii-Kuntz

6

Chinese American Families

The first Asian immigrants to arrive in the United States, the Chinese were attracted by the discovery of gold and other precious minerals in California and by jobs that became available as the American West developed. At the same time, they were forced to emigrate because of a poor economy and unstable political conditions at home. The Chinese were also the first group of Asians who faced insurmountable hostility in the United States, which culminated in institutional and legal discrimination against them. The formation and relationships of Chinese American families have been greatly influenced by these institutional barriers, as well as by cultural traditions and their home country's political and economic conditions. This chapter discusses how family structure and relationships among Chinese Americans have been shaped by the societal, cultural, and historical factors in the United States as well as China.

Historical and Cultural Background

The Chinese in the United States today are a diverse group of people whose ancestors originated in various parts of China. However, the Chinese U.S. population can be divided roughly into two major groups: Cantonese- or Toisanese-speaking Chinese and Mandarin-speaking Chinese. The former group is made up primarily of immigrants who came to the United States for economic reasons before World War II and the relatives of these early immigrants who have recently left Hong Kong and Guangdon (Kwangtung) Province in southern China. The majority of Cantonese-speaking immigrants are former peasants whose socioeconomic status in China was low. They settled in urban Chinatowns and worked as unskilled laborers (Sung, 1987). In contrast, most Mandarin-speaking Chinese are recent immigrants. They tend to be middle class and are more likely to be professionally oriented than entrepreneurial. To understand how early Chinese immigrants in the United States influenced various aspects of family life for contemporary Chinese Americans, we will focus on Cantonese-speaking Chinese immigrants in this section.

In the nineteenth century, when Chinese immigration to the United States began, the Chinese government strongly supported the values of the traditional family system, even when those values occasionally dictated that family needs take priority over state needs. The ideologies of the family system and the state were mutually supportive, both being based on **Confucianism** and the Confucian morality that held sacred a system of hierarchies based on generation, age, and gender. In terms of generation and age, traditional Chinese families emphasized **filial piety**, in which ancestors and elders were viewed with great reverence and respect. Within this value system, members of the older generations were regarded as deserving a higher status than individuals in the younger generation. The line of authority was clear, and the primary family unit exerted great control over its members.

Generation and age hierarchies were demonstrated in several aspects of the functioning of traditional Chinese families. First, in terms of property ownership, parents in traditional China retained the legal rights to family property. Members of the younger generation usually depended on the father or other close kinsmen for their occupations (Lee, 1956). Second, because of the scarcity of educational opportunities, personal experience was the major source of knowledge in traditional China. The strategic knowledge of the elderly ensured them a vital place, even after their physical strength had declined. Third, Chinese culture focused on the past. Ancestor worship was the central family religious practice. The elderly were seen as the link to the past, and when they died, they were believed to join the ancestors to be worshipped. Fidelity was reinforced by the belief that if descendants did not exhibit filial piety, the ancestors might return as vengeful ghosts (Adhern, 1973). Fourth, the extended family was central to the social organization of the Chinese village. Many southern Chinese villages were composed of just a few lineages (Freedman, 1979). In this situation, any unfilial behavior was an insult to everyone's ancestors and hence could jeopardize the relationships within the entire community. The community thus had a stake in ensuring filial behavior.

Gender hierarchy in traditional Chinese families was also evidenced by the power vested in the male family head. Strict division of labor existed in Chinese families; the husband assumed a breadwinner role, while the wife provided emotional support and physical care of the children. Gender and age hierarchies were clearly demonstrated in the system of inheritance. The family property was divided up among the sons, either before or upon the death of the father; in most cases, the eldest son, who was assigned the responsibility of caring for the parents, could expect to receive a larger share than his brothers.

Although these cultural values have been strongly embedded in the Chinese social and family systems throughout China's history, the country is far from a static state politically and economically. In fact, the Communist victory in 1949 brought about changes affecting various domains of the family, including mate selection, marriage, and **gender roles** (Wolf, 1984). In traditional China, marriage was a building block for the basic institution of society—the family. One of the most sacred duties of a son was to provide descendants for his and his father's ancestors. To do so, he must marry. Younger men and women were not usually consulted about whom they would marry or when, but were presented with a mate at the time deemed appropriate by the senior generations. After the Cultural Revolution, the first law the Communists promulgated was the Marriage Law of 1950, designed to intervene at a basic level in the intimate affairs of the family. For example, the opening paragraph of the law, aimed at guaranteeing equality between husband and wife, abolished the "supremacy of man over woman." Subsequent paragraphs ban **polygyny**, child betrothal, bride prices and dowries, and the coercion of either party to the union. In short, Communist policies focused on destroying the old family system and the patriarchal ideology that supported it, but not on destroying the family as a domestic unit.

In summary, the Confucian values of filial piety and gender hierarchy strongly influenced the traditional Chinese family. Chinese who emigrated to the United States during the nineteenth century left their country when it was under the strong influence of these Confucian principles; consequently, subsequent generations of Chinese Americans have also been influenced by these norms. At the same time, Chinese Americans have had to struggle with institutional and personal discrimination throughout their years in the United States. Thus, Chinese Americans have had to continue respecting their cultural heritage and practice, while adjusting to a hostile environment in which many legal and institutional barriers have restricted their lives and opportunities.

The Immigration Experience

Chinese emigration dates back to the seventh century, when people from Fujian (Fukien) Province in southeastern China started crossing the narrow Taiwan Strait to fish and settle in the small Penghu Islands and the larger island of Taiwan. During the following century, they were joined by people from the neighboring province of Guangdong. Eventually, inhabitants of these two provinces were sailing regularly to various regions in Southeast Asia. Virtually all the Chinese who went abroad throughout the later centuries came from five small regions in these two provinces and the island of Hainan (Chan, 1991).

A majority of Chinese came to the United States to search for gold, but there were also forces in their home country that encouraged their emigration. When Great Britain led the Western powers in "opening" China, the trade balance between Britain and China favored the latter. In an attempt to reverse the imbalance, the British exported increasing amounts of opium to China. As more and more Chinese became addicts, the balance of trade shifted. In the late 1830s, to curb the influx of this drug, a Chinese official confiscated and destroyed thousands of chests of opium stored in English merchants' warehouses in Canton. The conflict that ensued is known as the first Opium War (1839–1842), which China lost.

The Treaty of Nanjing (Nanking) ending the war cost the Chinese a great deal, including the island of Hong Kong and the opening of five ports to foreign commerce. The treaty also adversely affected the common people. Cottage industries, unable to compete with imported factory-manufactured goods, declined, depriving many peasant households of an important source of supplementary income. Taxes soared as the government tried to raise sufficient funds to cover the indemnity. And as opium continued to pour into the country, the number of addicts multiplied.

The financial difficulties of ordinary Chinese citizens were made worse by the loss of the Anglo-Chinese War (1856–1860), which resulted in English and French military occupation of Canton between 1858 and 1861. Along with the widespread social, economic, and political turmoil caused by the presence of Westerners, domestic uprisings such as the Paiping Rebellion, which lasted more than a decade and resulted in an estimated 10 million deaths, also created pressures for emigration. Although aspiring emigrants had many destinations to choose from, places where gold had been discovered—notably, California and Australia—were the most alluring.

Far more Chinese landed in California than in other parts of the country because of the gold rush (Takaki, 1990). In 1852, more than 20,000 Chinese passed through the San Francisco Customs House en route to the gold fields in the Sierra Nevada foothills. During the same year, the first 200 or so Chinese contract laborers arrived in Hawaii. In 1853, fewer than 5000 Chinese arrived, partly because California had imposed a Foreign Miners' Tax, greatly reducing the income of non-American miners, but also because news of the discovery of gold in Australia had by then reached Guangdong Province, causing thousands to rush southward instead of eastward (Chan, 1991). For the next decade, arrivals in California fluctuated between 2000 and 9000 a year. Then between 1867 and 1870, partly in response to recruitment efforts by the Central Pacific Railroad Company, which was building the western section of the first transcontinental railroad, some 40,000 Chinese poured into the United States.

Most Americans during the nineteenth century acknowledged that China had once had a magnificent civilization, but they also believed that the country had fallen into an advanced state of decay (Chan, 1991). In their view, China was a nation populated by starving beggars and opium addicts. Thus, even before Chinese people started immigrating to the United States, the American public had a negative—or at best, an ambivalent—impression of them. As a result, they were the targets of racial discrimination, as evidenced by violent outbreaks against the Chinese during the 1880s all over the American West. Because of Americans' negative perceptions about the Chinese, compounded by their fear of losing jobs to the immigrants, the U.S. government severely restricted Chinese immigration by the 1882 Exclusion Act and completely prohibited it by passing the 1924 Immigration Act.

As a result of the 1882 Exclusion Act and its subsequent extensions, special taxes were levied on Chinese immigrants, and discrimination in housing and employment limited the size of the Chinese population, forcing them into Chinatown ghettos. Because there were few Chinese women in the United States until the second half of the twentieth century, most of the Chinese men in the first wave of emigration, numbering over 300,000 (most of whom eventually returned to China), did not father children here. However, the small number of female emigrants did not mean that the majority of male emigrants were single and childless. In fact, many of these men had married shortly before they went abroad. Most also waited until they were sure their wives were pregnant before departing. Thereafter, whenever they could afford to do so, they would return to spend a few months with their families, in the hope of fathering additional children during their visits. Parents of emigrant sons believed that keeping the wives in China ensured the men would faithfully send money home to support their extended families. In the households of some emigrants, when sons became teenagers, they joined their fathers, brothers, uncles, or grandfathers across the Pacific. Some of these boys attended public schools run by Protestant missionaries in order to learn enough English to help their older relatives in business. Others went to work almost immediately upon arrival. Most of the wives and daughters, however, remained in the villages of China.

This **split-household family**, as Glenn (1983) named it, was maintained not only because elderly Chinese parents wished to keep their sons' wives and children at home, but also because the U.S. government imposed legal limitations on Chinese men. For example, an antimiscegenation statute in California forbade marriages between Chinese and members of other cultures, and in 1870, the Page Law, designed to curb the Chinese prostitution trade, was passed. The immigration application process for Chinese women was made difficult and arduous, and female applicants were subjected to repeated questioning and badgering. According to Pfeffer (1986), the effect of the application process was to discourage and bar laborers' wives, resulting in a decline in the proportion of women among the immigrant population. Because of the low number of children that Chinese immigrant men fathered in the United States, the proportion of Chinese Americans today who are third-, fourth-, and fifth-generation Americans is relatively small. (This differs from the Japanese American population, which consists of many descendants of early immigrants who came here around the turn of the twentieth century.)

A second wave of a few thousand Chinese came to the United States after World War II. During the war, the United States fearing that China might join forces with Japan, sought friendly relations with China and repealed the Exclusion Act, allowing a small immigration quota. After the war, when the Communists took control of China, the U.S. government encouraged Chinese scientists and professionals and their families to immigrate. Therefore, in addition to the descendants of the first wave of immigrants from China, the Chinese American population today includes the second group of immigrants, their children, and their grandchildren.

A third wave of Chinese came to the United States after the 1965 Immigration Act (and its 1990 extension), which gives priority to those who have special skills needed in the United States or who are joining their families here. Under the current quota, having relatives who are U.S. citizens or residents improves an individual's chances of immigrating. Thus, in the third wave of Chinese immigration, either entire families have moved to the United States together, or one family member has immigrated, has established himself or herself as a permanent U.S. resident or citizen, and then has sponsored other family members. The 1965 Immigration Act marked a radical change in U.S. immigration policy: Quotas were no longer based on race. Tens of thousands of Chinese have come to the United States every year since the 1965 Immigration Act became law. The fact that Taiwan, the People's Republic of China, and Hong Kong have separate quotas has further increased the number of Chinese who can immigrate to the United States.

In recent decades, Chinese have come to the United States to seek a better standard of living and a higher level of education for their children, and in the case of the Taiwanese, to help sons avoid the draft. These Chinese have primarily emigrated from Taiwan, Hong Kong, the People's Republic of China, and Vietnam. The last group of Chinese immigrated to Southeast Asia centuries ago. The increasing number of Chinese immigrants also has resulted in a gradual rise in the percentage of foreign-born Chinese in the United States. Using data from the U.S. Bureau of the Census, Barringer, Gardner, and Levin (1993) estimated that while only 14.8% of the Chinese population in the United States before 1960 was foreign-born, the comparable figure in 1980 was 63.3%.

Because some Chinese families have been in the United States for five or six generations (descendants of the first wave) and others have arrived as recently as last week (members of the third wave), there is a great diversity in the Chinese community. Consequently, some Chinese are almost completely embedded in American life, while others are much less fully assimilated. Some speak only English or only Chinese, while others are bilingual or trilingual (speaking Chinese, Vietnamese, and English). Some Chinese Americans grew up in the American middle class, while others experienced horrendous psychological and physical traumas before fleeing Southeast Asia.

It is clear that the experiences of Chinese people in the United States vary considerably depending on the dates of their immigration. Because of legal and institutional barriers, many early Chinese immigrant men were unable to form families. Those who came to the United States during the second and third waves either brought their families or formed families after their immigration. Consequently, the heterogeneity of contemporary Chinese American families must be considered in the context of their diverse immigration experiences.

Traditional and Emerging Family Systems

Because of the population's growing heterogeneity, today's Chinese American family cannot be described simply. Almost all the Chinese immigrants before the 1940s came from villages in Guangdong Province and thus shared a common language and culture. However, the situation changed dramatically following World War II. To understand the traditional and emerging patterns of the Chinese American family system, we must begin with the family experiences of early immigrants and see how they have influenced contemporary families.

Household Size and Composition

It is difficult to describe the size and composition of Chinese households in the United States from 1850 to 1920, because the vast majority of Chinese immigrants were men who were either never married or married but who had left their spouses and children in their home country. Glenn (1994) reports that in 1900, there were 18 Chinese men for every Chinese woman in the United States, and only 3.4% of the Chinese population consisted of children under the age of 14. Many immigrant men planned to return to China after accumulating enough money to acquire land and retire; in the meantime, they sent remittances to support their relatives in their homeland. At least two-thirds of these Chinese succeeded in returning to China, so the population of Chinese in America never exceeded 110,000.

The sojourning pattern of Chinese immigrants gave rise to the split-household family. In this arrangement, income earning was separated from the main household and carried out by a member living abroad, while keeping the family home, socializing children, caring for the elderly, and maintaining family graves were the responsibility of wives and other relatives in the home village. The family as an independent economic unit thus spanned two continents. The conventional definition of household size thus does not apply to early Chinese immigrants' split-household families.

In urban Chinatowns in the 1910s, families began to grow despite obstacles to their formation. This trend is evidenced by the increase of women and children in the Chinese American population. Between 1900 and 1930, the percentage of children age 14 and under rose from 3.4% to 20.4%. Glenn (1994) reports that most of these families were formed by small entrepreneurs who were former laborers who managed to accumulate sufficient capital to start a small business or shop. These men could register as merchants and send for wives.

The number of Chinese American families increased even more from the 1930s through the 1950s as a result of changes in immigration regulations. Openings for wives and children were expanded by the repeal of the Chinese Exclusion Act in 1943; the creation of the Brides' Act of 1946, permitting entry to wives and children of citizens and permanent residents; and the creation of the Immigration Act of 1953, which gave preferential entry to relatives of citizens. The vast majority who entered the United States under these agreements were women. Therefore, the size of Chinese American households steadily increased during the first half of the twentieth century.

Both family and household compositions of Chinese Americans today are similar to those of other Asian Americans and Whites. About 86.8% of Chinese American families consist of married couples with children under the age of 18, a figure that is comparable to Japanese Americans (84.1%), Filipino Americans (83.6%), Korean Americans (86.0%), and Whites (86.1%) (Barringer et al., 1993). In addition, only 20.9% of Chinese American households are characterized as "non-family" households, and this figure is not significantly different from other Asian American, as well as European American, households (29.2% for Japanese, 16.8% for Filipino, 16.8% for Koreans, and 26.5% for European Americans) (Barringer et al., 1993).

Because of the split-household family pattern, it is speculated that the fertility rates of Chinese wives who were left behind in China were relatively low, although some Chinese immigrant husbands were able to return to China to father more children. Instead of children, however, in-laws were frequently present in the split-household families. Therefore, the average size of split households was probably four or five.

Given the increase of women and children in the Chinese American population, it is easy to speculate that the rate of fertility among Chinese American women in the 1930s, 1940s, and 1950s soared dramatically. According to the U.S. Bureau of the Census, Chinese American women's fertility has reached a stable level: 1014 children were born per 1000 Chinese American women in

1990. Fertility also varies depending on a woman's place of birth, place of residence, and level of education. Fertility among contemporary Chinese American women who are native-born, reside in an urban area, and have completed a college education is 50% lower than those who are foreign-born, live in a rural area, and have completed high school (U.S. Bureau of the Census, 1990).

In summary, the composition of early Chinese immigrant families and households was determined by historical and legal factors that imposed constraints on family formation. Chinese American families today show similar patterns of family and household composition as their White and other Asian American counterparts.

The Socialization of Children

In traditional China, the line of authority was determined primarily by age and gender. Fathers or grandfathers exerted great control over their family members, including children. Parent-child relationships in Confucian China were characterized as formal (Sung, 1987). Behaviors that brought honor to the family involved achievement, obedience, and obligation to the parents. It was very important for the child to engage in activities that gave the family a good name. Problem behaviors were clearly spelled out; aggression, antisocial behavior, and disobedience brought shame to the entire family and were strictly discouraged. These values continue to be transmitted through the socialization process of Chinese children today.

The importance of these values is clearly evident among contemporary Chinese American families, as discussed in a study by DeVos and Abbott (1966). This study revealed that, among Chinese living in San Francisco, educational achievement is highly valued, a strong sense of responsibility toward relatives exists, a failure to live up to the elders' expectations results in self-blame, and respect for elders is equated with respect for authority. As was the case with traditional Chinese families, possibly the strongest value in Chinese American families is filial piety. Although mainstream American culture also stresses the importance of respecting the parents, filial piety among Chinese Americans requires a much stronger notion of obligation and parental respect that children are expected to display (Sue, Sue, & Sue, 1983).

The socialization practices of Chinese Americans are also influenced by the gender-hierarchical principles of Confucianism. The split-household prevalent among early Chinese immigrants is perhaps the ultimate form of gender segregation, with husbands and wives leading completely separate lives. This arrangement facilitated a strictly segregated gender-role socialization environment for children in several ways. First, under this system, children rarely had opportunities to interact with their fathers. Because many years passed between visits, children were spaced far apart, and the father was often middle-aged or elderly when the youngest child was born. The age difference increased the formality and distance of the relationship. Second, women were under the control of their husbands and in-laws, so their children grew up observing their mother's complete subservience to the male family head. Third, because the family lineage was maintained and inherited by sons, boys were given preferential treatment over girls. Girls, on the other hand, were expected to marry and bear male children. This was the essential reason for forming the split-household family.

As the numbers of women and children increased between 1920 and 1965, many Chinese American husbands and wives were, for the first time, raising their children together and by themselves. In contrast to the complete separation of men and women in the split-household, husband and wife were constantly together as partners. The relative egalitarianism among Chinese couples was maintained by their interdependence and by the absence of in-laws. The latter freed wives from subordination to their husbands' parents. Glenn (1983) reports that many Chinese Americans who grew up in families during these decades recalled their mothers as the dominant figures and as strong disciplinarians.

Parents and children interacted frequently, and language and cultural traditions were transmitted through daily contact and communication. Although there was a greater amount of egalitarianism between husbands and wives, they still adhered to the traditional values of obedience and harmony when socializing their children (Glenn, 1994). However, parental authority was limited because parents lacked proficiency in English and thus were often dependent upon their children in various ways. These Chinese parents arrived in the United States as adults, and they rarely acquired more than a rudimentary knowledge of English. Once they reached school age, the children rapidly learned to speak and write English, thereby becoming cultural facilitators and mediators for the family. Children age 8 or 9 accompanied their parents to the bank and translated notices in stores and notes from school. They were able to exercise considerable discretion in deciding what information to relay to their parents (Tan, 1989). These experiences of Chinese American families resulted in a role reversal and a reduction of parental power.

Chinese American children today are socialized by two parents, both of whom are likely to be in the labor force. These children also socialize with non-Chinese peers. These circumstances suggest that Chinese American boys and girls today are socialized in a more egalitarian environment—both at home and at school—than were children of previous generations. This trend is also reflected in data concerning the educational attainment of Chinese American women. Since 1960, the percentage of Chinese American women who have completed college has doubled to about 30%. Although this figure is still low compared with that of Chinese American men, the increase suggests that Chinese American women are encouraged by their parents to seek higher education. In fact, one observer claims that gender and generational relations among Chinese Americans are "American"—meaning egalitarian, with husband and wife sharing housework and child care, and both male and female children being allowed to make their own decisions (Glenn, 1994).

Intimate Relationships

In traditional China, the two people who were being wed were minor actors—in fact, they were not even consulted about whom and when they would marry. Parents of sons chose brides who met, first, the needs of the family and second, the needs of the sons. Out of poverty or callousness, some parents gave their daughters to whichever family offered the most for them, while others tried to avoid marriages that would cause their daughters grief (Wolf, 1984). Young people accepted this practice as the parents' decision and part of their own filial duty. Except among the highly Westernized Chinese, traditional attitudes toward marriage were not seriously questioned until the Communist victory in 1949. It is clear that mate selection among early Chinese immigrants entailed the process of families selecting their child's spouse in order to maximize the benefit for the entire family. Individual preference was given the least priority, and relationships based on love were virtually nonexistent.

Contemporary Chinese Americans are a diverse group of people, and more than half of them are foreign-born. Although parental pressure still remains a factor, most Chinese Americans born in the United States choose their own marriage partners based on love and compatibility. Not much is known about the mate-selection process of the foreign-born U.S. Chinese population. We know, however, that many of them are educated professional immigrants with urban backgrounds. After they arrive in this country, they live in middle-class neighborhoods in the city or in suburbs and are employed in mainstream institutions. Although they may socialize with other Chinese, their lives are quite Westernized even before immigration (Wong, 1985). Clausen and Bermingham (1982) also found that a high percentage of professionally employed immigrants in California had grown up in homes where members primarily spoke English and had been guests in Western homes or had part of their education in Western-style schools. These experiences of foreign-born Chinese in the United States today suggest that their mate-selection process is also based on the Western idea of romantic love.

As in other Asian American populations, the rate of **out-marriage** among Chinese Americans today is higher than in their parents' and grandparents' generations. The U.S. Bureau of the Census reports that 22.5% of Chinese

American men are married to someone from another cultural group, and the comparable figure for Chinese American women is 10.9%. The increase in out-marriage also suggests that contemporary Chinese Americans are free to choose their marriage partners, and that romantic love plays an important role in their mate-selection process.

Confucian principles had a strong impact on traditional Chinese families at the time when the first group of Chinese emigrants left for the United States. Confucianism teaches women to be obedient to their husbands' wishes and needs and to be sexually loyal to their husbands. This standard also applies to single women, and a strong emphasis is placed on virginity among single Chinese women. In contrast, men are expected to be sexually experienced, and their engagement in premarital sexual behavior is frequently accepted. This double standard was inherited by Chinese immigrants, many of whom left their wives in the hands of their elderly parents. The in-laws were responsible for safeguarding the wife's chastity and keeping her under the ultimate control of her husband.

By contrast, many immigrant husbands were not always faithful. The fact that the overwhelming majority of early Chinese female immigrants were prostitutes suggests that Chinese immigrant men had many opportunities to engage in extramarital sexual activity. The frequency of infidelity among Chinese immigrant husbands declined in **small-producer families**, where husbands and wives were constantly together as partners (Glenn, 1994). At the same time, with so many individuals working in close quarters for extended periods of time, it was difficult for many husbands and wives to have intimacy.

Aside from intimate adult relationships, members of Chinese American families express intimacy less frequently than members of European American families. Chinese American parents tend to teach their children to control their emotional expressions; thus, affection is not displayed openly (Uba, 1994). Although traditional Chinese accept public demonstrations of affection by non-Chinese, they consider such behavior by Chinese to be childish or in bad taste (Huang, 1981). When asked about their parents expressing intimacy, many Chinese American college students do not recall seeing their parents holding hands or hugging or kissing in front of them (Huang, 1981).

Work Relationships and the Family

The division of work and family roles among Chinese Americans has been shaped by structural as well as cultural forces. The split-household family is a clear example of the sharp division of labor that existed among early Chinese immigrant families. Chinese immigrant men in the United States were employed as laborers or engaged in small businesses, while their wives stayed with in-laws in China, taking responsibility for family affairs such as raising children and caring for elderly in-laws.

The small-producer family created an environment in which husbands and wives could work side by side. In this respect, their lifestyle was similar to that of Chinese peasant families, in that every family member contributed to productivity. In addition, the absence of in-laws freed women from the stress of caring for elderly relatives. Although the work environment in the small-producer family was much more egalitarian than in the split-household family, women suffered physically from long working hours added to caring for their children. As a result, tuberculosis and other diseases were rampant in Chinatown (Lee, Lim, & Wong, 1969).

Contemporary Chinese American wives have high rates of labor-force participation (almost 70% are employed). Many of these women are professionals, or white-collar workers. Approximately 28% of Chinese American women in the labor force occupy executive, administrative, and managerial positions. About 15% of them have professional specialty jobs. As is the case with Japanese American women, Chinese American women are best represented in the "administrative support" category (U.S. Bureau of the Census, 1990).

Husbands and wives in contemporary Chinese American families are frequently co-breadwinners. Together they earn an average of $46,780 a year, which is somewhat lower than the annual average earnings of Japanese American and Filipino American couples but still higher than that of European American couples (U.S. Bureau of the Census, 1990). Dual-earner families are common in urban centers, where housing and the cost of living are higher than in rural areas.

Despite the significant increase in labor-force participation of Chinese American women, there is still evidence of a gender gap in their levels of occupational attainment and their earnings. Although women are represented in professional and administrative categories, they are overrepresented in occupations of lower prestige. For example, a much higher proportion of Chinese American women than men are operators, assemblers, inspectors, and secretaries. The earnings of women are also lower across all types of occupations. For example, Chinese American women executives, administrators, and managers earn, on average, $5000 less each year than their male counterparts (U.S. Bureau of the Census, 1990).

Because the lives of contemporary Chinese Americans are regulated by the demands of their jobs, it is important for them to be able to balance work and family hours. Women are still responsible for caring for and educating their children. Although both parents are often employed, children still see their mothers more frequently than their fathers. Even women who work evening shifts make an effort to care for their children by cooking meals before returning to work (Chao, 1977; Ikels & Shang, 1979). With two working parents, many Chinese American children complain about the scanty amount of time they spend with their parents (Glenn, 1994).

Life-Cycle Transitions

Despite long periods of separation in split-household families and the stresses caused by overwork in small-producer families, most Chinese American marriages remained intact. The low divorce rate, however, does not say much about the quality of marriages. It is clear that marriages were looked upon by early Chinese immigrants as unions whose purpose was to produce offspring; the quality of the marital relationship was immaterial. Women who later joined their husbands or who were "hasty brides" suffered from many adjustment problems in their new environment. They often felt isolated because they spoke little English and had no supportive network of friends and relatives. Husbands were often too busy to pay close attention to the problems their wives faced. Long separations made even long-time mates strangers to each other. Brides who came to the United States after arranged marriages hardly knew their husbands, and their relationships were sometimes strained also by a disparity in age. In many cases, men in their forties, who had worked in the United States for years, married women in their teens or early twenties.

The low divorce rate, then, reflects the lack of choices Chinese American women have, rather than a high level of marital quality. In small-producer families, interdependence made it impossible for spouses to survive without each other. At the same time, divorced women were considered to be an embarrassment to the community; a stigma was attached to divorce. Some desperate Chinese American women even took their lives, believing there was no other way out of a miserable marriage and living conditions. In one study, Sung (1967) found that the suicide rate among Chinese Americans in San Francisco was four times that in the city as a whole, and that victims were predominantly women.

The Chinese American divorce rate continues to be low. In 1990, only 2.3% and 3.3% of Chinese American men and women, respectively, were divorced (U.S. Bureau of the Census, 1990). These figures are considerably lower than those of White men (7.5%) and White women (9.4%), and slightly lower than those of other Asian American groups (e.g., 4.2% and 6.5% for Japanese American men and women, respectively, and 3.7% and 5.1% for Filipino American men and women) (U.S. Bureau of the Census, 1990).

We know little about the prevalence of remarriage among Chinese Americans. However, because most White divorced people eventually remarry, there is no reason to think that this is not the case with Chinese Americans. A high remarriage rate among Chinese Americans can also be predicted on the basis of an increasing number of interracial marriages, the stigma attached to divorce, and the strong belief among Chinese Americans that children fare better with two parents.

There is little information about the frequency of single parenthood in the Chinese American population. According to the U.S. Bureau of the Census (1990), a vast majority of Chinese American children (87.6%) reside with two parents. This figure is slightly higher than that for Whites (77.2%) and considerably higher than that for African Americans (35.6%).

Traditionally, migration in China and overseas was a sequential process (Liu, 1966). Able-bodied young men migrated first and made preparations in the host society for the kin who migrated later. Although this was not a predominant migration pattern of the first wave of Chinese immigrants from Guangdong Province, the second and third waves of immigrants included a significant number of elderly parents.

Family Strengths and Challenges

Numerous strengths can be found in Chinese American family experiences, but three are central:

1. Cultural continuity, despite early immigrant adversities.

2. The absorption of extended family members.

3. The financial contribution of women.

First, Chinese American families have been able to maintain their cultural heritage despite the legal and institutional discrimination they have experienced. As previously discussed, Chinese Americans were one of the most vilified cultural groups in the United States. Even prior to their immigration, they were considered to be immoral and filthy opium-crazed heathens (Dower, 1986; Miller, 1969). Once their massive immigration began, they were looked upon as a group unable to assimilate, whose presence in the United States was justified by the exploitation of their cheap labor. At the same time, their willingness to work long hours for low pay threatened the livelihood of White working men.

Many aspects of Chinese immigrants' lives, including family formation, were hampered by a series of discriminatory laws. The ability of Chinese to earn a living in agricultural areas was affected by the Alien Land Laws, under which they could no longer buy agricultural land or lease it for more than 3 years. They were also targets of violent episodes: Chinese miners were attacked and robbed, and Chinese laundrymen in urban centers were singled out for discrimination. Eventually, violent outbreaks against the Chinese became more organized. Yet despite the hostile environment in the United States, Chinese immigrants endured and eventually succeeded in maintaining their cultural heritage and transmitting their cultural values to the younger generations. The family and community clearly played central roles in this continuity.

Second, Chinese American families have been able to absorb their extended kin without many internal conflicts. This absorption does not always mean that the extended family member lives under the same roof; instead, Chinese American families often successfully accommodate extended kin in separate households, while sharing some aspects of family functioning, such as economics. As the Chinese have adapted to the ways of American life, and as their children have become more nearly assimilated into the mainstream, the concept of filial piety has been reevaluated by contemporary Chinese Americans. This process of reevaluation means reformulating the concept, not abolishing it. Chinese American families who have successfully accommodated extended kin therefore have succeeded in adapting to a new environment while maintaining the traditional concept of filial piety.

Third, we need to recognize the central economic role of Chinese American women in family strength. Despite images of Chinese women as submissive and obedient, they have high rates of labor-force participation, regardless of socioeconomic status (Glenn, 1985). In 1990, 59.2% of Chinese American women age 16 and over were in the work force, compared with 56.8% of White U.S. women (U.S. Bureau of the Census, 1990). Chinese American wives are expected to contribute to family income, and their earnings are crucial to the family's economic survival. A high proportion of Chinese women in the labor force and their families' reliance on their earnings are important because women's resources have been found to contribute to an egalitarian division of household labor and child care.

Because Chinese Americans faced a tremendous amount of hostility in the early days of their immigration, they had numerous challenges in becoming an integrated part of the population of the United States. Today, opportunities for Chinese Americans are relatively abundant, and current immigration policies facilitate family formation.

Racism, however, is still an issue for Chinese American families. Middle-class Chinese Americans may feel relatively safe as long as they are in their own environment, but they are also aware of the increasing number of hate crimes and violence against their people. Although anti-Asian violence is directed mostly against new immigrants and students, no one with an Asian face is really safe because prejudice against all Asians generally exists, regardless of their citizenship and the length of their stay in the United States. Discrimination begins early in life: Chinese American children are often subjected to name-calling, taunting, and even beatings by White and other ethnic peers. Recent news coverage of illegal Chinese immigrants arriving on worn-out commercial ships is remembered vividly by the American public. In addition, protests against China's human rights violations and testing of nuclear bombs escalate the hostility against Chinese Americans. And Chinese Americans, many of whom don't even speak a word of Chinese, frequently become targets of anger when these images are shown on television. The challenges of Chinese Americans adjusting to the majority culture, and their fight against racism, will continue for the foreseeable future.

Another challenge for Chinese Americans exists in the workplace. Chinese professionals report that they still have to work much harder than their White counterparts to attain the same recognition, and they are unlikely to rise out of purely technical positions into managerial ones because Asians are not seen as managerial material (Glenn, 1994). This workplace discrimination is still very much alive and needs to be recognized as a problem hampering the opportunities of Chinese Americans.

Finally, the growing heterogeneity of the Chinese population, and its increasing dispersal beyond the boundaries of Chinatown, have altered the role of Chinatown as the center of family life. At one time, Chinatown communities provided much-needed support for newly arrived immigrants. Social life revolved around the activities of organizations in these communities. With the huge influx of new immigrants from many different backgrounds, along with the rise of suburbanization, family associations have lost membership and influence. Efforts need to be directed toward the revitalization of Chinatowns as key social, emotional, and family centers of support.

Misconceptions and Stereotypes

As is the case with Japanese Americans, Chinese Americans suffer from the so-called **model minority myth**, the belief that Asian Americans have high levels of educational attainment, low crime rates, and an absence of juvenile delinquency and mental health problems. When the academic achievements of Chinese American "whiz kids" are widely touted in the popular media, a subtle pressure is applied to all Chinese American youths to live up to those standards, leading to increasing emotional and social problems among those who cannot. These "dropouts" suffer from a tremendous loss of self-esteem that cannot be easily recovered. In addition, data from the U.S. Bureau of the Census make it clear that Chinese Americans still suffer from the **glass ceiling effect** at work—the illusion that one can reach the top, but in reality an invisible ceiling prevents it.

Many Americans believe that the Chinese American family is strongly influenced by Confucian principles. While this is partly true, family relationships and functions are influenced more strongly by the legal, structural, and institutional barriers that have existed throughout Chinese Americans' presence in the United States. For example, the low divorce rate among early Chinese immigrants can be interpreted as reflecting such cultural values as endurance and family integrity. A close look at married women's lives, however, indicates that the immigrant Chinese women had very few alternatives. In fact, staying in an unhappy marriage was the only option for many immigrant women because they lacked financial independence, and they did not have a supportive network of relatives and friends nearby. Considering the Chinese American family from legal, structural, and institutional points of view thus provides greater opportunities for understanding.

Personal Interview

Steve Wong (not his real name) is a married Chinese American in his mid-fifties. The owner of a picture-framing shop in southern California, he has two grown sons: an engineer and a graduate student studying business. Steve is a second-generation Chinese American whose father immigrated to the United States in the early 1920s and whose mother immigrated in the late 1930s.

How did your parents try to adapt to the American way of life when they came to the United States?

Steve: My father was 23 years old when he first arrived in the United States. Before he left his hometown of Canton, he had heard some of the horrible stories about how Chinese were treated in the United States. But I think he was too ambitious to listen to that. Once he told me that he had already dreamed of coming to the United States when he was younger. I don't think he was able to anticipate what was going to happen to him once he landed on foreign soil. So he came to San Francisco. But he never told me much about how he came. I once read about "paper sons" who were impostors of sons of American citizens of Chinese ancestry. They had pur-

chased the birth certificates of American citizens born in China and claimed they were citizens in order to enter the United States. I guess this was possible because the 1906 San Francisco earthquake destroyed all those immigration documents. So that was a big chance for Chinese who wanted to leave China for the United States. I remember my father telling us about him being detained at the immigration station on Angel Island in San Francisco. Although he never told me anything more, I kind of suspected that he had come to the United States as one of those "paper sons."

Instead of becoming a miner or going to the Sierra Nevada Mountains, my father went to the city and became a worker for a Chinese-owned factory. He used to say that he worked like a mule. His English wasn't that good at all, and his friends were mostly other Chinese men who came from the same region in China. San Francisco Chinatown was also a place to go to meet people and buy food. His social network never extended beyond Chinatown, not only because his English was poor but mostly because he wanted to avoid racist people outside of Chinatown. My father never really complained too much about his life being isolated from the mainstream. I think to him it was the way of life, and he felt there was nothing he could do to change Americans' attitudes toward the Chinese.

How about your mother? What experiences did she have when and after she arrived in the United States?

Steve: After living about 10 years in San Francisco and saving a little capital, my father decided to get married. Of course, marrying a White woman was prohibited, and there were not very many eligible Chinese women around where he worked. So he had his relatives back in China arrange a partner for him. I think it was pretty easy to find a wife that way. By then my father was in his thirties and my mother was only 19 or so. After the hastily arranged marriage, they started their lives together in San Francisco while my father continued working for the same factory. Although my mother was much younger than my father, she was a very strong-willed woman. I remember my mother as a strict disciplinarian. She also wouldn't give in easily to my father, which led to many arguments. Her English wasn't that good either, but somehow she seemed to have made many more non-Chinese friends than did my father, primarily through my friends at school. I think her experience in the United States was equally difficult, however, because Chinese women those days were considered to be "slave girls" or "prostitutes." My mother coming from the peasant background was used to a financially strained environment, but she never experienced such direct discrimination back in China. Although my parents' marriage was

not always a happy one, and despite the hostility they experienced in the United States, they and their marriage somehow survived. I think it is because of the sheer determination of my parents trying to make it in this foreign country.

How about your generation? Have you faced any difficult challenges when growing up and as an adult Chinese American?

Steve: In many ways, situations surrounding Chinese Americans got better when I was growing up. Soon after I was born, we moved out of our small apartment in Chinatown and moved into the suburbs. I had lots of non-Chinese friends in the neighborhood and at school. My parents, though, always made sure that I didn't forget our Chinese cultural heritage. Although we lived away from Chinatown, we would go there for shopping and for socializing. When I was a teenager, for a little while, I didn't want to go to Chinatown because I guess I tried to be an "American." I am sure that kind of attitude disappointed my parents, but it was my way of trying to gain independence from them. Unlike some of my Chinese friends, I was never interested in college and all the fascinating careers. So I decided to study art and learned how to frame paintings and photos. It wasn't easy to establish myself in this kind of job, which is far from being a doctor or lawyer. People always think that if you are Asian, you must be good at math or you must become a doctor or a scientist. Because of my own experience, I never wanted to pressure my sons into doing something they didn't want to. Strangely enough though, my sons turned out to be okay: One is an engineer, and the other is trying to get an M.B.A.

Questions for Discussion

1. Explain why so many early Chinese immigrants had to form split-household families.

2. Explain why Chinatowns in various parts of the United States were important places for Chinese immigrants. Relate this to other ethnic sections in cities. What are the advantages and disadvantages? How do Chinatowns compare to American Indian reservations?

3. The divorce rate among Chinese Americans is one of the lowest in Asian American populations. What are the reasons? How does this compare to the divorce rate in the Mormon American family and the majority culture? What accounts for the differences and/or similarities?

4. What are some of the social factors in China that encouraged the initial emigration of the Chinese? How does this compare to the experiences of other ethnic groups?

5. Summarize the misconceptions the American public has about the Chinese American population. What are the sources of these misunderstandings? How do they compare to misconceptions about other ethnic groups discussed in the book?

6. How are Chinese American families portrayed in literature and films? Read a novel or see a film that focuses on Chinese American family life, and evaluate how accurately or poorly it describes the family life of this first group of Asian immigrants.

7. How do the strengths of the Chinese American family compare to the strengths of other families discussed in the book? How do they compare to your own family strengths?

8. How does parental pressure shape the lives of Chinese American youths? How does this compare to your own experience? Are the outcomes similar or different?

Suggested Resources

Readings

Siu, P. C. (1987). *The Chinese laundryman: A study of social isolation.* New York: New York University Press.

Sung, B. L. (1987). *The adjustment experience of Chinese immigrant children in New York City.* New York: Center for Migration Studies.

Tan, A. (1989). *The joy luck club.* New York: Putnam.

Videos

Buena Vista Home Video (Producer). (1990). *The joy luck club.* (Available from Videofinders, 425 E. Colorado Street, Suite 10B, Glendale, CA 91205)

Gordon, R., Kline, K., & Sipe, D. (Producers), & Hunton, C. (Director). (1980). *Small happiness: Women in a Chinese village.* (Available from New Day Films Library, 22D Hollywood Avenue, Hohokus, NJ 07423)

References

Adhern, E. (1973). *The cult of the dead in a Chinese village.* Stanford, CA: Stanford University Press.

Barringer, H. R., Gardner, R. W., & Levin, M. J. (1993). *Asian and Pacific Islanders in the United States.* New York: Russell Sage Foundation.

Chan, S. (1991). *Asian Americans: An interpretive history.* Boston: Twayne.

Chao, R. (1977). *Chinese immigrant children.* New York: City College of the City University of New York, Department of Asian Studies.

Clausen, E. G., & Bermingham, J. (1982). *Chinese and African professionals in California: A case study of equality and opportunity in the United States.* Washington, DC: University Press of America.

DeVos, G., & Abbott, K. (1966). *The Chinese family in San Francisco.* Unpublished master's thesis, University of California, Berkeley.

Dower, J. W. (1986). *War without mercy: Race and power in the pacific war.* New York: Pantheon.

Freedman, M. (1979). The family in China, past and present. In M. Freedman (Ed.), *The study of Chinese society: Essays.* Stanford, CA: Stanford University Press.

Glenn, E. N. (1983). Split household, small producer and dual wage earners: An analysis of Chinese-American family strategies. *Journal of Marriage and the Family, 45,* 35–46.

Glenn, E. N. (1985). Racial ethnic women's labor: The intersection of race, gender, and class oppression. *Review of Radical Political Economy, 17,* 86–109.

Glenn, E. N. (1994). Chinese American families. In R. L. Taylor (Ed.), *Minority families in the United States: A multicultural perspective* (pp. 115–145). Englewood Cliffs, NJ: Prentice-Hall.

Huang, L. (1981). The Chinese American family. In C. R. Mindel & R. Habenstein (Eds.), *Ethnic families in America: Patterns and variations* (2nd ed., pp. 115–141). New York: Elsevier.

Ikels, C., & Shang, J. (1979). *The Chinese of greater Boston.* Washington, DC: National Institute of Aging.

Lee, L. P., Lim, A., & Wong, H. K. (1969). *Report of the San Francisco Chinese community citizen's survey and fact-finding committee.* San Francisco: Chinese Community Citizen's Survey and Fact-Finding Committee.

Lee, R. H. (1956). The recent immigrant Chinese families of the San Francisco–Oakland area. *Marriage and Family Living, 18,* 14–24.

Liu, W. T. (1966). Family interactions among local and refugee Chinese families in Hong Kong. *Journal of Marriage and the Family, 28,* 314–323.

Miller, S. C. (1969). *The unwelcome immigrant: The American image of the Chinese, 1785–1882.* Berkeley: University of California Press.

Pfeffer, G. A. (1986). *Forbidden families: Emigration experiences of Chinese women under the Page Law, 1875–1882. Journal of American Ethnic History, 6,* 28–46.

Sue, D., Sue, D. W., and Sue, D. M. (1983). Psychological development of Chinese-American children. In G. Powell (Ed.), *The psychological development of minority group children* (pp. 159–166). New York: Brunner/Mazel.

Sung, B. L. (1967). *Mountains of gold.* New York: Macmillan.

Sung, B. L. (1987). *The adjustment experience of Chinese immigrant children in New York City.* New York: Center for Migration Studies.

Takaki, R. (1990). *Strangers from a different shore.* New York: Plenum.

Tan, A. (1989). *The joy luck club.* New York: Putnam.

Uba, L. (1994). *Asian Americans: Personality patterns, identity, and mental health.* New York: Guilford.

U.S. Bureau of the Census. (1980). *Statistical abstract of the United States, 1980.* Washington, DC: U.S. Government Printing Office.

U.S. Bureau of the Census. (1990). *Statistical abstract of the United States, 1990.* Washington, DC: U.S. Government Printing Office.

Wolf, M. (1984). Marriage, family, and the state in contemporary China. *Pacific Affairs, 57,* 213–236.

Wong, B. (1985). Family, kinship, and ethnic identity of the Chinese in New York City, with comparative remarks on the Chinese in Lima, Peru, and Manila, Philippines. *Journal of Comparative Family Studies, 16,* 231–254.

Masako Ishii-Kuntz

7

Japanese American Families

Historical and Cultural Background

Japanese Americans have maintained a significant presence in the United States for more than a century. During the late 1800s, when the first group of Japanese began emigrating, Japanese society and culture were under the strong influence of **feudalism** and **Confucianism** (Reischauer, 1981). The prime virtue in the Japanese feudal system was loyalty to the ruler. Family lineage and honor were also of great importance in medieval Japanese society because inheritance determined power and prestige, as well as the ownership of property. Family continuity was also a matter of vital concern.

The hierarchical Japanese family system, or *ie*, is a concept handed down as inheritance in direct succession from generation to generation. The leadership role is inherited by the oldest son, who also inherits the family estate. The *ie* system gives absolute authority over individual family members to the father or to the family council, who make all the important decisions, including a child's occupation and a person's marriage partner. Feudal and Confucian values of loyalty are evidenced by the respect family members have for the household head under the *ie* system (Kitano, 1976).

Since the end of World War II and the adoption of a new constitution in 1947, the *ie* system has largely disappeared. The new system defined the family as consisting of husband, wife, and children; when the oldest son married, he and his wife formed a separate family. At the same time, husband and wife were accorded equal status and power (Steiner, 1950). These postwar legal changes, however, have not eradicated the influence of Confucianism and feudalism on the Japanese family. For example, according to Confucianism and feudalism, women's freedom was restricted and they were required to be completely subordinate to men (Reischauer, 1981). Although this form of subservience is rare in contemporary Japan, the current gender inequality in the labor market

(Brinton, 1988) and strong emphasis on women's roles as mothers and home-makers (Ishii-Kuntz, 1994a; Smith & Schooler, 1978) can be traced to these traditional beliefs.

The changes that have taken place among Japanese families over the last several centuries have little to do with religion, as religion has a more peripheral place in Japan than in Western, South Asian, and Middle Eastern countries (Reischauer, 1981). The secularism of Japanese society is the product of Confucianism, which emphasized a rational natural order, of which man was a harmonious element, and a social order based on strict ethical rules, governed by men of education and superior ethical wisdom.

Contemporary Japanese obviously are not Confucianists in the same sense that their ancestors were, but they still embody Confucian ethical values. Confucianism probably has more influence on them than do any of the other traditional religions or philosophies (Reischauer, 1981). Buddhism is the Japanese religion that comes closest to paralleling Christianity, for it, too, is concerned with the afterlife and with salvation of the individual. However, few people find solace in the Buddhist message of salvation. Shinto, the most distinctive of the Japanese religions, has also taken a background role in modern urbanized Japan.

To reiterate: Japanese cultural values of loyalty and harmony are strongly embedded in Confucianism and feudalism, yet Japanese lives are not strongly influenced by religion. In a recent survey, nearly half the Japanese polled felt that religion was unnecessary in their daily lives. Even those for whom religion was necessary indicated that it was important more as an expression of individual freedom than as a spiritual experience ("Do People Need Religion?" 1995).

It is difficult to assess how much these cultural values of the ancestral country have influenced Japanese American families. Most Japanese Americans today are grandchildren and great-grandchildren of Japanese who immigrated in the late 1800s and early 1900s. Yet a significantly smaller but steady flow of Japanese immigrants has arrived in the United States in recent years (Ishii-Kuntz, 1990). Some of the family experiences of the new immigrants may have been influenced, and continue to be affected, by cultural factors in their homeland. At the same time, their family lives have also been consistently challenged by a long history of legal and political discrimination in the United States.

The Immigration Experience and Internment

The Japanese immigration experience can be divided into two basic historical periods: early immigration, around the turn of the twentieth century; and post-1965 immigration, after a major revision of the U.S. Immigration Act. Earlier immigrants from Japan arrived in Hawaii in significant numbers beginning in the 1880s, and then in the United States a decade later (Takaki, 1989). This immigrant generation is known as the Issei (first generation); their children are referred to as the Nisei (second generation); their grandchildren make up the Sansei (third generation). A majority of the Sansei are now in their mid-adulthood and their children, the Yonsei (fourth generation), are school-age.

Following the 1868 Meiji Restoration, Japan began to pursue a program of modernization and Westernization in order to protect against European and American imperialist powers (Takaki, 1989). To finance industrialization and strengthen the military, the Meiji government imposed a new system of land taxation. Farmers had to pay taxes based on the assessed value of their land, rather than on the size of their harvest. Most of them were unable to pay their taxes, and farmers all over Japan faced economic hardship.

In addition to the economic changes, another reform undertaken during the Meiji era helped make emigration attractive. In 1873, a national conscription law was enacted because the *samurai*, the warrior class obligated to bear arms, no longer existed. A series of amendments to the original law excused students studying abroad and emigrants from military service, at first until age 26, and later until age 32 (Takaki, 1989).

The above "push" toward emigration was reinforced by the "pull" that was generated mostly as a result of the Hawaiian recruitment program. Because of anti-Chinese sentiment and subsequent legal discrimination, the number of Chinese laborers on Hawaiian sugar plantations had declined dramatically. The Chinese labor supply had to be replaced by other cheap labor from Asia.

Beginning in the 1890s, Japanese migrants were also attracted to the U.S. mainland. A higher American wage was one of the most important factors for these immigrants. Between 1885 and 1924, 200,000 Japanese went to Hawaii and 180,000 to the U.S. mainland. They were predominantly young men who were relatively well educated, as the result of Japan's system of compulsory education. The average Japanese male immigrant arrived in America with more money than his European counterpart (Chan, 1991). In order to avoid the problems of prostitution, gambling, and drunkenness generated by a bachelor society, and to bring greater stability to American immigrant communities, the Japanese government promoted the emigration of women. Japanese women began trickling into the United States around the turn of the century and arrived in sizable numbers around 1915.

Between 1910 and 1920, when the majority of Japanese women emigrated, they could not make the independent decision to leave their homeland. A Japanese woman could emigrate only if she already had a spouse living in America, if an immigrant returned to Japan to marry her, or if she had married an immigrant by proxy. These proxy marriages became known as *shashin kekkon*, or "photograph marriages," by the Issei, and as "picture-bride marriages" by others. From the Western point of view, these picture-bride marriages might have seemed quaint at best and immoral at worst. For the Japanese, however, they were not that far removed from traditional marriage practices. As Ichioka (1988) notes, marriage was never an individual matter, but always a family affair in Japan.

Americans were concerned that immigrants were experiencing a population boom and were now purchasing acreage in the names of their citizen children. In an attempt to quell this rising clamor, the Japanese government ceased issuing passports to picture brides altogether in 1920. This measure, however, was followed by a harsher one. In 1924, the U.S. government passed the U.S. Immigration Act, which effectively closed the door on any further immigration from Japan. Because Japanese immigration would not be allowed again until after World War II, these restrictive laws set the generational pattern that would distinguish the future Japanese American population (Nakano, 1990).

The family was the central institution defining Issei women's place and social identity (Glenn, 1986). Issei women brought to the new country traditional family values strongly embedded in the *ie* concept. In particular, two features of the *ie* system remained strong in the immigrant family: the practice of collective effort, and the pattern of male dominance and privilege (Nakano, 1990). Male dominance in the Issei family was illustrated by the husband's ultimate authority and breadwinning role and, in contrast, the wife's responsibility for the house and children (Kitano, 1976).

Initially, Japanese immigrants were considered to be sojourners who, after accumulating capital, intended to return to Japan. However, the arrival of U.S. citizen children in the Issei households marked a change of plans for the immigrants. In spite of the hostility they were encountering, they considered the prospect of putting down roots in America.

The absence of the mother-in-law in the household gave the wife more authority in raising the children. But Glenn (1986) contends that the Issei family was oppressive for women. There was little love between Issei partners, and many of the Nisei women's childhood memories reveal a history of parental alcohol abuse, domestic violence, and long hours of working in the family business (Thomas, 1952).

One of the key forces that shaped the lives of Japanese Americans was the wholesale evacuation of West Coast Japanese communities during World War II. As soon as the United States declared war on Japan, following the bombing of Pearl Harbor in Hawaii on December 7, 1941, more than 40,000 Japanese living on the Pacific Coast, along with their 70,000 American-born children—who were U.S. citizens—were removed from their homes and incarcerated in "relocation camps." Once the Japanese were in the relocation camps, the War Relocation Authority (WRA), created by President Franklin Roosevelt, took over supervision of the internees, though the army retained control over the camps. Camps were divided into blocks, each with 14 barracks subdivided into apartments. Since these camps were located in the semiarid desert, sand seeped through the cracks into the apartments whenever the wind blew. Summers were blistering hot, and winters were freezing cold (Takaki, 1989).

Relatively little is known about Japanese immigrants who arrived in the United States after the revised 1965 Immigration Act, which abolished the national origin system. The paucity of Japanese immigration—only about 3% of all Asian immigrants since 1965 have been Japanese—may be the reason scholars have done very little research on this group. Japanese Americans are the only Asian American population that has more native-born than foreign-born members (Barringer, Gardner, & Levin, 1993). The U.S. Bureau of the Census (1991) reports that while 63.3% of Chinese Americans, 64.7% of Filipino Americans, 81.9% of Korean Americans, and 90.5% of Vietnamese Americans are foreign-born, the comparable figure for Japanese Americans is 28.4%.

Although Japanese constitute a minor proportion of the stream of contemporary Asian immigrants, an annual total of 3000–5000 Japanese were admitted to the United States as immigrants during the 1970s and 1980s (Immigration and Naturalization Service, 1988). Today, there are more than 100,000 Japanese in the United States who have been granted permanent resident status since 1965. During the same period, an additional 39,000 Japanese have become naturalized U.S. citizens. Most recently, the U.S. government lottery, or "green-card sweepstakes," for 40,000 permanent visas has surprisingly attracted many Japanese applicants, most of whom are members of younger families.

The experiences of new immigrants cannot be compared directly with those of contemporary Japanese Americans because the historical and social environments in which each group was raised are vastly different. Ishii-Kuntz (1990) proposes that many of the post-1965 immigrants from Japan are "social-psychological refugees" from their home country—that is, the primary reason for their immigration is not necessarily to seek better economic conditions but rather to escape from a country in which a rigid code of behavior and expectations exists. After emigrating, many Issei who find support or a niche in America are satisfied with their lives here; although their children face numerous challenges outside the home, they generally adjust to the new environment (Ishii-Kuntz, 1994b).

Although it is also important to understand the family experiences of recent immigrants from Japan, the focus of this chapter is on Japanese American families. As previously discussed, in many ways family formation, structure, and generational relationships among Japanese Americans were shaped by their immigration and subsequent internment experiences. At the same time, we cannot understand the departure from the traditional family among Japanese Americans unless we have a grasp of the various legal and institutional barriers they faced.

Traditional and Emerging Family Systems

The political and legal history that shaped the character of Japanese immigration to the United States created relatively discrete, nonoverlapping generations (Thomas, 1950). Therefore, describing traditional and emerging family systems among Japanese Americans involves presenting the family experiences of the Issei, Nisei, and Sansei.

Household Size and Composition

The postwar Japanese family is structurally similar to the American nuclear family. However, the **stem family** still exists, in which retired parents are likely to live with the child who inherits the leadership role, whether or not there has been a farm or business to pass on. Those families who can afford to may have a separate but adjoining house or wing of the family residence for the elders. This situation is a reflection of old customs and necessitated in part by inadequate retirement income and social security benefits, which make retired Japanese more dependent on their children for support than elders in the West.

Many Nisei men and women experienced a measurable transformation in their lives with the changing times—the period before World War II, during the war, the postwar period, and the period after the 1960s—all of which had various effects on fertility. For example, in the camp environment, conjugal relations were severely limited by the lack of privacy. Young Nisei couples occupying a room with their children—or worse, with people outside the family—found little opportunity for intimacy. This factor alone may have contributed to the declining birth rates among the Nisei women compared to their parents' generation. Accordingly, the fertility rate of Issei women was almost twice that of Nisei women (Watanabe, 1977).

Today, the Japanese American fertility rate of 0.9% is much lower than that of earlier generations (U.S. Bureau of the Census, 1990). It is also lower than that of other Asian American groups, European Americans, African Americans, and Hispanics. Since foreign-born women tend to have higher birth rates than native-born women, the relatively low number of foreign-born Japanese American women is considered to be a factor (Barringer et al., 1993). The decreasing size of Japanese American households over the generations is due primarily to declining fertility rates among Japanese American women.

Upon marriage and the subsequent birth of their first child, many Issei couples formed a nuclear family in which the wife was "free" from her mother-in-law. However, a substantial proportion of Issei families also had grandparents and parental siblings who immigrated to the United States (Yanagisako, 1985). Thus, some Issei marriages were far from being "free" from kin relationships.

Parental involvement in the lives of prewar Nisei was not much different from that of the previous generation. Many of the Nisei were economically dependent upon their parents, who were almost always involved in marriage arrangements before the engagement was announced. During internment, many Nisei reached marriageable age, and the internment itself brought greater opportunities for meeting potential spouses. In addition, the Issei had less control over their children's marriage decisions. Some Nisei moved to the Midwest or East Coast to avoid discrimination during internment, and afterward continued to enjoy more freedom from their parents.

The internment experience also significantly influenced the residential patterns of married Nisei. Using a Seattle sample of Issei and Nisei, Yanagisako (1985) found that during the war years, stem family residence was more prevalent than in the prewar or resettlement periods, primarily because of the lack of space for separate residences during internment.

Many contemporary Japanese American families are nuclear, consisting of the father, mother, and their children. According to the U.S. Bureau of the Census (1990), only 4.8% of Japanese American households contain "other relatives." The fact that very few Japanese American households are made up of extended families compared to those of other Asian American groups is due to the small number of recent Japanese immigrants (Gardner, Robey, & Smith, 1985).

Although Japanese American households used to contain more **consanguineal relationships**, over the years, the Nisei and Sansei gained more independence in their decision making and formed separate households. Thus, recent Japanese American families are most likely to be nuclear, with much more emphasis on **conjugal relationships**.

The Socialization of Children

With the decision to permanently settle in America, Issei parents felt it was important for their children to assimilate into the mainstream culture. Therefore, Nisei children were encouraged to speak English almost exclusively to their peers, and their educational achievement was considered by the parents to be an indication of their children's successful acculturation (Nakano, 1990). Interestingly, however, Issei parents also adhered to many family values that were prevalent in Japan in socializing their children (Yamamoto & Kubota, 1983). For example, Issei parents instilled in their children values that tended to bind the family together, so that the conflicts in their daily lives were usually short-lived and superficial. In addition, Glenn (1986) notes that Issei women tried to preserve and pass on everyday aspects of Japanese culture, including cooking, folk medicine, peasant lore, and family customs.

The family values the Issei attempted to preserve stem from the Confucian ideal that places great emphasis on hierarchical relationships, including deference to and respect for elders and for the male head of the household. These hierarchical gender relationships are reflected in the different expectations of Issei parents in socializing their sons and daughters. The Issei customarily designated their eldest son the successor to the family business (Chan, 1991). Accordingly, the eldest Nisei son usually received special treatment and privileges from his parents. In many Issei families, he was the second to be served at meals, after his father, and he was generally indulged by his mother (Nakano, 1990; Yanagisako, 1985). Younger siblings were instructed to obey his directions, and even older sisters were expected to defer to him.

Issei parents were far more likely to send their eldest son, rather than any other child, to live in his grandparents' household in Japan (Takaki, 1989). These sons were educated in Japan and eventually returned to America after finishing high school. Known as *Kibei*, these Nisei children fulfilled their parents' wish to continue the heritage of the Japanese family. However, because the education they received in Japan during the 1920s and 1930s was infused with militaristic and chauvinistic values, upon their return to the United States, many *Kibei* found it difficult to get along with their highly Americanized siblings (Chan, 1991).

As Nisei sons and their siblings reached adolescence and young adulthood, they were expected to contribute to the household economy through work in the family business or through the wages they earned doing outside work. However, the eldest sons were often specifically groomed to take over the family business. In some cases, only the eldest son worked in the family business, while other sons and daughters were encouraged to find work elsewhere. In other cases, all children worked in the family business as soon as their labor became useful, but only the eldest son was taught about its finances and management.

Caudill (1952) also observes that Japanese American children were valued in terms of both their potential for helping parents in the future and, in the case of male children, their ability to carry on the family line. It should be noted, however, that this type of strict adherence to traditional filial relations was more common among Japanese American families before World War II than in the postwar generation (Nakano, 1990).

The Nisei, many of whom were born between 1915 and 1940, reached young adulthood and formed families just before and just after World War II. There are several differences between Issei and Nisei families in terms of gender expectations. In large part, the traditional family organization of the Issei broke down as the result of internment and the subsequent geographic dispersion. Yanagisako (1985) notes that Issei women's experiences were primarily inside the family, whereas men's experiences were outside the family. In contrast, Nisei men's and women's experiences were both based on the kind of work they did, rather than on the inside/outside dichotomy of family experiences. Glenn (1986) also notes that the eldest Nisei cohort (statistical group) retained traditional elements in family life such as gender hierarchy, while younger Nisei families were characterized by relative egalitarianism, shared decision making, and companionship between husband and wife.

Intimate Relationships

The level of involvement of Issei parents in their children's mate selection differs considerably before and after World War II and the internment experiences. Before the war, Issei parents were heavily involved in their offspring's mate-selection process (Nakano, 1990). However, in the camps, Issei parents found themselves earning the same low wages as their Nisei sons or daughters. Because their children no longer depended on them, Issei parents' authority and power over their children declined, and Nisei children made more independent decisions about mate selection.

Internment also dictated the kinds of activities the Nisei could engage in. Because their home was a small barrack with little privacy, many Nisei teenagers and young adults spent most of their leisure time away from home with friends. Thus, younger Nisei had a greater opportunity to make friends and meet potential marriage partners than had their prewar counterparts. These structural factors changed the traditional roles of parents in selecting their children's mates. Because of reduced parental supervision, the Nisei had a much longer period of dating than their Issei parents, and the selection of their marriage partners was based more on love and individual compatibility than on family concerns (Nakano, 1990).

Another difference between the Issei and the Nisei is the average age at marriage. Nisei men married at an average age of 27.8 years, compared to their Issei fathers, who were on average 1.4 years older. Nisei brides, on the other hand, were on average 3 years older than their Issei mothers, who had married at an average age of 21.4 (Yanagisako, 1985). The higher average age of Issei men reflects the fact that some Japanese immigrant men were remarried after divorcing their wives who were left in Japan.

The freedom to choose one's marriage partner, which started with the Nisei, clearly continued with the next generation, the Sansei, who selected their mates based on individual preferences and after a period of courtship. According to the U.S. Bureau of the Census (1990), the percentage of early marriages was lower among Japanese Americans than in any other Asian American group. For example, only about 20% of Japanese American women were married at ages 20–24, compared to about 50% of Korean American and 40% of Filipino American women. For men, while 30% of Japanese Americans were married at ages 25–29, nearly 60% of Korean American and Filipino American men in the same age groups were married. Although these are comparisons among Asian American groups, we can speculate that fourth-generation Japanese Americans will marry at older ages than did their parents and grandparents.

One of the major differences between Nisei and Sansei in terms of mate selection and marriage is the trend toward cross-cultural marriage. The anti-miscegenation laws prohibiting cross-cultural marriages were repealed in the 1950s, resulting in a dramatic increase in **out-marriage** among Japanese Americans during the 1960s. Kitano and Kikumura (1976) report that Sansei intermarriage rates were 50%, compared with rates of 15% for the Nisei and 5% for the Issei. A three-generation survey of Japanese Americans by the Japanese American Research Project (JARP) at the University of California, Los Angeles, revealed that 40% of married Sansei had wed non–Japanese Americans (Levine & Rhodes, 1981). Using 1980 census data, Jiobu (1988) also confirms that observed rates of Japanese American intermarriage were five times higher than the expected rate. It was also found that intermarriage rates were gender-specific: women were a little over twice as likely to intermarry as men (Jiobu, 1988; Kitano & Kikumura, 1976).

Certain studies (Kikumura & Kitano, 1973; Tinker, 1973) offer the following possible explanations for the higher incidence of cross-cultural marriages for Japanese American women:

▲ Cross-cultural marriage offers a more appealing status for women than the traditional female role in the Japanese patriarchal family.

▲ Because of the importance of family continuity, men are pressured to marry Japanese women to carry on the family name and "pure" ethnicity.

If current **exogamy** (out-marriage) trends persist, more than 50% of Japanese American married-couple households will soon contain either wives or husbands who are non-Japanese. The most recent data, however, reveal that the rate of Japanese American cross-cultural marriage has stabilized at around 50–60% (Kitano, 1994).

Traditional Japanese values on intimate relationships have a strict double standard that allows sexual freedom for men but not for women. Traditionally, Japanese women were expected to remain pure, and sexual permissiveness or infidelity on the part of women was considered socially disruptive and was carefully guarded against. Men, however, in their greater freedom, could develop a broader social and sexual life, as long as they did not let it impinge on family duties.

Little has been written about the sexual behavior of Japanese immigrants. However, it is conceivable that a strict double standard also existed among Japanese men and women who immigrated to the United States in the late 1800s. Japanese women who came as brides of Issei men were expected to be sexually inexperienced. In particular, picture brides, many of whom were in their late teens, got married without any prior sexual experience. Upon their arrival and marriage, many Issei women perceived sex to be a means of procreation only. Therefore, although many Issei couples had contraceptives available, they rarely used them (Nakano, 1990). Sexual expression was also a very private matter, and intimate emotions such as love and affection were not openly demonstrated by Issei couples. In fact, many Nisei children never saw their parents hug or kiss each other, and they usually cannot remember when one of their parents hugged or kissed their grandchildren (Uba, 1994).

Some evidence suggests that this may have influenced the Nisei in their pursuit of intimate relationships. Toward the end of the prewar era, the Nisei began to adopt a more Westernized appearance (Yanagisako, 1985). By the late 1930s, the largest Nisei birth cohorts were beginning to reach young adulthood. The sheer size of these statistical groups gave the Nisei numerical strength to construct their own version of American adolescent social life. As they were usually excluded from the social circles of their White classmates, they developed their own parallel social clubs and activities. Prior to the outbreak of World War II, a proliferation of social events was sponsored by Nisei clubs, many of which were attached to Japanese churches (both Buddhist and Christian). Although the extent of sexual activity among the young Nisei is not known, they had more opportunities to engage in intimate relationships than did their parents.

Wartime internment severely restricted intimacy among younger Nisei couples. In Nakano's research on three generations of Japanese American women, one Nisei woman recalled putting up sheets to partition off her bed from her children's beds. But even then, she was always aware that the children could hear everything, even a whisper (Nakano, 1990). Therefore, structural limitations placed on the wartime Nisei also influenced their levels of intimacy and sexual activity.

To the extent that there is still a double standard in American society, Japanese Americans are affected. However, Sansei and Yonsei Japanese Americans probably have much more liberal attitudes toward sexuality in general, including premarital sex. At the same time, the low birth rates among Japanese American women indicate that sexual activities are no longer considered solely procreational, and that there is a greater use of contraceptives among Japanese American couples.

Work Relationships and the Family

Traditionally, Japanese women had an overwhelmingly subservient position in the broader society, while men enjoyed superior social status. Accordingly, men's primary role was breadwinning and women's was homemaking. Although this gendered pattern of work and family roles existed among Issei couples, Issei women were more likely than their Japanese counterparts to engage in some type of labor. For example, many wives of Japanese farmers labored in the fields from dawn to dusk (Nakano, 1990). These women also may have worked until the day their children were born, rested for a few days, and then resumed work with their babies strapped to their backs. In urban areas, women worked alongside their husbands in family-owned enterprises such as laundries, cleaners, small hotels, plant nurseries, and catteries.

Contemporary Japanese American families, many of whom are Sansei, tend to be more egalitarian than the Issei and Nisei (Osako, 1980; Takagi, 1994). At the same time, there is much greater labor-force participation among Japanese American women today. According to the U.S. Bureau of the Census (1990), 38.6% of Japanese American workers in 1960 were women, whereas almost half (47%) of the Japanese American labor force was occupied by women in 1990.

The increase in women's work-force participation and the trend toward egalitarianism in the family do not necessarily mean that Japanese American men and women today enjoy equality in terms of their earnings. In fact, Japanese American women still lag far behind men in median earnings. In 1959, men's annual median income was $10,035 and that of women, $4893. In 1990, the annual median income for Japanese American men was $28,563, while the comparable figure for Japanese American women was $15,155 (U.S. Bureau of the Census, 1990). This earning gap also reflects the type of employment held by Japanese men and women. For example, while Japanese American men are concentrated in such occupations as executive, administrative, managerial, and professional specialties, Japanese American women are almost three times as likely as men to be employed in administrative support, clerical, and sales categories (U.S. Bureau of the Census, 1990).

Increasing numbers of Japanese American women in the work force also imply that there is a demand for dual-earner households. Most Japanese American women are employed because they need to contribute to the family financially, not because they wish to pursue a professional career. This is obvious from the gender gap in educational and occupational statistics. According to the U.S. Bureau of the Census (1990), there is still a discrepancy between Japanese American men and women in educational attainment. For example, although a similar proportion of Japanese American men and women graduate from high school, men are more likely than women to graduate from college

(42.5% and 28.2%, respectively). This discrepancy has persisted over the last 40 years.

Higher household expenses are another reason for dual-earner Japanese American families. Census data show that the average annual household income for Japanese Americans in 1990 was $50,367, of which almost 20% went to paying the mortgage. Because 90% of contemporary Japanese Americans live in urban and suburban areas where housing tends to be expensive, both the husband's and the wife's incomes are necessary to maintain the standard of living. In addition, approximately 7% of Japanese American households are at the poverty level, despite a relatively high household income (U.S. Bureau of the Census, 1990).

Life-Cycle Transitions

Japanese Americans have one of the lowest rates of divorce of any group in the United States. Using U.S census data, Kitano (1976) reports that only 1.6% of Issei marriages end in divorce. The low divorce rate, however, does not reflect unrecorded desertion and separation cases, and it does not reflect the quality of Issei marriages because many Issei retained the Japanese cultural value of *gaman*, perseverance in the face of adversity (Glenn, 1986). Levine and Rhodes (1981) observe that Japanese Americans share a generalized wish not to bring shame on the family or on the community, and divorce can be defined as a shameful act.

Unlike their parents, Nisei men and women have most likely chosen their mates, although older Nisei (born before 1920) often accepted arranged marriages. Because of the dissimilarity between the Issei and Nisei mate-selection processes, their beliefs and attitudes toward marriage also differ. The Issei belief that it is better to remain married for the sake of the children is thought by the Nisei to be ill-conceived, because in the end the children will suffer from the absence of love and from the tensions that inevitably pervade such a family (Yanagisako, 1985). Indeed, in the eyes of the Nisei, a family without conjugal love and solidarity is no family at all, but merely an empty facsimile of one. Even though the Nisei conception of marriage differs from that of the Issei, the Nisei divorce rate is still low, as reported in the Nisei sample of the JARP (Levine & Rhodes, 1981).

Regarding single parenthood, the U.S. census provides some figures related to single motherhood but little on single fatherhood. According to Barringer et al. (1993), the proportion of Japanese American female heads of household without husbands is 11.9%, slightly higher than that of Whites (10.8%).

Because divorce, remarriage, and single parenthood among Japanese Americans are not prevalent, scholars have not rigorously studied the impact of these family life-cycle transitions on the Japanese American family. Furthermore, the emphasis on family in the traditional culture has contributed to the belief that Japanese American marriages are long-lasting. However, when divorce, remarriage, and single parenthood do occur, the consequences on the family system and its relationships are probably wide-ranging. A divorce probably still brings shame to the family, and the parent–adult child relationship may suffer as a result. As happens in other cultural groups, single parenthood has grave economic consequences for many Japanese American households.

Although internment experiences have altered various relationships between the first and second generations of Japanese Americans, the Nisei retained much of the traditional value of respect for elderly family members (Nakano, 1990). Therefore, it is not surprising that research generally indicates that Japanese Americans tend to have strong commitments to family and to caring for elderly parents (Connor, 1974). Research has also found that, compared with European Americans, Japanese Americans tend to live closer to their parents, feel more obligated to their parents, provide more financial aid to their parents, and interact more frequently with them (Osako, 1976). In addition, younger Japanese American adults are expected to live with their families until they marry, elderly parents tend to live with family members rather than in nursing homes, and members of all age groups participate in family activities (Johnson, 1977).

Because of improved longevity, low birth rates, and low levels of recent immigration, the Japanese American population is aging rapidly. One of the major consequences of the changing age composition of a population is economic dependency—how many nonworking people there are for each working person. The Japanese American population shows a relatively high old-age dependency ratio: about 11 aged per 100 workers (Barringer et al., 1993). Because of the aging population and higher dependency ratio among contemporary Japanese Americans, we need to carefully assess the increasing demand for taking care of the elderly and the stress associated with such caregiving.

Family Strengths and Challenges

Family strengths of the Japanese American family can be summarized as follows:

1. Strong family solidarity, despite adverse historical experiences.

2. Strong feelings of obligation and commitment toward parents.

3. Tolerance toward family diversity.

For many years prior to World War II, a strong anti-Japanese sentiment had been developing, evidenced by various forms of discriminatory legislation, including immigration laws and antimiscegenation laws. Japanese Americans also faced other types of hardship and discrimination, including housing shortages, hostility, and outright violence after their return to the West Coast. In spite of these assaults, evidence strongly suggests that families typically held together. For example, during internment, the quality of marriage deteriorated somewhat, but the traditional pattern of family solidarity remained strong (Kitano, 1976). Not surprisingly, women shouldered the bulk of the responsibility (Nakano, 1990). Following the archetypical model of their foremothers, Nisei women tended to the physical and emotional needs of the children, made and cemented social ties, and often acted as intermediaries between their husbands and the children.

The Japanese American internment experience influenced the relationship between parents and adult children. History shows the transformation of the Japanese American family from the traditional hierarchical family system based on *ie* into one based more on egalitarian relationships. Despite this transformation, one strength that can be drawn from Japanese American family experience is their commitment to, and high degree of obligation toward, their elderly parents. Although the internment experiences profoundly weakened the hierarchical parent-child relationship, the sense of responsibility toward parents remained strong. Nakano (1990) argues that parent-child bonding in the Issei-Nisei family had already occurred, so the relationship weathered the buffeting conditions of the internment camp. When, for example, the Nisei migrated to cities outside the military zone, they called for their parents as soon as they became established. Many provided economic support to their parents during this resettlement period, and continued to provide for their care and well-being for the remainder of their lives. This family strength continues among later generations of Japanese Americans.

Finally, Japanese American families today tend to reflect a greater diversity within them. This is primarily the result of the high rate of cross-cultural marriages in the Sansei generation. Divergence from traditional families to nontraditional types, such as female-headed households, also contributes to this diversity. Takagi (1994) states that it is now difficult to speak of a singular Japanese American family experience. Given this diversity, today's Japanese American families are more tolerant and understanding of various family forms than were early immigrant generations. Japanese American children are now also being socialized in a much more diverse environment. It is no longer rare for the Japanese American family to include children and young adults of **dual heritage**. One study reports that many dual-heritage children show the same level of self-esteem as children with a single heritage (Nakano, 1990). This finding indicates that Japanese American families are able to provide an environment that facilitates positive development for children of mixed heritage. It also indicates Japanese Americans' high level of acceptance of cross-cultural marriage in their offspring.

Many values—such as politeness, the importance of family, and hard work—are shared by Japanese Americans and other Americans alike. In fact, Connor (1974) argues that the reason Japanese Americans succeeded in the dominant society was that the value of hard work was shared by Japanese immigrants and the White middle class. But certain American values, such as assertiveness and individualism, sometimes conflict with Japanese American values based on Confucianism or on the experiences of Japanese Americans in the United States. Research suggests that such cultural conflicts can be sources of psychological stress, personality problems, and intergenerational disagreements (Carlin & Sokoloff, 1985; Sue & Chin, 1983). However, these conflicts seem to have more influence on immigrant families with children who are born or raised in America. In particular, cultural conflicts arise when children become more Americanized than their foreign-born parents (Uba, 1994).

The Sansei, today, have taken giant steps toward assimilation by absorbing various values and practices of the majority culture. Yet they neither appear to be, nor wish to be, completely assimilated. While the lives of the Sansei and Yonsei do not seem to be different from those of European Americans, studies have found that contemporary Japanese Americans still maintain varying degrees of cultural values and identity inherited from previous generations. Several accounts of Sansei women reported by Nakano (1990) show this mix of dominant and traditional Japanese culture in their daily routine. One Sansei woman noted that she eats Japanese food frequently, but she hardly discusses Japanese topics with anyone, including her Sansei friends. Many Sansei and Yonsei reportedly feel fortunate being bicultural because it enhances a multicultural global perspective, which is rapidly becoming the norm in many occupations (Nakano, 1990).

While many Japanese Americans continue to maintain a bicultural identity, they still face challenges imposed by society. Japanese Americans have achieved economic parity with European Americans (Barringer, Takeuchi, & Xenos, 1990; Wong, 1982; Wong & Hirschman, 1983). However, although this finding usually holds, it is also the case that those at upper occupational levels do not fare as well as European Americans. For example, among native-born American men with a college degree and 20 years of experience, only 8% of the Japanese Americans became managers, compared to 20% of the European Americans (U.S. Commission on Civil Rights, 1988). In addition, there is little political representation among Japanese Americans. These facts show that Japanese Americans today still suffer from the **glass ceiling effect**: They are encouraged to be as successful as possible, but it is virtually impossible to reach the top.

Finally, the Japanese American family system will continue to change as out-marriage continues, women's participation in the labor force increases, and the number of single-person and female-headed households continues to rise. The diversity in family experiences already evident among Japanese Americans will continue to grow in future generations. It should be recognized, however, that no matter what changes occur, Japanese American families will always recognize how historical factors have influenced their ancestors and the way they were raised. The redress movement, which culminated in the passage of a resolution seeking monetary compensation for each Japanese American incarcerated during World War II, was initiated primarily by the Sansei in the 1970s. This is a prime example of later generations of Japanese Americans recognizing the importance of such a historical event as wartime internment.

Misconceptions and Stereotypes

Perhaps the most frequent misunderstanding about contemporary Japanese Americans comes from the so-called **model minority myth**, which first surfaced in the mid-1960s when journalists began publicizing the high educational attainment levels, low crime rates, and absence of juvenile delinquency and mental health problems among Asian Americans. This thesis served an important political purpose during the Civil Rights movement in the 1960s by reminding other cultural and ethnic groups to work hard to improve their situation, rather than protesting. The model minority thesis also influenced the view of Japanese American families as ideal families with high median income, low divorce rates, and strong bonds.

Without question, the socioeconomic status of Japanese Americans has improved since the early 1940s. Schmid and Nobbe (1965) used 1960 census data to show that Japanese Americans ranked above European Americans in educational attainment, as measured by the percentage who had completed 4 years of college, the median years of schooling, and the percentage of high school graduates. This trend has also been confirmed with the 1980 and 1990 census data, as reported by Barringer et al. (1993). It is also true that the family income of Japanese Americans is higher and the rate of divorce is lower than among European Americans. The conclusion that Japanese Americans are a model minority is drawn primarily from census figures. However, a closer look at some numbers and at the lives of Japanese Americans makes the image of model minority and ideal family largely a myth.

In terms of the Japanese American family being ideal, we can also examine several facts that debunk the myth of the strongly bonded, stable, and financially and emotionally healthy family. First, statistics on suicide show that Japanese American families do not always raise emotionally healthy and stable individuals. For example, the suicide rates among Japanese Americans age 15–24 and after the age of 74 are higher than those of European Americans. In fact, the suicide rate of Japanese American youths and young adults is almost twice that of Whites. Second, the proportion of female-headed households without husbands is higher for Japanese Americans than for Whites. Although the divorce rate for White females is much higher than for Japanese American women, both groups have a similar rate of marital separation. Third, one study found that elderly Japanese American parents are less likely than Whites to want to live with their adult children (Osako, 1980). Fourth, Japanese American families are far from conflict-free. Much of the conflict seems to come from the parent-child gap in expectations for children's educational and occupational attainment. There are also signs of spousal abuse and other forms of domestic violence, which have been neglected in the research on Japanese American families (Rafu Shimpo, 1994).

It is thus important to recognize that Japanese American families do suffer from problems similar to those encountered by the dominant culture. However, in general they seem to have healthy family functioning and relationships.

Personal Interview

Sharon Shimizu (not her real name) is a married Sansei woman in her early forties. A full-time nurse in an emergency room at a large hospital in southern California, she has two daughters, ages 16 and 12.

How did your grandparents try to adapt to the American way of life when they came to the U.S.?

Sharon Shimizu: Let me talk about my mother's side of the family, since I was much closer to them than to my father's. My mother's father was born and raised in Wakayama. He was only 19 when he arrived in San Francisco in 1902. My grandmother came to the U.S. in 1910 as one of the picture brides. When they were alive, they used to tell me some interesting stories of their earlier days in

this country. Their marriage through exchanging photos didn't go well initially. My grandmother was a very strong woman and my grandfather was somewhat disappointed at first about not receiving the gentle woman he had been promised. My grandmother, who only knew limited words of English such as "yes," "no," and "thank you," resented coming to the U.S. after realizing the difficulty communicating in English. Despite these initial resentments on both sides, their marriage survived more than 50 years! Many challenges awaited them in their efforts to adjust to the American way of life, ranging from food to new customs. My grandfather worked for a farmer, and my grandmother was a domestic worker. My grandmother learned to set table, fry bacon, bake cookies, and make coffee from the woman she worked for. Although both of my grandparents had to learn so many new things, they were never allowed to assimilate into the dominant culture. They spent lots of time with other Japanese, my grandfather playing cards with the Issei neighbors, and my grandmother exchanging ideas and talking about child care with her Issei women friends.

How did the internment experience change the way your grandparents viewed adjustment to the majority culture?

SS: My grandparents endured much emotional and physical pain when they were incarcerated. They had given up the idea of trying to adjust to America. Instead, various limitations in their new lives forced them to adjust to the new familial relationships. Although there was a lot of caring for each other, my grandparents were no longer the final authority in deciding the fate of their family members. To them, adjustment to the majority culture became an unthinkable issue.

How did your Nisei parents try to adjust to the dominant culture?

SS: My parents were late teenagers when they were interned. They met at the camp and married soon after their return to San Francisco. After living with my father's parents for a year, they found their own apartment. My parents' attitudes toward their own family were very different from their Issei parents. They had much more egalitarian attitudes toward each other and in raising us. My parents have lots of friends, many of whom are *ha-*

kujin (European Americans), and they seem to be quite integrated in the dominant culture. But they are still active in the Japanese American Citizens League (JACL). My mother has been a president of the local chapter, and they really enjoy getting together with their friends and families through JACL-sponsored Easter picnics, banquets, and other events.

How about your generation? What are some of the challenges you faced growing up as a Sansei in American society?

SS: I think most of my generation feels fortunate after growing up listening to our parents' stories about camp. I chose my college, occupation, and my spouse. My parents were not really involved in any of the decision-making process but simply trusted me. In reflecting more deeply, I believe that we, Sansei, can freely choose to do and be whomever we want to be because of what our grandparents and parents endured. When I was growing up, most of my friends were non-Japanese, many were *hakujin* and Mexicans. During these formative years, I wasn't even aware that I was different from my friends. This was probably the biggest contributing factor to my identity crisis. I think I unconsciously suppressed my Japanese American identity until college when I became involved in the Japanese Student Association and the JACL. I was pretty active in the redress movement. I also tried to get our two daughters involved in learning *Obon* (ancestor worship) dance. It's not that we tried to go back to our ancestors' tradition, but I think it is important to be familiar with our cultural heritage. I want our daughters to be proud of their Japanese American heritage.

Questions for Discussion

1. What stereotypes and misconceptions about Japanese American families are described in this chapter? What are the sources of these stereotypes? How do they compare to Chinese American family stereotypes?

2. Describe how Japanese American families have been influenced by the Japanese traditional culture. What other cultures have had the same type of influence?

3. How did the immigration experience shape the family structure and relationships of Japanese Americans?

4. Describe how Japanese American internment during World War II influenced family relationships between Issei and Nisei generations. How does this compare to the slavery experienced by African Americans? How does it compare to the persecution of American Indians? What are the root causes of all three of these experiences?

5. Summarize the strengths found in Japanese American families. What are the sources of these strengths?

6. Japanese American divorce rates have increased over the past 20–40 years. What are some of the causes of this increase? How does this compare to the divorce rate of other ethnic groups discussed in this book? What accounts for the differences and similarities across groups?

7. What differences exist between the Chinese American family and the Japanese American family? Why is it important to understand the differences between these groups?

8. What similarities exist between your life and the life of Sharon Shimizu in the interview? What similarities exist between Sharon Shimizu and Alice, the African American interviewee?

Suggested Resources

Readings

Nakano, M. (1990). *Japanese American women: Three generations, 1890–1990.* Berkeley, CA: Mina Press.

Yanagisako, S. J. (1985). *Transforming the past: Tradition and kinship among Japanese Americans.* Stanford, CA: Stanford University Press.

Videos

Doelger, F. (Producer). (1985). *War between the classes.* (Available from The Learning Corporation of America, 1440 S. Sepulveda Boulevard, Los Angeles, CA 91602)

Library Video Company. (Producer). (1993). *Japanese Americans: A multicultural people.* (Available from Videofinders, 425 E. Colorado Street, Suite 10B, Glendale, CA 91205)

Public Broadcasting Services. (Producer). (1989). *Family gathering.* (Available from Videofinders, 425 E. Colorado Street, Suite 10B, Glendale, CA 91205)

References

Barringer, H. R., Gardner, R. W., & Levin, M. J. (1993). *Asian and Pacific Islanders in the United States.* New York: Russell Sage Foundation.

Barringer, H. R., Takeuchi, D. T., & Xenos, P. (1990). Education, occupational prestige, and income of Asian Americans. *Sociology of Education, 63,* 27–43.

Brinton, M. C. (1988). The social-institutional bases of gender stratification: Japan as an illustrative case. *American Journal of Sociology, 94*(2), 300–334.

Carlin, J., & Sokoloff, B. (1985). Mental health treatment issues for Southeast Asian refugee children. In T. Owan (Ed.), *Southeast Asian mental health: Treatment, prevention, services, training, and research* (pp. 91–112). Washington, DC: U.S. Department of Health and Human Services.

Caudill, W. (1952). Japanese-American personality and acculturation. *Genetic Psychology Monographs, 45,* 3–102.

Chan, S. (1991). *Asian Americans: An interpretive history.* Boston: Twayne.

Connor, J. W. (1974). Acculturation and family continuities in three generations of Japanese Americans. *Journal of Marriage and the Family, 36,* 159–165.

Do people need religion? (1995, September 20). *Hiragana Times,* pp. 12–16.

Gardner, R. W., Robey, B., & Smith, P. C. (1985). Asian Americans: Growth, change and diversity. *Population Bulletin, 40,* 1–44.

Glenn, E. N. (1986). *Issei, nisei, war bride: Three generations of Japanese women in domestic service.* Philadelphia: Temple University Press.

Ichioka, Y. (1988). *The Issei.* New York: Free Press.

Immigration and Naturalization Service. (1988). *Immigrants admitted to the United States.* Washington, DC: U.S. Department of Justice.

Ishii-Kuntz, M. (1990, April). *Structural and psychological adaptation of immigrants: A case of post-1965 Japanese immigrants in the U.S.* Paper presented at the Pacific Sociological Association meeting, Spokane, WA.

Ishii-Kuntz, M. (1994a). Paternal involvement and perception toward fathers' roles: A comparison between Japan and the United States. *Journal of Family Issues, 15*(1), 30–48.

Ishii-Kuntz, M. (1994b). *Shin* Issei and their adaptation to American society. *Orange Network, 2*(7), 1–20.

Jiobu, R. M. (1988). *Ethnicity and assimilation: Blacks, Chinese, Filipinos, Japanese, Koreans, Mexicans, Vietnamese, and Whites.* Albany: State University of New York Press.

Johnson, C. L. (1977). Interdependence, reciprocity and indebtedness: An analysis of Japanese American kinship relations. *Journal of Marriage and the Family, 39*, 351–363.

Kikumura, A., & Kitano, H. (1973). Interracial marriage: A picture of Japanese Americans. *Journal of Social Issues, 29*, 67–81.

Kitano, H. H. (1976). *Japanese Americans: The evolution of a subculture* (2nd ed.). Englewood Cliffs, NJ: Prentice-Hall.

Kitano, H. H. (1994, November). Recent trends in Japanese American interracial marriage. Paper presented at the Center for Family Studies Lecture Series, University of California, Riverside.

Kitano, H. H., & Kikumura, A. (1976). The Japanese American family. In C. Mindel & R. Habenstein (Eds.), *Ethnic families in America: Patterns and variations* (pp. 41–60). New York: Elsevier.

Levine, G. N., & Rhodes, D. (1981). *The Japanese American community: A three-generation study.* New York: Praeger.

Nakano, M. (1990). *Japanese American women: Three generations, 1890–1990.* Berkeley, CA: Mina Press.

Osako, M. M. (1976). International relations as an aspect of assimilation: The case of Japanese Americans. *Sociological Inquiry, 46*, 67–72.

Osako, M. M. (1980). *Aging, social isolation and kinship ties among Japanese Americans: Project report to the administration on aging.*

Rafu Shimpo. (1994, November 15). Domestic violence on the rise. p. 1.

Reischauer, E. O. (1981). *The Japanese.* Cambridge, MA: Harvard University Press.

Schmid, C. F., & Nobbe, C. E. (1965). Socioeconomic differentials among nonwhite races. *American Sociological Review, 30*, 909–922.

Smith, C. K., & Schooler, C. (1978). Women as mothers in Japan: The effects of social structure and culture on values and behavior. *Journal of Marriage and the Family, 40*(3), 613–620.

Steiner, K. (1950). The revision of the civil code of Japan: Provisions affecting the family. *Far Eastern Quarterly 9*(2), 169–184.

Sue, S., and Chin, R. (1983). The mental health of Chinese-American children: Stressors and resources. In G. Powell (Ed.), *The psychological development of minority group children* (pp. 385–397). New York: Brunner/Mazel.

Takagi, D. Y. (1994). Japanese American families. In R. Taylor (Ed.), *Minority families in the United States: A multicultural perspective* (pp. 146–183). Englewood Cliffs, NJ: Prentice-Hall.

Takaki, R. (1989). *Strangers from a different shore: A history of Asian Americans.* New York: Penguin Books.

Thomas, D. S. (1950). Some social aspects of Japanese-American demography. *Proceedings of American Philosophical Society, 94,* 459–480.

Thomas, D. S. (1952). *The salvage: Japanese-American evacuation and resettlement.* Berkeley: University of California Press.

Tinker, J. N. (1973). Intermarriage and ethnic boundaries: The Japanese American case. *Journal of Social Issues, 29*(2), 49–65.

Uba, L. (1994). *Asian Americans: Personality patterns, identity, and mental health.* New York: Guilford Press.

U.S. Bureau of the Census. (1980). *Statistical abstract of the United States, 1980.* Washington, DC: U.S. Government Printing Office.

U.S. Bureau of the Census. (1990). *Statistical abstract of the United States, 1990.* Washington, DC: U.S. Government Printing Office.

U.S. Bureau of the Census. (1991). *Statistical abstract of the United States, 1991.* Washington, DC: U.S. Government Printing Office.

U.S. Commission on Civil Rights. (1988). *The economic progress of Americans of Asian descent: An exploratory investigation.* Washington, DC: Clearinghouse Publications.

Watanabe, T. (1977). *A report from the Japanese American community study.* Seattle: University of Washington, Department of Anthropology.

Wong, M. G. (1982). The cost of being Chinese, Japanese, and Filipino in the United States: 1960, 1970, 1979. *Pacific Sociological Review, 25,* 59–78.

Wong, M. G., & Hirschman, C. (1983). Labor force participation and socioeconomic attainment of Asian-American women. *Sociological Perspectives, 26,* 423–446.

Yamamoto, J., & Kubota, M. (1983). The Japanese-American family. In G. Powell (Ed.), *The psychosocial development of minority group children* (pp. 237–247). New York: Brunner/Mazel.

Yanagisako, S. J. (1985). *Transforming the past: Tradition and kinship among Japanese Americans.* Stanford, CA: Stanford University Press.

Hector Carrasquillo

8

Puerto Rican Families in America

Historical and Cultural Background

The story of Puerto Rican migration to the United States is one of sharp contrast: trading a lush tropical island for the blustery cities of the northeastern United States, abandoning steady but low-paying jobs in favor of unstable industrial employment, and leaving a society whose traditional values emphasize family and community for one where the aspirations of the individual often take precedence over those of the group.

In attempting to adapt the values of a traditional culture to the pressures of a modern, economically advanced society, Puerto Rican migrants in the United States have experienced many of the same problems—poverty, family breakup, or a sense of isolation, for example—reported by members of other ethnic groups who have settled in America. However, the Puerto Rican experience is set apart by two major factors: the timing of migration, and the status of Puerto Ricans as U.S. citizens.

Because the greatest thrust of Puerto Rican migration to the United States has occurred over the last half-century, advances in telecommunications and transportation have made it possible for migrants to retain close ties with the country and culture they left behind. As U.S. citizens, all Puerto Rican Americans have the right to travel between the island and the mainland as they please. As a result, visits between friends and family members, who might otherwise have been perpetually separated by distance or by national boundaries, are frequent. This ongoing close contact has provided Puerto Ricans living in the United States with the support they need to maintain much of their traditional culture.

Thus, the Puerto Rican migrant experience—the extent to which acculturation and assimilation into the dominant culture has occurred—has differed in important ways from that of other ethnic groups. **Acculturation**, or learning to live in an environment with others whose cultural values differ from one's own, has played an important role for Puerto Ricans for centuries. Like many of the cultures of the Americas, including that of the United States itself, Puerto Rican culture evolved as Europeans, Africans, and indigenous Indians mixed with and influenced each other over hundreds of years.

When Christopher Columbus first set foot on Puerto Rico, the island was occupied by the Taino Indians. Columbus claimed the island for the King and Queen of Spain, and as the age of exploration and colonialism advanced, the Spanish recognized both the military importance of Puerto Rico's position in the Caribbean and its economic potential as a rich agricultural producer of exotic and expensive goods such as sugar, coffee, and tobacco. These products were most efficiently produced using the labor-intensive plantation system, supported by the work of slaves from Africa. This economic exploitation of the land would play a critical part in Puerto Rico's future.

The colonization of the island also established an ethnic mix that gave birth to a dynamic new Puerto Rican culture. Although the Spanish did not engage in the wide-scale emigration and formation of permanent communities typical of the British in North America, they did bring the Spanish language and Catholicism to Puerto Rico. African slaves also contributed to the culture, as is primarily evident in the distinctive rhythms of Puerto Rican music and in the African-based folk religion that exists alongside the officially sanctioned Catholicism. The Taino influence is perhaps less obvious, but the indigenous people also left their mark on Puerto Rican food, music, and spiritual practices.

Another major influence on Puerto Rican culture came from the island's larger neighbor to the north. As the United States grew into a large, rich, and powerful nation during the nineteenth century, it began to supplant Spain as a trading partner for the plantation owners of Puerto Rico. And after the Spanish-American War of 1898, the United States replaced Spain as the ruler of the island and assumed a more important role in the development of Puerto Rico's economy and culture. European Americans brought their own influence, particularly their religion, to Puerto Rico, resulting in the rise of Protestantism on the island during the twentieth century. The establishment of Puerto Rico as a commonwealth of the United States, and the consequent status of Puerto Ricans as U.S. citizens with the right to travel freely to the mainland, set the stage for the migration of large numbers of Puerto Ricans following World War II.

Despite the influence of the United States on Puerto Rico, the island's native culture retained many distinctive characteristics. And despite the rapid changes brought about by the technological revolution, Puerto Rican culture has maintained the community orientation that is part of its Spanish and African heritage. This sense of community grew out of a society consisting primarily of small agricultural groups whose survival depended upon solidarity and cooperation. The high status accorded to the elders of the family, particularly the **patriarchs**, and the prevalence of traditional **gender-role expectations**, indicate that Puerto Rican culture still features a rigid social system in which hierarchies are respected, within both the family and the larger community.

The Migration Experience

Although Puerto Rico began as a Spanish colony, its economy and its culture have long been linked to those of its closest powerful neighbor, the United States. Even before it took possession of the island in the late nineteenth century, the United States had emerged as the most important trading partner for Puerto Rican agriculture. This commercial necessity led to the establishment of small groups of Puerto Rican traders and political exiles in Brooklyn and other American communities. In time, these groups grew, as the unbalanced colonial economy caused social and economic conditions on the island to worsen. Unable to find enough traditional agricultural work to support themselves, Puerto Ricans increasingly looked to the mainland for employment opportunities that were absent in their homeland.

The most significant factor contributing to the massive migration of the mid–twentieth century was the Jones Act of 1917, which granted U.S. citizenship to native residents of Puerto Rico, giving them the right to travel freely to and from the mainland without the papers required of other immigrants. Many Puerto Ricans availed themselves of this opportunity and moved to the mainland in search of unskilled industrial or service jobs. It was World War II, and the consequent need for labor on the mainland, that led to the most significant Puerto Rican emigration. At the beginning of the war there were fewer than 75,000 Puerto Ricans living mostly in the New York City area, but by 1950, over 300,000 were living on the mainland. By 1970, their number had grown to nearly 1.5 million, not including those who had been born in the United States but still remained associated with Puerto Rican culture. By the year 2000, it is estimated that there will be about 7 million men and women of Puerto Rican ancestry living in the United States (U.S. Bureau of the Census, 1994).

These figures, however, do not tell the entire story. Many Puerto Ricans who emigrated prior to World War II hoped to live in the United States only temporarily, while they saved enough money to return to their homeland on a firmer financial footing. In most cases, the migrants were unable to fulfill this dream, and, particularly after starting families in the United States, they reconciled themselves to living permanently on the mainland.

The extent to which individual Puerto Ricans have adapted to American life varies. Some Puerto Ricans, particularly those who have established themselves in professional roles, have chosen the values and customs of the dominant society, leading lives that are, on the surface, indistinguishable from those of other middle-class Americans. Typically, however, they have retained their connection to the Puerto Rican communities on the mainland and on the island, and continue to observe many of their culture's traditions.

Other Puerto Ricans have decided not to immerse themselves in mainstream American society, preferring to adhere to the traditional customs of their culture. They live, either by choice or of necessity, in the more exclusively Puerto Rican environments of the **barrios**, or ghettos, of the United States. To cope with the difficult economic circumstances in the *barrios*, they have established distinct new cultural forms that adapt elements of Puerto Rican culture to American life. The language of the *barrios*, for example, demonstrates the creative response of Puerto Ricans to their social and cultural situation. While many residents are bilingual, using Spanish as their primary language, the *barrio* form of Spanish is not strictly identifiable with the Spanish traditionally spoken on the island. Instead, *barrio* speakers have established a dialect that incorporates many English words and phrases. Some purists look down on this "Spanglish," while others consider the blending of the languages a positive and natural evolution to a form that is more appropriate to the immigrants' new situation.

Puerto Ricans in the *barrios* have adapted much more than just the Spanish language to suit their changing needs. Such diverse aspects of everyday living as diet, clothing, music, and religion reflect a unique merging of American culture with that of the island. *Barrio* residents are comfortable eating frijoles or hamburgers, listening to salsa or rock music. This ability to assimilate elements of the American lifestyle without losing their own cultural identity has been vital to Puerto Rican migrants.

Traditional and Emerging Family Systems

Our notion of culture often assumes that traditional cultures are static, but change and adaptation are part of every culture. This section discusses the Puerto Rican family as it existed in the premigration period and how it has adapted to the social environment of the United States.

Household Size and Composition

The "ideal" mainstream American family is often perceived as a **nuclear family** consisting of father, mother, and children living in a single household, separate from other relatives, who play a secondary role in the family. Although this model no longer describes most American families today, it does express the dominant culture's conception of the ideal family structure. Many Puerto Rican families conform to this model, and many others do not; on the surface, the diversity of Puerto Rican family structures does not significantly differ from that of the United States.

This similarity, however, belies important differences in family structure that are not apparent from household composition. The difference is most obvious in the context of the **extended family**, an arrangement in which grandparents, aunts, uncles, and cousins live together in close proximity to each other. This structure is a characteristic feature of the traditional Puerto Rican household; for the Puerto Rican, the family is an extended social unit that encompasses a wide variety of relationships. The extended family functions as a primary agent of socialization, as a safety net for its members in times of need, and as a means for obtaining protection, companionship, and social and business contacts. Although the members of the extended family do not always reside in the same house, they generally live close to each other and, most importantly, remain in frequent contact with each other (Blatt, 1979).

In addition to blood kin, the extended family includes people linked by a variety of informal, but culturally important, roles that are not based on biological relationships (Padilla, 1987). For example, when an adult informally adopts another's child as an *hijo de crianza*, thereby accepting special emotional ties to the child and to the child's family, each becomes part of the other's extended family (Sánchez-Ayéndez, 1988). A better-known relationship is that of godparent—*compadrazgo*—which has its roots in Catholicism, but which, in Puerto Rico, has developed a secular meaning as well as a religious one. Those linked by the *compadrazgo* relationship are under special, and emotionally important, obligation to help each other in times of need (Fitzpatrick, 1987). The relationship thus acts as an important survival strategy in a culture where extreme poverty is common. Moreover, families often use the *compadrazgo* relationship to associate themselves with other extended family groups, allowing the larger society to grow out of, and be embedded within, the basic social unit of the extended family.

Generational relationships play both a symbolic and a practical role in the survival of the extended family and its members. Elders are treated with a special respect, or *respeto*, which serves as the foundation on which the entire familial system is based. By virtue of their lifetimes of experience, the elders are regarded as repositories of wisdom, and it is to them that both the young and the middle-aged traditionally go for advice.

The importance of the extended family in traditional Puerto Rican society cannot be overstated. The family is the root from which the rest of society grows, and it is the matrix that provides the basis for the identity of the individual. In a very real sense, a Puerto Rican is only fully a person insofar as he or she is a member of a family. To lose or abandon one's family is to detach oneself from one's social identity and to become uprooted from one's source of emotional support. It is not surprising that Puerto Ricans believe that someone detached from a family cannot lead an adequate life (Bastida, 1979).

This strong orientation to the family as both the root of one's identity and a conduit to the outside world represents a value system that social scientists call **familialism** (Rogler & Cooney, 1984). According to this viewpoint, that which exists within the family has a stronger reality than that which stands outside it; it is only within the family, with its close and highly personal relationships, that one can feel full security and trust (Mintz, 1966).

This strong familial orientation had an important impact upon emigration practices and the structure of life within the new American urban environments into which Puerto Ricans typically moved. What was practical in a small island village was not necessarily possible in the tenements of a city like New York. While members of extended families often emigrated as a group and took up residence close to each other, in some cases crowding together into tiny apartments, separations and disruptions of the pattern of constant contact were inevitable. Although Puerto Rican migrant families have experienced a shift toward the American norm that emphasizes the importance of the nuclear family, close contact (often by telephone) between family members has continued, and the family remains a critical resource for social and economic survival.

Inevitably, changes since migration have weakened many Puerto Rican families in the United States. Perhaps the most important change has been the erosion of intergenerational respect. Young Puerto Ricans, particularly those who have lived their entire lives in the United States, tend to adapt and/or assimilate more readily into American culture than their elders did. Thus, immigrant families often experience a generational role reversal. Because the elders must come to the young for advice and guidance in this new situation, they may be perceived as antiquated or irrelevant. Although they still receive formal deference, their role in the family has changed as a result of the loss of the traditional environment. An element of instability has thereby been introduced into Puerto Rican American families, leading many older immigrants to consider the move to the mainland as a mistake. This perception, in turn, has persuaded large numbers of migrants to return to Puerto Rico, seeking out their old way of life.

The Socialization of Children

Because of the centrality of the family in Puerto Rican American life, child rearing is of special importance. After all, one is both raising an individual and maintaining an institution that extends back into the distant past and will extend into the future. Not only an individual life, but the whole culture, depends on making certain that children are raised in the right way so they will be able to assume their proper social roles in the next generation.

Although raising children is primarily the mother's responsibility, the father is also involved. Particularly in the traditional family, the goal of socializing children is to develop boys and girls into adults who conform to traditional masculine and feminine gender roles. Because men and women have different gender-role expectations in Puerto Rican culture, boys and girls are raised differently.

Boys, taught to be aggressive and extroverted, are allowed to play outside the household much earlier than girls are, and are encouraged to take risks and to participate in neighborhood activities. Girls, on the other hand, are expected to stay close to the home, to assume domestic responsibilities at an early age, and to behave in a restrained and obedient manner. Although the pressure to conform to these socially accepted roles is diminishing, it is still formidable, and young Puerto Ricans who refuse to conform pay a high price for their independence. In contrast to mainstream American parents who raise their children to be much more individualistic, Puerto Rican American parents tend to reinforce the norms of family closeness and respect for authority (Harwood & Miller, 1991; Okagaki & Sternberg, 1993; Zayas & Solari, 1994).

Especially in rural areas, however, childhood in the traditional Puerto Rican culture is not as carefree as it is in modern Puerto Rican culture in the United States. Often living in subsistence conditions, boys and girls are both expected to contribute to the family's financial health by working. Play is important, but it does not have the central role that it tends to have in mainstream American culture. The transition from childhood to adulthood comes rather quickly.

Intimate Relationships

Gender-based behavioral differences continue as Puerto Rican American children become teenagers and begin looking for marriage partners. Given the culture's emphasis on maintaining female virginity until marriage, and the protective measures taken by parents on behalf of their daughters, the relatively open dating patterns characteristic of mainstream American adolescents are not acceptable in traditional Puerto Rican American families.

Selecting one's future mate is a key part of one's personal life and, particularly in a family-oriented culture, the larger life of the family unit. Where the norms of the family are emphasized more than the desires of the individual, courting behavior is controlled by strict rules; the mate-selection process is simply too important to be left up to the person involved. Courting in traditional Puerto Rican families in America occurs under the watchful eyes of the parents, whose duty it is to preserve the virtue of their daughters and to ensure that an appropriate marriage is made for both sons and daughters.

Although personal affection plays an important role in mate selection, it is also true that a marriage constitutes an alliance between families; consequently, the family elders have a certain degree of influence over a young person's decision. Although young people are generally allowed a certain degree of choice in selecting mates, they must choose their partners from within an appropriate social group. In marriage, as in other aspects of life, the interests of the family and those of the individual within the family are considered to be so tightly joined as to be inseparable.

For this reason, the American dating patterns in which groups of young people and couples get together to engage in social activities are not characteristic of traditional Puerto Rican culture. The process of meeting and evaluating potential mates occurs in a much more controlled and ritualized manner. Traditionally, rather than meeting prospective marriage partners in relative isolation, unmarried men and women met while promenading through a central area of town; they could look at and speak to each other, but the public character of the meetings prevented any kind of intimacy. When a tentative selection was made and a couple began courting in earnest, they typically still were not left alone. They were allowed to socialize in order to get to know each other better, but such "dates" occurred under the watchful eye of an adult chaperone. Within this context, relationships formed slowly, and control over mate selection was maintained by the family leaders. Today, not all adolescents unconditionally accept these constraints, and some premarital sexual activity does take place. However, the culture as a whole still places great value on the traditional norms.

Because the family is the central social unit of Puerto Rican culture, there is great concern for familial continuity, and thus for children. For this reason, traditional Puerto Ricans living in the United States consider it inappropriate to delay childbearing. Believing that raising a family is a central part of everyone's role in life, they assume that role as soon as they can. Thus, Puerto Ricans traditionally tended to marry while still adolescents and to begin having children as soon as possible. Being a teenage parent was accepted. A man or woman who did not become a parent at an early age would be going against the cultural ideal and therefore subject to significant social pressure. A marriage that did not produce children was by definition a failed marriage. Because of the importance of child rearing in traditional Puerto Rican culture, and because of the influence of the Catholic Church, using contraceptives has been traditionally discouraged, although it is becoming a more popular practice in the United States and even on the island today.

Gender differences are deeply embedded within the cultural ideals of *machismo*, manliness, and *marianismo*, femininity. The term **machismo** has been incorrectly interpreted in the United States to mean insensitivity and extreme aggressiveness, particularly in sexual matters. While the ideal of *machismo* does emphasize the importance of sexual potency, aggressiveness, and risk-taking, the stereotype of the "macho" male as one who brutalizes women and who takes no interest in domestic affairs distorts the actual norm considerably. The ideal Puerto Rican male is capable of demonstrating a high degree of sensitivity, and he participates actively in the domestic life of the family. He is the head of the household and should be involved in all significant decisions (Stycos, 1955). His aggressiveness in dealing with those outside the family stems in part from his responsibility to protect his family from the hostile world that exists outside its boundaries (Mussen & Beytagh, 1969). It is acceptable for a macho male to have extramarital sexual relations, but within the family he is expected to treat each person, particularly each female, with a high level of respect.

The term **marianismo** derives from the devotion accorded in Latin American Catholicism to the figure of the Virgin Mary. The Puerto Rican female is expected to reflect the modesty and chastity associated with the Virgin, and to retain a highly domestic orientation. Traditional Puerto Rican women have few relationships outside the extended family, and their lives center on the home and the raising of their children (Landy, 1959; Safa, 1974). In traditional society, the costs of openly violating this norm (by losing virginity before marriage, for example) are very high. Deviant behavior is considered an attack on basic family values and therefore is not tolerated. For a woman not to conform is for her virtually to take on the status of a prostitute, leaving her vulnerable to the sexual aggressiveness of males in a way that "respectable" women are not. At least in part, the sexual aggressiveness expected of Puerto Rican men can be interpreted as a social control mechanism that serves to differentiate between respectable and unrespectable women, and to ensure that most women act in a manner that does not undercut the stability of the family.

In both traditional and contemporary Puerto Rican American cultures, the basic family unit is not necessarily limited to pairings that have been formalized through marriage ceremonies. There is a long tradition of men and women, particularly those of low socioeconomic status, living together in informal relationships that resemble marriage more than cohabitation. Entering into such a relationship does not necessarily bring about a loss of respectability (Landale & Fennelly, 1992). However, even among those who engage in this practice, the ideal remains a formalized relationship.

Relationships and the Family

The Puerto Rican American family functions as a cooperative social unit, within which the roles assigned to men and women are precisely drawn. Unlike the emerging egalitarian norm for middle-class families in the United States, in which gender roles and status differences are minimized, the traditional Puerto Rican family in America accords males higher status and more freedom of action, particularly outside the home (Landy, 1959; Safa, 1974). Women are expected to remain close to the home and maintain most of their social relationships within the extended family. They are supposed to be subservient to men and to allow men to establish the family's direction. Although women have always indirectly asserted considerable informal power within the family, they have been able to do so only insofar as they have acknowledged the formal power of the men in the family.

In general, the male role involves responsibilities within the family and in the outside world. Men are expected to venture out of the household to provide for the family and even to engage in such domestic duties as shopping (Blatt, 1979). While in traditional Puerto Rican society it was often necessary for women to participate in the economic life of the family, ideally their role was to be totally devoted to the household and the children.

Today, the role of women in the family is changing. The primary reason is the influence of the dominant culture. In America, women are exposed to female role models, in life and in the media, who play an important role in the economic survival of the family. As in many non–Puerto Rican families, the financial security of Puerto Rican American families often depends on the woman's contribution.

Another reason for the economic participation of women is the fact that their traditional skills, particularly sewing, provided an easier entry into the working world than those of men, whose farming skills were not of great use in most northeastern U.S. cities. Thus, while Puerto Rican women managed to establish themselves in the New York garment industry, albeit as exploited sweatshop employees, Puerto Rican men had few skills that were valuable in their new economic environment.

Life-Cycle Transitions

The entry of Puerto Ricans into relatively high-paying jobs in the United States has not occurred. This has led to increasing instability in poor Puerto Rican American families, and the consequent dramatic rise in the number of female-headed households has placed tremendous strain on a culture grounded in patriarchy and a strong family orientation. In 1987, 43.7% of all Puerto Rican American families were headed by women (U.S. Bureau of the Census, 1990). Such female-headed families typically have less access to resources traditionally provided by the extended family, and this loss of support has led to an increase in destructive (and self-destructive) behavior among children and adolescents.

Closely associated with escalating numbers of single-parent households has been an increase in informal unions among migrants (Landale, 1994). Changing circumstances have also dictated a shift away from some traditional values. The rate of sterilization among poor Puerto Rican women in New York City, for example, has increased dramatically in recent years, signaling a movement away from previously high levels of fertility.

Although there is no single reason for this disintegration of the family, psychological factors probably play a significant role. Self-worth is to a large extent determined by one's ability to live up to the expectations of society. Failing to live up to accepted norms tends to lead to a sense of defensive apathy and rationalization of one's perceived shortcomings. Rather than trying to fulfill a role in an environment where one seems doomed to fail, one will very often stop trying. In the case of men, coming into a situation where they are unable to play the role of dominant breadwinner, and seeing their wives assuming that role, can lead to a serious sense of inadequacy and subsequent withdrawal from family life. This inevitably leads to tensions and to failed marriages, and ultimately to female-headed households. The situation is exacerbated by the economic incentives for single mothers provided by the current welfare system.

Thus, the problems of families are deeply rooted in social conditions. Even among intact Puerto Rican American families, significant changes are occurring. Not only have Puerto Rican American women been exposed to the influences of modern feminism, but, because they have often had more success finding employment than their male counterparts, they have achieved an economic status unavailable to them in the traditional society. Many Puerto Rican American women find traditionally structured gender roles too constraining; they desire greater authority in making household decisions, as well as a home environment that emphasizes mutual participation rather than male dominance (Leavitt, 1974; Rogler & Cooney, 1984; Rogler & Procidano, 1986). While in the past Puerto Rican women sought their primary emotional relationships among the women of their extended families, the trend toward modernization has led to a strengthening of emotional relationships primarily within the nuclear household (Rogler & Cooney, 1984).

Family Strengths and Challenges

Despite the changes imposed upon it by the shifting environment, the Puerto Rican American family retains many of its traditional strengths. Although increasing numbers of Puerto Rican Americans live in nuclear and/or disrupted families, most continue to rely on the extended family for emotional and practical support. Over 75% of Puerto Rican American families in New York City have adult children who visit their parents at least weekly (Rogler & Cooney,

1984). This is especially important for those living in poverty, insofar as grand-parents, as well as aunts and uncles, can provide such services as child care to help cope with financial hardship. Those who are isolated from their families tend to lose their personal and social bearings.

The Puerto Rican family in the United States appears to be moving in two directions. Those who have not prospered tend to be subject to high levels of fa-milial instability, which is also destructive of the traditional Puerto Rican val-ues and family system. For those able to obtain an education and gain an economic foothold in the dominant culture, there is a shift from the traditional extended family structure toward a nuclear family, featuring the close egalitar-ian relationship between husband and wife that characterizes many American marriages. However, even more nearly assimilated middle-class Puerto Rican Americans continue to have close relationships with members of their ex-tended families, to downplay what they often see as excessive individualism in themselves or their children, and to look to the past as well as to the future.

Puerto Rican culture, despite the difficulties it encounters on the main-land and on the island, remains vital, and there are few indications that most Puerto Ricans will lose their distinctive cultural identity. Puerto Rican Ameri-cans continue to remain in contact with the island, and the *barrios* themselves have become important Puerto Rican cultural centers within the United States. Given these factors, it seems likely that the Puerto Rican family in America is in transition rather than decline, and that we will eventually see not one but several adaptations of the traditional culture to the modern envi-ronment.

The traditional life-cycle patterns of families arose in the rural villages of Puerto Rico, and they have been difficult to maintain—both on the mainland and on the modern island itself. It is much more difficult to exercise control over children and adolescents in urban environments, particularly in the face of strong influences that tend to subvert traditional norms and gender roles. Thus, while many Puerto Rican American families exert pressure on their daughters to act in a manner traditionally deemed appropriate, young people tend to conform more to the openness of modern society than to the con-straints of traditional society. This is a major factor in the changing tenor of in-tergenerational relationships in the Puerto Rican American family. As Puerto Ricans adapt to new urban environments in the United States, they tend to rely on those who have lived in the *barrios* more than on those whose experience was contained in the very different world of Puerto Rican rural life.

The modification of the traditional Puerto Rican family has also been in-fluenced by the poverty endemic to some sectors of the Puerto Rican American population. Puerto Ricans migrated to the northeastern United States follow-ing World War II, in hopes of obtaining jobs that were unavailable in the poor economy of the island. The war had ended the Great Depression in the United

States, and many people believed the new economic growth would last indefinitely. Manufacturing jobs for unskilled and semiskilled workers provided opportunities for both men and women, promising them the better lives they sought in the United States. However, the decline in American manufacturing and the movement of jobs from northeastern to southern and western regions of the country left many immigrants unemployed. Those Puerto Ricans who had gained a foothold on the economic ladder of the mainland became part of the American middle class. Many who were less fortunate became trapped in a cycle of long-term underemployment and unemployment.

The United States has always been a land of opportunity and has prided itself on the people who have come here in search of a better life. Puerto Ricans came to the United States for the same reason as did most earlier ethnic and cultural groups, and thus they are a part of the great current of the nation's history.

Misconceptions and Stereotypes

Like members of many immigrant cultures, Puerto Ricans in the United States have been subjected to a variety of stereotypes that misrepresent them. In spite of the fact that they migrated to the mainland in search of jobs, Puerto Ricans are widely perceived as being lazy and unwilling to work because they have been forced to rely on welfare. The antisocial nature of the activities of a minority of Puerto Ricans receives more media attention than does the cultural vitality of the wider community, and the economic roots of those disruptive activities are often ignored. Although they are American citizens with the right to travel freely into and out of the United States, they are often viewed as unassimilated foreigners.

This misperception is particularly pervasive in the stereotypes about the Puerto Rican family. Because they are different from the coherent nuclear families that are the American ideal—an ideal that has become more an exception than the rule—Puerto Rican American households are sometimes perceived to be unstructured collections of people who are gathered together as a manifestation of social disorganization rather than as a reaction against it.

This stereotype mistakes a traditional strength of the Puerto Rican family—its extended, multigenerational character—for a weakness, merely because it varies from the norm of the dominant culture. Certainly, poverty has forced many Puerto Ricans to live in inadequate apartments. But these circumstances have made them develop cooperative ways of living that in turn help them cope with their poverty. Whether working in the island's fields or in New York's sweatshops, most Puerto Ricans have always been poor and have always used their extended families to help them survive that poverty.

Personal Interview

Immigrants come to the United States seeking freedom and prosperity, and with hard work they, or at least their children, often improve their socioeconomic status. This ideal, however attractive, is not necessarily reflective of reality, as evidenced in the story of the Rivera family.

The Riveras are a middle-aged couple living in New York City with two daughters, ages 18 and 14, and a son, age 15. Although Mrs. Rivera resisted their move to the United States 5 years ago, her husband, who had lived with his first wife on the mainland in the 1950s, felt a need for a change. He was convinced that a move to the United States would be best for the entire family; however, both the parents and the children now regret making the decision to relocate.

Mr. Rivera obtained a fairly good position as a building inspector for New York City, although he lives with the constant threat that the city budget crisis will result in his termination. Mrs. Rivera has been much less lucky. Although she speaks fluent English, she was fired from a clerical job because her employer felt it was inappropriate to have someone with an accent answer the telephone.

Discrimination has been a problem for the Riveras in more areas than just employment. In a particularly blatant case, which occurred during the 1960s, Mr. Rivera sought to buy a house but was shown only substandard houses in bad neighborhoods. When he finally located an appropriate house, the real estate agent told him that it was already sold; his lighter-skinned Italian American wife, however, was informed that the house was still available.

Not only discrimination has led this family to regret their move. Overall, they feel that the life they left, even considering the depressed economic environment of the island, was superior to the one they found. Reacting to the insularity and individualism inherent in North American life, Mrs. Rivera notes that on the island people are community-oriented and are not as isolated from each other as are New Yorkers. The Riveras appreciate the many activities New York offers, but they also recognize that the cost of these activities makes it impossible for a family of five to participate in them regularly. Feeling quite isolated, Mrs. Rivera takes comfort in her family, in a friend from her home town, and in the services at the Spanish-language evangelical church she attends. Still, she has felt the need to seek treatment for depression.

The daughters also would like to return to Puerto Rico with its less enclosed life and the greater educational opportunities it affords for those who are still not entirely comfortable speaking English. Only Pedro, their teenage son, prefers the mainland, with its greater freedom and access to sports. The family looks forward to returning to Puerto Rico in 5 years, when Mr. Rivera retires.

The Riveras are relatively well off in comparison with many New York Puerto Ricans. Although they are not wealthy, they have established a middle-class existence for themselves. Yet their regrets represent the difficulties that immigrants of many nationalities have faced as they moved from their traditional cultures to the more formal and distant world of urban America. Their loss of contact with the environment and extended family, both of which give meaning to life, can cause for Puerto Ricans, like Mrs. Rivera, a sense of uprootedness and depression.

Questions for Discussion

1. How have differences in the social and physical environment affected the adaptation of the Puerto Rican family to the mainland?

2. Compare the changes that have occurred in the Puerto Rican family since migration to those experienced by the Mexican American family. How have the immigration experiences of these two groups differed? How are they similar?

3. How has colonialism affected the structure and stability of the Puerto Rican family? Can these effects still be seen?

4. How have modern developments in communication and transportation affected the Puerto Rican family after migration to the mainland?

5. What differences and similarities can you see between the Puerto Rican family and the "ideal" American family?

6. What do you see as the role of the extended family in traditional Puerto Rican culture? What advantages and disadvantages might that structure have in helping Puerto Ricans adapt to life in the mainland?

7. What are the gender roles within the Puerto Rican family, and how can they be expected to help or hinder adaptation to contemporary American society? How do these gender roles compare to those in American Indian and Mormon American families? What accounts for the differences and similarities?

8. It is sometimes claimed that the breakdown of the traditional family and traditional family values is responsible for much of the poverty in our society. Is this true for poor Puerto Ricans? Are there other factors that may contribute to the high incidence of poverty among Puerto Rican Americans? How does this situation compare to African American families?

9. What is the relationship between the individual, the family, and the larger group in Puerto Rican culture?

10. Can the Puerto Rican American family retain its distinctive identity as it adapts to the modern world in the United States? How does this affect the development of Puerto Rican culture?

11. What are the differences between the Puerto Rican American family and the Mexican American family?

Suggested Resources

Readings

Rivera-Batiz, F., & Santiago, C. (1994). *Puerto Ricans in the United States: A changing reality.* Washington, DC: National Puerto Rican Coalition.

Rodriguez, C. (1991). *Puerto Ricans born in the U.S.A.* Boulder, CO: Westview Press.

Salvo, J., Ortiz, R., & Lobo, A. (1994). *Puerto Rican New Yorkers in 1990.* New York: Department of City Planning.

Sanchez-Korrol, V. (1994). *From colonia to community: The history of Puerto Ricans in New York City.* Berkeley: University of California Press.

Videos

Production Multimedia Entertainment (Producers). (1993). *PR.* (Available from Films for the Humanities, P.O. Box 2053, Princeton, NJ 08543)

Rights Home Group (Producer), & Bird, S. (Director). (1980). *Retratos (Portraits).* (Available from Cinema Guild, 1697 Broadway, Suite 802, New York, NY 10019)

Rivera, P., & Zeig, S. (Producers). (1986). *Manos a la obra: The story of operation bootstrap.* (Available from Cinema Guild, 1697 Broadway, Suite 802, New York, NY 10019)

Research Centers in the United States

Center for Puerto Rican Studies
Hunter College
New York, NY 10021
(212) 772-5689

The Puerto Rican Cultural Heritage House
1230-5th Avenue, Room 458
New York, NY 10029
(212) 722-2600

Center for Latino Studies
Brooklyn College
Brooklyn, NY 11210
(718) 951-5561

References

Bastida, E. (1979). *Family integration and adjustment to aging among Hispanic American elderly.* Unpublished doctoral dissertation, University of Kansas, Lawrence.

Blatt, I. B. (1979). *A study of culture change in modern Puerto Rico.* Palo Alto, CA: R & R Research Associates.

Fitzpatrick, J. (1987). *Puerto Rican Americans: The meaning of migration to the mainland* (2nd ed.). Englewood Cliffs, NJ: Prentice-Hall.

Harwood, R. L., & Miller, J. G. (1991). Perceptions of attachment behavior: A comparison of Anglo and Puerto Rican mothers. *Merrill-Palmer Quarterly, 37,* 583–599.

Landale, N. S. (1994). Migration and the Latino family. *Demography, 31,* 133–157.

Landale, N. S., & Fennelly, K. (1992). Informal unions among mainland Puerto Ricans: Cohabitation of an alternative to legal marriage. *Journal of Marriage and the Family, 54,* 269–280.

Landy, D. (1959). *Tropical childhood.* Chapel Hill: University of North Carolina Press.

Leavitt, R. R. (1974). *The Puerto Ricans: Cultural change and language deviance.* Tucson: University of Arizona Press.

Mintz, S. W. (1966). Puerto Rico: An essay in the definition of a national culture. In *Selected background papers.* San Juan: Puerto Rico Commission on the Status of Puerto Rico.

Mussen, P., & Beytagh, L. (1969). Industrialization, child rearing practices and children's personality. *Journal of Genetic Psychology, 115,* 195–216.

Okagaki, L., & Sternberg, R. J. (1993). Parental beliefs and children's school performance. *Child Development, 64,* 36–56.

Padilla, F. M. (1987). *Puerto Rican Chicago.* Notre Dame, IN: University of Notre Dame Press.

Rogler, L. H., & Cooney, R. S. (1984). *Puerto Rican families in New York: Intergenerational processes.* Maplewood, NJ: Waterfront Press.

Rogler, L. H., & Procidano, M. E. (1986). The effect of social networks on marital roles: A test of the Bott hypothesis in an intergenerational context. *Journal of Marriage and the Family, 48,* 693–701.

Safa, H. I. (1974). *The urban poor of Puerto Rico.* New York: Holt, Rinehart, & Winston.

Sánchez-Ayéndez, M. (1988). Puerto Ricans in the United States. In C. Mindel, R. Habenstein, & R. Roosevelt, *Ethnic families in America* (pp. 173–198). Boulder, CO: Greenwood Press.

Stycos, J. M. (1955). *Family and fertility in Puerto Rico.* New York: Columbia University Press.

U.S. Bureau of the Census. (1990). *Current population reports, Series P-20, No. 444, The Hispanic population in the United States: March, 1989.* Washington, DC: U.S. Government Printing Office.

U.S. Bureau of the Census. (1994). *Statistical abstract of the United States, 1994.* Washington, DC: U.S. Government Printing Office.

Zayas, L. H., & Solari, F. (1994). Early childhood socialization in Hispanic families: Context, culture, and practice implications. *Professional Psychology: Research and Practice, 25,* 200–206.

Shobha Pais

9

Asian Indian Families in America

Historical and Cultural Background

The name Asian Indian refers to people who are originally from the subcontinent of India. Asian Indians are a subgroup of the larger Asian American group. The name Asian/Pacific Islander (Asian American), established by the U.S. Immigration and Naturalization Service, includes all South Asians and Southeast Asians; however, it overlooks ethnic and cultural variations that exist both within and among the different nations of Asia.

Among the many Asian populations in the United States, Asian Indians are one of the fastest-growing groups. According to the U.S. Bureau of the Census, 815,447 Asian Indians lived in the United States in 1990, comprising approximately 0.3% of the nation's total population. Asian Indians are the fourth-largest Asian population in the United States, after Chinese Americans (1,645,427), Filipino Americans (1,406,770), and Japanese Americans (847,562) (U.S. Bureau of the Census, 1990). By the year 2000, the Asian population in the United States is expected to increase to 10 million, of which Asian Indians will comprise close to 1.7 million (U.S. Bureau of the Census, 1994).

As a nation that consists of 83% Hindus, 11% Muslims, 3% Christians, and 2% Sikhs, India is a land of religious diversity (*World Almanac and Book of Facts*, 1991). In addition, Indian society is divided into many castes, tribes, languages, and subcultures, resulting in a variety of traditional practices. Religion and family are two major institutions that migrants carry with them wherever they go (Saran, Varma, & Embree, 1980).

Hinduism, a 2500-year-old religion, forms the basis of Asian Indian psychology and philosophy. Hindus believe that the self, *atman*, is a part of the cosmic absolute, *Brahman*. Through the study of scriptures and meditation, one understands that reality is *maya*—that knowledge and physical satisfaction are illusions and that life consists of impermanence, suffering, and the absence of the ego. Ideally, then, Hindus forfeit their desire for life and seek salvation (*Nirvana*) from the cycle of reincarnation in order to become one with *Brahman*.

Hindus also believe that an individual's destiny, or *karma*, is the result of present actions, and they adhere to codes of conduct appropriate for different stages of human life (Sodowsky & Carey, 1987). Four major concepts—*dharma, artha, kama*, and *moksha*—underlie this attitude toward life and daily conduct.

Dharma, perhaps the most influential concept in Indian culture and society, refers to actions characterized by considerations of righteousness and duty. Activities whose object is material gain are referred to as *artha*; those whose end is love or pleasure are called *kama*. Finally, *moksha* describes a devotion to spiritual pursuits in order to liberate the self from worldly life.

Indian Hindu society is divided into **castes**, into which individuals are born; caste membership restricts a person's choice of occupation and social group. The virtue (*punya*) and vice (*pap*) of one's actions in each lifetime determine one's caste in the succeeding life. Therefore, it is important to perform one's duties as prescribed by one's caste. The notion of *karma* teaches Hindus that they are born into particular castes because they deserve to be born there, while *dharma*, the code of duties or rules of the caste, identifies the responsibilities of the individual that cover a lifetime and all life events, including contingency behaviors for exceptional circumstances.

The Immigration Experience

For political and economic reasons, U.S. immigration laws have been altered to accommodate or discourage immigration from other countries. Before 1965, quota restrictions allowed only about 100 Indians to immigrate annually to the United States. The U.S. Immigration Act of 1965 abolished the discriminatory practices that limited immigration based on place of birth and national origin, allowing Indians to enter the country in large numbers for the first time. Between 1965 and 1970, over 26,000 Indian immigrants entered the United States (U.S. Immigration Service, 1975). During the 1980s, approximately 20,000 Indians entered the country each year, causing the Asian Indian population to increase by an estimated 56% between 1980 and 1990 (O'Hare & Felt, 1991).

Migration is not a new phenomenon for Asian Indians. According to one study, Asian Indians have moved to different parts of the world whenever they found the right opportunity (Saran, 1985). While in the past most Asian Indians came to the United States to work on farms, in construction, and in industry, today a large percentage immigrate in search of educational or professional opportunities (Leonhard-Spark & Saran, 1980). Many cite career advancement as an important motivation for immigration (Kaul, 1983; Shribman, 1981). Asian Indians have come to be viewed as a **model minority**, largely because of their high levels of education and privileged socioeconomic status, which enable them to find employment fairly easily and maintain income levels that provide a buffer against many of the challenges other groups of immigrants face.

Another important characteristic of Asian Indian immigrants is their exposure to Western values and beliefs. The Indian educational system is distinctly Western European, particularly British, in orientation. As a result, most Asian Indians are fluent in English, and many speak English frequently at home. Fluency in the language and familiarity with the culture facilitate and enhance their entry into American society (Leonhard-Spark & Saran, 1980).

A study by Saran, Varma, and Embree (1980) of Indian immigrants in the New York area indicated that religious observance did not decline after migration; in fact, for many Asian Indians, the move to a different culture spurred them to a more conscious cultivation of their religious identity. The practice of traditional rituals provides Hindu individuals, families, and communities with a strong sense of cultural identity. Many Hindu parents take the time to instill religious and cultural values in their children to ensure that they do not lose their inherent "Indianness." Families regularly visit temples, and most Hindu homes include a prayer room with pictures and statues of divinities. Some families have regular offerings (*poojas*) and prayers. In spite of the efforts of the parents, however, the indoctrination of Hindu children is difficult and not always successful (Gokulanathan & Gokulanathan, 1980). Although children participate in the family's religious activities, the dominance of Western culture may render them unable to internalize these religious beliefs.

Traditional and Emerging Family Systems

Traditionally, Indians live in a **joint family**, which includes the married couple, their unmarried children, and their married sons with their spouses and children. Three or more generations may live together in a joint family system. Interdependence, group solidarity, and conformity are highly valued. Behavior and roles are governed by age, gender, and generational status (Sue, 1981). The social roles of family members are rigid and formal, and they are enforced by using shame and guilt as agents of control.

As head of the family, the father is responsible for enforcing family rules and discipline. He may, therefore, be seen as stern, distant, and less approachable than the mother (Shon & Ja, 1982). The mother is the nurturing parent, who minds the household and is the primary caretaker of the children. In joint families, all family members help care for the young. Although infants are sometimes overindulged, young children are raised in an authoritarian atmosphere that discourages autonomy (Whiting, 1961). Children live with their parents into adulthood and remain submissive to them even after leaving the parental home, marrying, or becoming employed (Sue, 1981). They are expected to contribute to the finances of the family and to take care of their parents in their old age.

Household Size and Composition

Rapid economic changes, industrialization, and urbanization in India have affected the size, structure, and role of Indian families (Sinha, 1984). Among the middle class, family structure is slowly evolving toward the **nuclear family** model. However, the essence of the joint family continues to prevail through the **extended family**, an arrangement in which two or more nuclear families affiliate through the extension of the parent-child relationship. For example, a married son may live with his spouse, his children, and his parents under the same roof. In spite of the shift toward extended and nuclear families, Asian Indian immigrants are finding ways to maintain links with each other through visiting, providing financial support, helping with household chores, and cooperating in business ventures.

A notable consequence of Asian Indian migration to the United States has been a shift in the structure and size of the family. Saran and Eames (1980) point out that the American culture serves as a framework within which Asian Indians have developed their own unique pattern. Because a large number of Asian Indians are middle-class professionals and business entrepreneurs, their families reflect a middle-class structure. A typical Asian Indian family is nuclear, consisting of two parents and two or three children (Nandan & Eames, 1980). Social security, pension plans, and savings accounts have replaced the desire for a large number of children to support parents during their old age. However, most Asian Indians feel a cultural conflict between the traditional, Indian form of elderly support and the American system of elder care.

Although Asian Indian families are unable to remain connected in ways similar to urban Indian families, they maintain personal and ethnic ties through regular visits to India (Nandan & Eames, 1980). But because of conflicting work schedules, it is not always possible for the entire family to visit together. Sometimes a spouse (often the wife) visits with the children, or relatives from India visit their families in the United States.

The Socialization of Children

Traditionally, child rearing in India has encompassed the physical, psychological, and spiritual aspects of life. Important milestones in child development and growth have been identified even in Hindu mythology. Mythological stories about infancy and childhood not only provide a framework for child development, but also serve as guidelines for parenthood.

While traditional and cultural factors may underlie the basic care of Asian Indian children in the United States, most Indian families seek the same prenatal and delivery care as Americans. According to Gokulanathan and Gokulanathan (1980), contrary to the Indian tradition of children being born in their mother's parents' community, Asian Indian children are usually born in hospitals near where their parents reside. Since they can rely on little help from friends and relatives, parents may have a difficult time looking after infants. Sometimes, the infant's maternal grandmother visits her daughter for a considerable length of time to share the housework, care for the infant, and help in the process of transition. This arrangement gives the new mother an opportunity to learn the techniques of child care under experienced supervision. The father may also stay at home to help with housework and child care. Working mothers sometimes leave infants and young children with babysitters, preferably Indians.

Compared to American youths, Asian Indian children are often docile and reserved, and obedient to American teachers, probably as a result of their role in the traditionally authoritarian Indian household. Parents are supportive of their children's scholastic endeavors and apply a great deal of pressure on them to succeed.

Adolescence can be a particularly troublesome time for Asian Indian families. Traditionally, Indian culture does not recognize an "adolescent" stage in the life cycle (Segal, 1991). Research conducted by Segal (1991) on adjustment difficulties of Indian teenagers in the United States concluded that issues such as control, communication, prejudice, and expectations of excellence cause emotional difficulties. Parents of Asian Indian American teenagers feel that their children are unable to make sound judgments, and their need to do so is perceived as deviant and the result of "cultural contamination." They also worry that their children will lose respect for their elders and will experiment with sex and with different lifestyles. Communication between parents and children tends to be hierarchical and one-sided. Children are expected to listen to and obey their parents without question. Since family hierarchy and chronological age play an important part in the Indian family, open dialogue and discussion between parents and children can easily be viewed as insolence.

Despite economic and occupational success, Asian Indians tend not to integrate socially, probably in an effort to retain their ethnic identity, culture, and religious values. Parents often limit their children's contact with American children. An unintended consequence is that the children may develop negative attitudes toward their own Indian culture. Overall, the conflict between parents pushing their children to achieve while inhibiting their autonomy is a source of confusion to Asian Indian adolescents. The tension between their parents' traditional Indian values and the mores of the dominant culture renders the processes of socialization and acculturation extremely stressful for both children and parents.

The degree of selectivity in immigration criteria and the model minority image create an expectation of high achievement and success. Asian Indians are known for their strong desire for upward mobility and recognize that education is necessary in order to get ahead in the United States (Nandan & Eames, 1980). However, Asian Indian children have been found to be less achievement-driven than their immigrant parents.

Intimate Relationships

Although arranged marriages are not the norm in the United States, they are still prevalent in India, despite rapid urbanization and the geographic dispersal of community members (Bhargava, 1988; Rao & Rao, 1982). Arranged marriages in India today allow the prospective husband and wife some input in the process of mate selection. A couple may be allowed to meet formally, to determine mutual suitability, before the marriage. Asian Indian immigrants follow a similar system for marriage and mate selection (Dworkin, 1980; Rao & Rao, 1982). Menon (1988) studied arranged marriages among Asian Indian immigrants and found that ads in newspapers serve as surrogate marriage brokers, since parents cannot depend upon their own contacts or upon those of a marriage broker. Immigrant parents often select mates for their children who are of the same ethnic origin, and place less emphasis on caste or language (Wakil, Siddique, & Wakil, 1981). Almost half the women in Menon's study had their marriages arranged. Men usually self-sponsored their marriage inquiries. Marriages arranged in such a way are not much different from American personal ads and dating services. However, Menon (1988) predicts that arranged marriages among Indian immigrants will slowly diminish as each generation assimilates into the dominant American culture.

Because the marriages of a high proportion of immigrant parents were arranged, these parents often assume their children will also prefer to have their mates selected for them. This can be distressing for teenagers and young adults who have been raised in a culture in which individuals choose their spouses themselves. Indian immigrants discourage their children, particularly their daughters, from dating. Parents disapprove of intimacy and sexual contact before marriage, and fear that dating may lead to sexual involvement (Segal, 1991). In most cases, dating someone from a different ethnic background is forbidden, for fear of losing one's cultural identity and values (Ballard, 1978; Gibson, 1988; Wakil, Siddique, & Wakil, 1981). There is also the observation that a large number of American marriages end in divorce.

Because sexuality is not an easy topic of discussion for Indians, it is difficult to accurately assess the sexual attitudes of Asian Indian immigrants. In their 1980 study, Saran and Leonhard-Spark drew some inferences based on the attitudes of adult immigrants toward marriage and the upbringing of children. They found that a large number of adult males at American educational institutions had sexual relations before marriage, but that most of them had traditional attitudes toward female sexuality, expecting women to remain virgins until marriage. Not surprisingly, many Indian men return to their native country, where female sexual activity prior to marriage is strongly discouraged, to select mates. The researchers also found that, where sexuality is concerned, Asian Indian parents are more protective of their daughters than of their sons (Leonhard-Spark & Saran, 1980). These traditional sexual mores continue to be the norm among Asian Indian families.

Traditionally, weddings are large and expensive and include a variety of rituals that begin several days before the formal ceremony. A Hindu bride often dresses in a silk *sari* extravagantly trimmed in gold. Her hair interwoven with flowers, heavy gold jewelry adorning her wrists and neck, and her hands and feet painted with henna in an intricate design, she is expected to sit quietly—a passive presence at her own wedding. When the groom arrives (often late, although this is accepted by the bride's family), the guests congratulate the couple, eat, and depart, leaving only the immediate relatives and close friends to participate in the ceremony. The bride and groom sit for several hours under a canopy in front of a sacred fire, while a priest chants Sanskrit prayers and pours sandalwood powder into the flames. Following the prayers, the couple circle the fire, taking seven steps, each of which represents one of the seven sacred blessings: food, strength, wealth, happiness, progeny, cattle, and devotion. On the seventh step, the marriage becomes irrevocable.

Asian Indians place a high value on marriage and the family, and parents instill these values in their children at an early age. Most Asian Indian parents hope their children will choose Indian mates; when Asian Indians marry people from other cultures, their families often respond by partially or totally rejecting the spouse (Saran, 1975).

The traditional pattern of male dominance in spousal relationships is common in Asian Indian families, particularly those in which both spouses are of Indian origin. In the Indian culture, love and passion are not necessary components of marriage. In a traditional Indian marriage, the presence of members of the extended family, especially the parents, often inhibits the development of intimacy and attachment between the couple. The husband and wife are left alone for only brief periods of time, and are restrained by cultural taboos from publicly expressing affection or love for each other. This does not mean, however, that the Indian marriage lacks intimacy; closeness develops between the couple as they become householders and parents.

The pattern of male-dominated marriages continues to be the norm among Indian immigrants in the United States, but some important changes have begun to occur. As large numbers of Asian Indian women hold jobs or pursue education, their exposure to the more liberal American environment encourages them to seek a more nearly egalitarian husband-wife relationship (Nandan & Eames, 1980). In general, Indian women find their experience in the new country empowering. In addition to the educational and career opportunities available to them, they are spared the age-old struggles involved in entering, or establishing their status in, a joint family. On the other hand, the greater freedom experienced by women through their increased contact with the outside world can become a source of conflict for Asian Indian couples.

Work Relationships and the Family

Many Asian Indians are highly trained professionals. And many Asian Indian women are employed outside the home, not necessarily because of financial necessity (Leonhard-Spark & Saran, 1980). Their educational and occupational skills generally enable them to find employment fairly easily.

Although it is difficult to accurately determine the number of Asian Indian women in the work force in the United States, it seems reasonable to assume that it has increased significantly over the last two decades. As more Asian Indian women are employed in professional capacities—as doctors, scientists, engineers, partners in family-owned businesses—a major shift in household roles has begun. A study focusing on patterns of social and psychological adaptation among Indian immigrants in the United States determined that wives' employment outside the home tended to induce husbands to take on a larger share of household responsibilities, resulting in the development of more nearly equal relationships (Saran, 1985). Responsibilities like child care, shopping, and cooking, which in India were typically the domain of the extended family or paid help, now rest on the couple. Dual-earner couples often employ babysitters or use day-care services for their infants and children, and husbands take on nontraditional levels of responsibility for raising the children. Nevertheless, the wives generally continue to take primary responsibility for child rearing and domestic tasks, and some report feeling a "sense of guilt" when they see their husbands doing housework (Leonhard-Spark & Saran, 1980).

For dual-earning Asian Indian families in a new environment, stress and strain are highly likely to exist. Balancing work and family roles can be stressful for a newly married couple who are also adapting to a different culture. The couple may face changes in their roles both at home and in the workplace, compared to their early gender-role socialization standards. As in most dual-earning families, Asian Indian husbands and wives experience the difficulties of blending their individual career cycles with the family life cycle. And because of their new roles and lifestyle, they may have less time to interact with friends and relatives. This can be both isolating and extremely stressful for people who consider extended family and friends an important part in the development of their individual identity.

Single-earner families usually follow a comparatively more traditional pattern of role division. In these circumstances, the wives are more involved in child rearing and household responsibilities, which creates lower expectations and pressure on the husbands, compared to husbands in dual-earner families.

Life-Cycle Transitions

Despite legislation that permits divorce, the dissolution of the family unit in India is still rare. However, it is difficult to assess the stability of marriages in the Asian Indian community in the United States. While couples who have migrated together may adapt to life in the new country, strain often develops in the marriages of Indian students who return to their homeland to marry and bring their spouses back to America. In such instances, the spouse (usually the husband) who has adapted to an American lifestyle may find his wife too traditional and conservative. There are fewer barriers to divorce in America than in India, but because Indian culture stigmatizes it, the process of divorce is not an easy one, particularly for the woman. Due to the taboo against divorce, remarriage among Asian Indians rarely occurs.

Single parenthood is uncommon in families of Indian origin for two reasons: Divorce is rare, and there is a strong taboo against parenthood without marriage, particularly for women. In cases where a spouse has died, a single parent may return to India to find a more supportive environment. However, if the surviving spouse is well established financially and socially in the United States, or if there are children who are well integrated into American society, moving to India is less likely.

Respect for elders and for the wisdom they have gained through experience is instilled in children at an early age. Typically, as aging parents become unable to care for themselves, their children support them. This tradition, which has made a system of organized social security unnecessary in India, has been maintained by Indian immigrants. Although the Asian Indian immigrant population in the United States as a whole is fairly young and is presently raising the next generation, some families have their elderly parents living with them, either permanently or for extended periods of time. While the proximity of family members is comforting to elderly Asian Indians, they may not be able to adapt to life in the United States as easily as their children can—a situation that often results in increased stress for the entire household.

Family Strengths and Challenges

Family plays an important role in linking the individual to the larger community. Particularly for middle-class Asian Indians in America, the family facilitates the development of ties with the dominant culture and provides stability for its individual members as they struggle to maintain their ethnic identity while adapting to the new culture. While single Asian Indians, particularly students, often lack the presence and support of their immediate families, they assemble networks of Indian friends and relatives to help them make the transition to life in the United States.

Like the traditional Indian family, Asian Indian families in the United States are characterized by closeness among family members. While this form of cohesiveness may be perceived as overinvolvement with or overresponsiveness to one another by the dominant American culture, Asian Indian families exhibit clear role divisions, a clear hierarchy, and a high tolerance to stress. Thus, familial closeness is culturally sanctioned.

There is a strong sense of concern for everyone's general well-being among the members of the Asian Indian family. For example, parents are often quite involved in their children's lives and support them economically. To continue such support well into adulthood is not considered overbearing on the part of the parents. In return, children are expected to maintain a strong commitment to the family and its values. Pride and loyalty are virtues that every family cherishes, even in a new environment.

At times of crisis, family members, relatives, and friends are expected to provide emotional and other kinds of support. In a culture that emphasizes hierarchy and formality, the roles of family members are very clear and defined. The individual experiencing the stress can rely on the immediate as well as the extended family for support and direction.

Leonhard-Spark and Saran (1980) studied the behavioral patterns of Asian Indians in the New York City area and found that they were highly similar to American sociocultural behavior. Culturally, there was even a preference for

American-style activities over traditional ones. Yet this degree of assimilation was balanced by participation in Indian activities and organizations.

The process of adaptation for Asian Indians takes place primarily in two realms, economic and cultural, while the maintenance of ethnic identity is provided by the Indian community and various Indian associations. Economic adaptation for Asian Indians is supported by a strong educational background and occupational skills that are highly rewarded in America. The process of assimilation is highly dependent on the level of occupational skill (Desai & Coelho, 1980). In the cultural realm, adaptation is facilitated by knowledge of the dominant language of the host country and familiarity with Western values.

Usually, Asian Indian immigrants have two characteristics that are important in enabling the process of assimilation: they are urban, and they are partially Westernized. Whether in India or any other part of the world, most middle-class Indians are familiar with the pattern of being "Western" on the job and traditional at home (Fornaro, 1984). For example, they are comfortable in Western clothing in the professional realm but often wear Indian clothing on social occasions and in religious celebrations.

Furthermore, the English language is not a barrier, as it can be for other immigrant groups. Most Asian Indians are partially, if not fully, familiar with and fluent in English before coming to the United States. The knowledge of the dominant language is a big advantage in assimilating into the community at the professional level, and to some extent at the social level.

Despite successful adaptation, Asian Indian families have faced ongoing conflicts for many years. The primary conflict often manifests itself in the ambivalence that most Indians experience about living in the United States. Desai and Coelho (1980) believe that in addition to switching their life orientation between work and home, Asian Indian immigrants balance an appearance of being foreigners and adapting to a new culture, while being in a constant state of ambivalence, which occasionally develops into a desire to return to India. Thus, they remain psychologically connected to India and their culture at all times. The ability to remain outwardly involved with one's surroundings without an internal commitment has been identified as the Hindu ideal of life, an essential quality of the Indian psyche (Desai & Coelho, 1980). Hence, while Asian Indians may dress, eat, and socialize in American ways outside the home, inside their home, social interactions, food, and traditions continue to be Indian.

Whether new or old immigrants, Asian Indians often feel lonely and isolated. It is not unusual for them to find that their attempts to share confidences are not reciprocated by their American friends. The lack of long-lasting friendships and connectedness within a social environment can become major sources of stress. And conflict about adaptation is not just related to the new culture, but also to what no longer exists. One may mourn the loss of family and friends, as well as familiar personal and social ways of behaving (Desai & Coelho, 1980).

Misconceptions and Stereotypes

Because Indian society itself is not homogenous, Asian Indian immigrants are not a homogenous group. This makes the process of understanding Asian Indians a complex one. Most of the factors that apply to the nonacceptance of Asian immigrants among European Americans also apply to Asian Indians. While most Asian Indians in the United States speak English, they have a foreign accent. Besides physical appearance, including skin color, the Indian style of dress may seem peculiar to Americans (Buchignani, 1980). For example, the Sikhs from Punjab (a state in northern India) who continue to have beards and wear turbans have been called "rag heads" or "carpet flyers." Women who wear a *sari* or a *salwar kameez* (an Indian pantsuit), particularly at social gatherings, may be perceived as being strangely attired. These perceptions can affect the thinking and behavior of members of the host community, thereby hindering the acceptance of these immigrants into the professional, educational, and social domains of American society.

In the United States, where assertiveness, independence, and competence are encouraged and valued, an Asian Indian who has been raised to be submissive to authority may be perceived as being servile, dependent, passive, and too eager to please. Although cultural expectations may be clear to immigrants, their personal predispositions and the individual traits that result from socialization make it difficult to meet those expectations.

At a social level, while a sense of privacy is very important to Americans, this concept is not familiar to most Indians. It is not unusual for an Indian to simply drop by a friend's house unannounced; this is not considered intrusive, but inclusive. For an Indian, a house symbolizes security and the prestige of the family; it is often likened to a shrine, and it is open to anybody. Also, friendship represents close interdependence, reciprocity of favors and benefits, and a long-lasting relationship (Desai & Coelho, 1980). This pattern may be considered a sign of overinvolvement, overdependence, and enmeshment to Americans.

Although affection between men and women is not expressed publicly in Indian culture, the spontaneous expression of friendship, such as a hug or an embrace, between members of the same sex is permitted. This can be easily mistaken for homosexual behavior in American culture.

Because cooperation is a dominant Indian value, Asian Indians are uncomfortable with confrontation as a style of problem solving in the competitive environment of America (Desai & Coelho, 1980). According to Desai and Coelho (1980), two interpersonal strategies that replace competition and confrontation among Asian Indians are envy and collusion, behaviors that might be perceived as being two-faced. For example, Asian Indians may envy the achievement of their colleagues. But instead of actively pursuing their own success through competition, they may hide their envious feelings and become resentful. Instead of confronting the problem directly, they may become sullen and sarcastic and resort to forming alliances with the opposition. It is obvious how these coping styles, which are culturally instilled, can easily be misunderstood by members of the dominant culture.

Personal Interview

Mr. and Mrs. Barua live in a small midwestern American town. They have two children: a son, age 11, and a daughter, age 9. A 42-year-old entrepreneur, Mr. Barua came to the United States as a student nearly 20 years ago. After earning a master's degree in engineering, he returned to India, where he worked briefly for nearly a year. Somewhat dissatisfied, he returned to the United States and joined an engineering firm. After working a couple of years, he returned to India to marry a girl whom he had not met before.

"It was an arranged marriage," he said, and "my family arranged it for me."

When asked about the wedding arrangements, Mrs. Barua replied, "I knew my parents wanted me to marry this young man who lived in the United States. I was a little worried about leaving home and going so far away, but that was okay." Mr. Barua admits that life was much better for him after he was married. He was not as lonely and did not miss home as much.

"Living here after marriage is much easier," he said. While Mr. Barua had already become somewhat acculturated, everything was new to Mrs. Barua. She remembers being very scared when she came here for the first time, not knowing what to expect. "Many of his [her husband's] friends and their wives took care of me. I am grateful for that. Later, as I had my children and learned more about this society, I began to like living here, although I still miss home. Did you know that I called home almost every week?" She continued, "When I had my son, my mother came to help me and lived with us for seven months. But when my daughter was born, I was able to manage on my own. Of course, my husband helped a lot. Also, my friends in the Indian community helped out."

After a few years of experience, Mr. Barua started his own engineering consulting firm. Meanwhile Mrs. Barua, who had an undergraduate degree from India, spent most of her time raising her two children and managing the household. Once the two children were old enough to be independent, she decided to return to school. She decided to enhance her occupational skills and enrolled in computer and accounting training so that she could help with the business.

When asked about how they like it in the United States, and what were some of the challenges they faced as immigrants, Mr. Barua replied, "I am quite happy here, although I have to work very hard. Most of my friends and family believe it has been easy for me. They don't really know. Of course there is discrimination sometimes, but that is a larger problem that is pervasive in this society. Being different makes one realize that you are from a different culture. I think one is more conscious of his identity here in the United States. In India you take it for granted."

Mrs. Barua said that she likes it here since she is with her husband and children. She misses home, her relatives, and her community at times, because she is unable to visit India often. She said, "It is very expensive for the family to go home for a long time. Besides, it has to be during the summer months when the children are out of school. Often, I go with the children for at least two months and then in the last four weeks my husband joins us."

"The biggest struggle for me has been to maintain our culture. I have to teach the children our language at home. They have learned it quite well, but do not speak it unless I ask them to." Her son said that it was easier to speak English. He said that he could only speak their regional language if they had Indian friends and guests who spoke the same language. However, he speaks it with his maternal grandmother on the phone. The daughter enjoys trying to speak their regional language. While both the children are American citizens by birth, the parents are permanent residents of the United States. They have chosen to remain so, because it is easier to travel to India as Indian citizens.

At home the Baruas lived very traditionally, although they most often dressed in Western clothes. "This is common for most Asian Indian families in America," said Mr. Barua. "We only dress in Indian clothes for Indian gatherings, and then too it's mostly women who wear *saris* or *salwar kameez* and Indian jewelry." "We meet socially with other Indians almost every weekend," Mrs. Barua said. Meeting other Asian Indians is a very important part of community building and connectedness. The food they eat for most of the family meals is ethnic. "We are able to get most of the Indian groceries and spices at a larger city, particularly if there is a fairly large Indian population there," Mrs. Barua said. However, the children take American foods to school.

The Baruas shared their concern for their children and how assimilated they would become. Both the children socialize primarily with other Indian children at social gatherings. They have American friends at school and in their neighborhood. Although a strong value is placed on educational and scholastic performance for the children, it appears that both the parents want to make sure their son succeeds.

When asked about their plans for the future, Mr. Barua replied, "I am not sure. Once the children grow up we can decide what to do. I am building a house in India. So, if I think of retiring and returning to India we have that option. The children can decide whatever they want."

In a strange way, the Baruas had explained how most Asian Indians feel once they come to the United States, and how they are able to successfully maintain a level of split-consciousness. While they did not commit to living in the United States, they did not seem to plan to move anytime in the near future.

Questions for Discussion

1. What are the reasons for Asian Indian migration, and what are the major characteristics of this group of immigrants?

2. Traditionally, Indians live in a joint family system. What is the common family structure of Asian Indians in the United States? How is it different from the traditional system? How does the joint family compare to the split family among Chinese Americans and the stem family among Japanese Americans? What purposes do these three family systems serve?

3. In what ways are the patterns of socialization of children among Asian Indians similar to and different from those in your culture? How do Asian Indian socialization patterns compare to those of other cultures discussed in this book?

4. Do you know any Asian Indian teenagers or young adults? Are they allowed to date? Why or why not?

5. How is the relationship between Asian Indian men and women different from that of European American men and women in the United States? How does this compare to other ethnic groups discussed in the book?

6. In what ways have household roles for Asian Indian men and women changed from the traditional pattern? Why?

7. How does the Asian Indian family differ from the Chinese American and Japanese American family?

8. Compare the caste system in India to racial discrimination in the United States. Describe similarities and differences.

9. In what ways can the family support an Asian Indian immigrant during the process of adapting to the new culture?

10. How do Asian Indians maintain their ethnic identity in the United States? How could this lead to misunderstanding or discrimination?

Suggested Resources

Readings

Jung, A. (1990). *Unveiling India: A woman's journey.* New Delhi: Penguin Books India.

Seth, V. (1993). *A suitable boy.* New York: HarperCollins.

Videos

MacDonald, J., & Camereni, M. (Producers), & Camereni, M., & Gill, R. (Directors). (1995). *Dadi's family.* (Available from Public Broadcasting Services, P.O. Box 4030, Santa Monica, CA 90411)

Vithal, H. (Producer), & Nair, M. (Director). (1988). *Salaam Bombay.* (Available from Image Entertainment, 9333 Oso Avenue, Chatsworth, CA 91311)

Wong, W. (Producer), & Stone, O. (Director). (1993). *City of joy.* (Available from FACETS Media, 1517 W. Fullerton Avenue, Chicago, IL 60614)

References

Ballard, C. (1978). Arranged marriage in the British context. *New Community, 6,* 181–197.

Bhargava, G. (1988). Seeking immigration through matrimonial alliance: A study of advertisement in an ethnic weekly. *Journal of Comparative Family Studies, 19,* 245–259.

Buchignani, N. (1980). The social and self identities of Fijian Indians in Vancouver. *Urban Anthropology, 9,* 75–97.

Desai, P. N., & Coelho, G. V. (1980). Indian immigrants in America: Some cultural aspects of psychological adaptation. In P. Saran & E. Eames (Eds.), *The new ethnics: Asian Indians in the United States* (pp. 318–341). New York: Praeger.

Dworkin, R. J. (1980). Differential processes in acculturation: The case of Asiatic Indians in the United States. *Plural Societies, 11,* 43–57.

Fornaro, R. J. (1984). Asian-Indians in America: Acculturation and minority status. *Migration Today, 12*(3), 29–32.

Gibson, M. (1988). *Accommodation without assimilation: Sikh immigrants in an American high school.* Ithaca, NY: Cornell University Press.

Gokulanathan, K. S., & Gokulanathan, I. U. (1980). Child health care of Asian Indians in the United States: Conflict and compromise. In P. Saran & E. Eames (Eds.), *The new ethnics: Asian Indians in the United States* (pp. 318–341). New York: Praeger.

Kaul, M. L. (1983). Adaptation of recently arrived professional immigrants in four selected communities in Ohio. *Journal of Applied Social Sciences, 7,* 131–145.

Leonhard-Spark, P. J., & Saran, P. (1980). The Indian immigrant in America: A demographic profile. In E. Eames & P. Saran (Eds.), *The new ethnics: Asian Indians in the United States* (pp. 136–162). New York: Praeger.

Menon, R. (1988, February). *Marrying a green card: Motivations underlying marriage among South Asian immigrants.* Paper presented at the meeting of the American Sociological Association, Atlanta, GA.

Nandan, Y., & Eames, E. (1980). Typology and analysis of the Asian Indian family. In E. Eames & P. Saran (Eds.), *The new ethnics: Asian Indians in the United States* (pp. 136–162). New York: Praeger.

O'Hare, W. P., & Felt, J. C. (1991). Asian Americans: America's fastest growing minority group. *Population Trends and Public Policy, 19,* 1–17.

Rao, V. V., & Rao, V. N. (1982). *Marriage, the family, and women in India.* Columbia, MO: South Asia Books.

Saran, P. (1975). *Indian immigrants in and around New York City.* Paper presented at the meeting of the Eastern Sociological Society, New York, NY.

Saran, P. (1985). *The Asian Indian experience in the United States.* New Delhi, India: Vikas Publishing House.

Saran, P., & Eames, E. (Eds.). (1980). *The new ethnics: Asian Indians in the United States.* New York: Praeger.

Saran, P., Varma, B. N., & Embree A. T. (1980). Hinduism in a new society. In P. Saran & E. Eames (Eds.), *The new ethnics: Asian Indians in the United States* (pp. 216–232). New York: Praeger.

Segal, U. A. (1991). Cultural variables in Asian Indian families. *Families in Society, 72,* 233–242.

Sinha, D. (1984). Some recent changes in the Indian family and their implications for socialization. *Indian Journal of Social Work, 45,* 271–286.

Shon, S. P., & Ja, D. Y. (1982). Asian families. In M. McGoldrick, J. K. Pearce, & J. Giordano (Eds.), *Ethnicity and family therapy* (pp. 208–228). New York: Guilford.

Shribman, D. (1981, December 20). Congress finally acts to stem the flood of foreign doctors. *The New York Times,* p. E1.

Sodowsky, G. R., & Carey, J. C. (1987). Asian Indian immigrants in America: Factors related to adjustment. *Journal of Multicultural Counseling and Development, 15*(3), 129–141.

Sue, D. W. (1981). *Counseling the culturally different.* New York: Wiley.

U.S. Bureau of the Census. (1990). *Statistical abstract of the United States, 1990.* Washington, DC: U.S. Government Printing Office.

U.S. Bureau of the Census. (1994). *Statistical abstract of the United States, 1994.* Washington, DC: U.S. Government Printing Office.

U.S. Immigration Service. (1975). *Annual report*. Washington, DC: U.S. Government Printing Office.

Wakil, S. P., Siddique, C. M., & Wakil, F. A. (1981). Between two cultures: A study in socialization of children of immigrants. *Journal of Marriage and the Family, 43*, 929–940.

Whiting, J. W. M. (1961). Socialization process and personality. In F. L. K. Hsu (Ed.), *Psychological anthropology: Approaches to culture and personality*. Homewood, IL: Dorsey Press.

World Almanac and Book of Facts. (1991). New York: Scripps-Howard.

Zulema E. Suárez

10

Cuban American Families

Historical and Cultural Background

Geographically, Cubans have not had to travel far to get to the United States. Emotionally, however, their journey has been long and arduous. Migration has meant giving up family, friends, property, a way of being, a lifestyle—and their paradise island home. It has meant learning to live with longing and displacement. Still, since 1959, the start of the Cuban Revolution, hundreds of thousands of Cubans have been compelled to flee the island, by air or by sea, to preserve their personal, political, and economic freedom.

Today, numbering about 1 million, Cuban Americans comprise the third largest, and most prosperous, group of people of Hispanic descent living in the United States. Despite sharing a common language, Hispanic heritage, and Catholic ideology, Cubans are also distinct from other Hispanics in terms of their history of migration, their geographic clustering, and their demographic characteristics.

Cuban culture is a blending of Spanish, African, and Amerindian cultural patterns (Bernal, 1982; Jimenez-Vasquez, 1995). The Spaniards who colonized the island brought African slaves to its shores, after the indigenous inhabitants died by the hand of the conquerors or from diseases introduced by the foreigners. Yet the legacy of Amerindian culture remains in Cuba through the names of cities and in the daily diet (Jimenez-Vasquez, 1995). While the Spanish cultural foundation is reflected in both the language and the strong influence of Catholicism, the African influence is also clearly evident in Cuba's music, poetry, colloquial expressions, and spirituality. For example, **Santería**, an African-Cuban religious and folk-healing method, evolved from the fusion of Spanish colonialist Catholic beliefs and African world-view rituals; it is "the product of an identification between the gods of the slaves and the Catholic saints of their masters" (Sandoval, 1979, p. 137).

The belief in *espiritismo*, another faith-healing method that predominates in Puerto Rico, may also be found in segments of the Cuban community, particularly those coming from the Oriente region of the island (Bernal, 1982). The practice of *espiritismo* is led by a medium or spiritual counselor, who helps clients through the exorcism of spirits that cause physical illness or mental or emotional distress (Bernal, 1982). Both *Santería* and *espiritismo* have been successfully used at times by health-care practitioners providing mental health services for Hispanics in the United States (Fields, 1976; Garrison, 1977; Sandoval, 1979).

Despite the proliferation of *Santería*, especially among those in lower socioeconomic levels because of their need for support in coping with the problems of migration, and an increasing exodus from the Catholic Church, Cuban Americans remain predominantly Catholic (Rogg & Cooney, 1980). The Catholic Church still plays an important role in the lives of Cuban American families in crisis and in the lives of elderly Cuban Americans (Bernal, 1982).

Research on the value system of Cuban Americans in Miami has identified this group as tending to value lineality, subjugation to nature, and a present-time orientation (Szapocznik, Scopetta, Arnalde, & Kurtines, 1978). In cultures having a tendency toward **lineality**, the locus of accountability is defined by the social structure, and relationships are hierarchically ordered; "reciprocal roles are based on a dominance-submission mode of interrelationship" (Papajohn & Spiegel, 1971, p. 260). This implies deference to authority and to age, particularly the seniority of parents, teachers, and professionals in general (Queralt, 1984).

People who value subjugation to nature and have a present-time orientation demonstrate a "fatalistic acceptance of life's circumstances and a belief that little can be done to counteract the forces of nature to which human beings are subjugated" (Szapocznik, Scopetta, Arnalde, et al., 1978, p. 961). This philosophy does not mean that Cubans just passively allow things to happen to them; it means that they are aware of their human and external limitations and of the forces outside their control and understanding that are influencing their lives. The tendency to be oriented to the present correlates with a conviction that the future is unpredictable. Although this does not preclude Cuban Americans from having a vision of the future, they are less likely than European Americans to live for the future and more likely to live in the present.

Familialism, the belief in and valuing of the nuclear and extended family systems and members, is a central value of Hispanic culture in general. In traditional families, members are expected to be very much involved with the extended family and family affairs. Consequently, what is generally considered an ordinary degree of involvement among Cuban family members may be perceived as **enmeshment** by cultural outsiders.

A value considered to be the basis of the Cuban national character is that of *personalismo*, a concern for personal dignity, combined with a personal, rather than conceptual, approach to social relationships. It also includes a distaste for impersonal associations (Bernal, 1982; Queralt, 1984).

Personalismo is the perception "that life is nothing but the flow of interactions with other people, in which case the attainment of trust, respect and warmth in relationships become desirable goals" (Jimenez-Vasquez, 1995, p. 1229).

Finally, a cultural value that is believed to have helped Cubans adjust to life in the United States is that of individualism. According to Queralt (1984), Cubans have not been "traditionally known for their collective spirit or social consciousness" (p. 118). This individualism is manifested through personal pride and self-confidence that are often perceived by non-Cubans as arrogance.

When considering Cuban values, however, Bernal (1982) cautions that this should be done in light of the migration experience, and that "of particular importance are the values and principles transmitted to the children and how these values may have been influenced by migration" (p. 193). Queralt (1984) further warns that

> values are not fixed attributes; rather, they are always evolving. The degree of acculturation to this society, for example, determines in part the extent to which Cubans will exhibit purely traditional Cuban-Hispanic values or variations that incorporate aspects of the dominant culture. (p. 117)

The Immigration Experience

Cuban migration to the United States is relatively recent and has been primarily politically motivated. Although Cuban migration to this country can be traced as far back as the mid-1800s, prior to the Cuban Revolution in 1959, there were only 50,000 Cubans living in the United States. While the earliest immigrants came fleeing from the Spanish regime, Fidel Castro's rise to power and his declaration in 1961 that his regime would follow Marxist-Leninist ideology stimulated the sudden exodus of thousands of Cubans, despite strict government restrictions. This exodus, which consisted of as much as 10% of the island population, occurred in what scholars call "waves." Today there are approximately 1 million people of Cuban descent living in the United States.

Immigration became very difficult after 1961, when the United States severed diplomatic ties with Cuba (Wenk, 1968). The first wave, which occurred between January 1961 and October 1962, the time of the Cuban Missile Crisis, included more than 150,000 refugees. Because of restrictions imposed by the Cuban government, the second wave brought an estimated 75,000 Cubans between November 1962 and November 1965. The third wave, spanning December 1965 through March 1972, brought an additional 275,000 refugees. Most of these arrived via Freedom Flights, an airlift initiated by the Johnson administration, that brought 3000–4000 passengers per month. Unlike the earlier waves of immigrants, who were primarily escaping political persecution, about 40% of the airlift group were students, women, and children, who were reuniting with their relatives (Bean & Tienda, 1988). The fourth wave took place during 1978–1980 and consisted of approximately 20,000 former political prisoners and their families (Szapocznik & Hernandez, 1990).

After these early waves, Cuban migration to the United States has been very controversial. Between April and September 1980, more than 125,000 people left Cuba under extremely hazardous and chaotic circumstances through a disorganized boatlift via the port of Mariel. Although many came voluntarily to join family members, a significant portion were forced to leave by the Castro government (Gil, 1983). This wave was characterized by an overrepresentation of gay men and lesbians, people with criminal records, and other institutionalized individuals who had been forced into exile (Bach, Bach, & Triplett, 1981; Jimenez-Vasquez, 1995). Although they came to be known as "social undesirables," this wave was undeserving of that stereotype.

Knowing what wave a Cuban American belongs to is important because it informs us of the contextual and historical aspects of his or her migration to this country. For example, the early refugees were mostly of European stock, and from the upper, middle, and professional socioeconomic sectors of the population (Bernal, 1982). Because of their skin color, their education, and the strength of the U.S. economy at that time, this wave was greeted with open arms and treated like "golden exiles." Moreover, Cubans embodied the anticommunist sentiment of the period and were used as symbols of the danger of communism. Hence, a massive Cuban Refugee Program was established by the U.S. government to help with resettlement and retraining (Hernandez, 1974; Pedraza-Bailey, 1980).

The program retrained selected groups of skilled and professional workers (i.e., teachers, college professors, doctors, optometrists, and lawyers). This program aided about 70% of the immigrants, greatly facilitating their adjustment to America. Despite the fact that each successive wave brought people of lower socioeconomic, educational, and occupational levels than the preceding ones, the newest arrivals were able to ride on the reputation of the earlier waves and were greeted with the same goodwill.

Subsequent immigrants, starting with the Mariel boatlift of 1980, however, have been treated with contempt. Cubans exiting through the port of Mariel found themselves estranged not only from the host country but also from the exile community (Fradd, 1983). Arriving one month after the Refugee Act of 1980 was signed, the Mariel entrants were not eligible for refugee status. This law "put an end to the assumption that all Cubans are persecuted in Cuba and should be granted political refugee status" (Jimenez-Vasquez, 1995, p. 1224). While this wave of immigrants was permitted to enter the country, the details of their stay remained pending for a while; since that time, Cubans coming to the United States have had to provide evidence of political or religious persecution. Because of their uncertain status, limited health and social services were available to the newcomers (Gil, 1983). Moreover, the negative publicity they received and the status of the economy greatly jeopardized the Mariel entrants' chances of employment. Their adjustment was also made more difficult by the radical difference between their communist society and the United States. Earlier Cuban immigrants were aided by the fact that having come from a capitalist society, the upper and middle socioeconomic sectors of prerevolutionary Cuban society shared the American ethos of individualism (Portes, 1969).

Immigration has resulted in considerable upheaval for Cuban families. One of the greatest tensions has come from the intergenerational conflicts between old-world Cuban parents and their American or Americanized children. As with other immigrant groups, problems occur when second-generation and Cuban-born youths adopt American attitudes and behaviors at a faster rate than their parents, who either were born and raised on the island or still adhere to traditional Cuban values. According to one study, the development of marked intergenerational differences within the nuclear family has been the source of widespread behavioral disorder and family disruption among Cuban immigrants (Szapocznik, Scopetta, & Kurtines, 1978). This situation is less true today because Cuban parents, now in their forties, were teenagers in this country and are giving their children more freedom ("For Cuban Americans," 1988).

Another source of tension in Cuban families came from the transition of early immigrant women, from being nonworking mothers in Cuba to being working women in the United States. Prior to the revolution, the majority of women were not employed outside the home, but as immigrants they were forced to take full-time jobs in order to survive economically. Having greater economic independence, they were less apt to condone their husbands' chauvinist behavior (Rodriguez & Vila, 1982).

Mariel entrants experience tension with their extended families because of value differences. While they are a product of a communist society, their relatives fully embrace capitalism and complain that the people from Mariel feel entitled and do not want to work. The Mariel wave, on the other hand, complain that their relatives "are too busy making money and shopping to care about the latest book, the new foreign film, or the next concert of classical guitar" ("Mariel Generation," 1988, p. 22).

Traditional and Emerging Family Systems

The Cuban value of familialism makes the family the most important social unit in Cuban society. The Cuban family, characterized by loyalty and unity, includes the **nuclear family**, the **extended family**, and a network of friends, neighbors, and the community (Bernal, 1982). This familial tendency may become more or less pronounced with migration and **acculturation**, however. For example, while the retention of the extended family is an economic necessity for Cuban families when they first arrive in the United States, their use of the extended family network occurs primarily during the first 3 years after migration (Chavira-Prado, 1994; Jimenez-Vasquez, 1995).

Although Cubans tend to be actively and emotionally involved with the family, extended families do not necessarily live under the same roof, but they usually live nearby. A **fictive kin** relationship that has lost significance among Cuban Americans is that of *compadres*, a child's godparents (Queralt, 1984).

Household Size and Composition

Cuban Americans tend to live in two-parent nuclear family households, the predominant norm in Cuba since the 1930s (Queralt, 1984). In fact, the 1953 Cuban census showed that only 14% of the population lived in extended family households (Gil, 1968). The majority of Cuban Americans live in married-couple families (76.1%), with 19.4% living in female-headed households (U.S. Bureau of the Census, 1992). Cuban Americans also tend to live in small families, averaging 2.81 persons per household. About 65% of this group lives in two- and three-person households. Following tradition, however, never-married Cuban Americans between ages 18 and 24 are more likely to live with their parents than their counterparts in other Hispanic groups or among European Americans (Bean & Tienda, 1988).

Despite originating in a predominantly Catholic country, Cuban American families in exile have uncharacteristically low fertility rates because of careful family planning. The lowest birth rate among all Hispanic groups, it is even lower than that of non-Hispanic White women (Bean & Tienda, 1988). Unlike other Hispanic groups, Cuban Americans reflect a pattern of delayed childbearing. For example, in 1980, fertility rates for Cuban American women between ages 20 and 24, a period of heightened childbearing for other Hispanic subgroups, were equal to those of women between ages 25 and 34.

It is not exactly clear why Cuban American women have such low birth rates. A possible explanation is their immigrant status (Bean & Tienda, 1988). Since most Cuban American women tend to be concentrated in the first generation of immigrants, their lower fertility rates may be a reflection of the disruptive impact of migration. (Groups of immigrant women have lower birth rates than do their generational counterparts.) That most Cuban American women are also refugees may compound the situation even further. However, although first-generation immigrant women have lower fertility rates than their second- and third-generation counterparts, the latter also have lower fertility patterns than women in other ethnic groups, suggesting that some factor other than the disrupting effects of migration is contributing to this phenomenon.

The Socialization of Children

Not surprisingly, the socialization of Cuban children has changed with migration to the United States. The need for mothers to work has meant greater independence for their children. Nonetheless, children are often pampered in Cuban American families, and despite busy work schedules, mothers manage to do a lot for their offspring. For example, mothers often cook, clean, and wash, even though their children are capable of doing these chores for themselves. Indeed, parents tend to indulge their children by catering to their desires materially and emotionally.

There are differences between male and female children's socialization, however (Queralt, 1984). In traditional Cuban families, boys are waited on by their mothers and the other women in their families because of their privilege of being male or "*macho*." As they grow older, they are given the freedom to explore and act out their manhood sexually. A young man's sexual escapades may be viewed with pride, as a sign of masculinity and prowess.

Females, on the other hand, are overprotected in order to preserve their sexual purity (Bernal, 1982). They may have strict curfews, are discouraged from going away to school, and are generally prohibited from exploring their sexuality outside a marital relationship. The ideal of female virginity is reinforced from childhood and throughout the life of a Cuban woman, as she is encouraged to emulate the Virgin Mary (Bernal, 1982). Many Cuban girls are introduced into society through a celebration, *la quinceañera*, on their fifteenth birthday. A traditional party may be as extravagant as a formal wedding, consisting of 15 couples, including the birthday girl, dressed formally. The party begins with a choreographed and rehearsed dance performed by the 15 couples. After that, friends and family join in the festivities, sharing music, dance, drink, and lots of food.

Despite years of living in the United States, Cuban American children are expected to live in the parental home until they get married. Although these adult children may make financial contributions to the household, it is not necessarily expected.

How Cuban children in the United States are socialized, however, ultimately depends on a number of factors, including the parents' levels of acculturation and education, socioeconomic status, and where they live regionally. Cuban children growing up in Miami will have more exposure to Cuban traditions because of the density of the Cuban community there. But no matter where they live, parents encourage their children to learn Spanish and develop pride in being Cuban.

Intimate Relationships

Migration has resulted in a relaxation of traditional sexual mores. Nonetheless, female virginity is still valued as an ideal among Cuban American families. Traditionally, young women were never allowed to be alone with a man in public or in private unless they were married. In prerevolutionary Cuba, couples were always accompanied by a chaperone. Although families tried to cling to this tradition during the early years in the United States, the use of a chaperone seems to have disappeared. Because of the need to work, family members are not available to constantly supervise the courtship behaviors of their children. Moreover, young Cuban Americans' exposure to the less-restrictive dating practices of their American peers has caused them to rebel against their parents' strict and outdated rules. Still, young couples are expected to observe respectful behavior. Parents will generally impose curfews. And although holding hands and embracing in public are acceptable, any other displays of affection are frowned upon.

Despite the increased freedom that younger Cuban Americans enjoy, their parents remain disturbed if their daughters engage in premarital sex. While males may become sexually active in their middle to late teens, females are more likely to do so in their late teens to early twenties because of the greater restrictions placed on them by their parents and by Cuban society. Still, there is a recognition that young women in the United States cannot be controlled and protected the way they were in prerevolutionary Cuba. And although by now parents may have become reluctantly resigned to their daughters' premarital sexual activity, young women and their partners are expected to be discreet about their sexual relationship. Sex is not discussed with parents, and unmarried couples are not allowed to stay in the same room when visiting relatives.

Because of the strict rules against sexual activity for young adolescent girls, teenage pregnancy does not occur frequently among Cuban Americans. But if a girl does become pregnant, it is considered disgraceful and, in a traditional Cuban family, a reflection of the father's inability to control his daughter. She is likely to marry the baby's father. But if for some reason she does not, she will not be turned away by her family, despite their shame and pain.

Although Cuban Americans are traditionally Catholic, on the whole they are not against using contraceptives. The fact that Cuban Americans have the lowest birth rate of the three largest Hispanic groups in the United States reflects this openness to family planning.

Despite rising divorce rates and changing customs, marriage continues to be a very important **rite of passage** in the Cuban American family. It is expected that young men and women will get married and have children. Although individuals choose their mates, the family may be very much involved in the courtship process—especially if the son or daughter is still living at home. A suitor is expected to visit regularly and to interact with the family. The degree of family involvement is determined by the family's level of acculturation. For example, in a more traditional family, dating is not expected to occur unless it will result in marriage. Church weddings are highly desirable, not only for religious reasons, but also because they serve an important social function in that they reflect the family's economic well-being.

In 1980, the average age at first marriage for men was 24 and for women, 22 (Bean & Tienda, 1988). Cuban Americans are increasingly likely to marry; the rate of never-married Cuban Americans declined from 26.4% in 1980 to 22.4% in 1990 (U.S. Bureau of the Census, 1990). Marriage between Cuban Americans and White non-Hispanics was necessary during the 1960s and 1970s, because the number of women in exile was greater than the number of men—a result of Castro's refusal to permit the migration of military-age males to the United States. However, this trend has begun to level off, as the ratio of men to women becomes more balanced in the second generation ("For Cuban Americans," 1988).

Marriages and **gender roles** among Cuban Americans vary according to socioeconomic status, level of acculturation, stage of migration, and religion (Bernal, 1982). Cultural elements from the Spanish heritage, such as *machismo*, female virginity, and female marital fidelity, may still underlie contemporary marital relationships. ***Machismo***, a largely misunderstood and misused concept, was "originally intended to describe the male role as **patriarch** or autocratic ruler of women and children within the culture" (p. 193). Women are expected to be pure and chaste before marriage. They are also expected to maintain marital fidelity at all times. While adultery by a man may be forgiven, the same behavior in a woman would be scandalous. This double standard may result in unbalanced and oppressive marital relationships.

Although the image of the "macho" male persists, particularly among lower-income Cuban Americans, second-generation Cuban Americans, having been raised in the United States, do not necessarily embrace such traditional gender roles ("For Cuban Americans," 1988). Younger couples seem to be moving toward increasingly egalitarian relationships, as more and more young women pursue professional careers (Jimenez-Vasquez, 1995).

Work Relationships and the Family

With migration and acculturation, Cuban families have by necessity become less traditional with regard to work and family relationships. Whereas most women in prerevolutionary Cuba devoted themselves to being homemakers and mothers and therefore did not work outside the home, this drastically changed upon their arrival in the United States. Cuban women were able to find work more easily than the men, and they were not as threatened by doing menial jobs (Boswell & Curtis, 1984). This increase has persisted. In 1991, the rate of labor-force participation of Cuban American women (55.1%) was similar to that of European American women (57.4%) (U.S. Bureau of the Census, 1991).

Queralt (1984) observes that the higher rates of employment for Cuban American women may have been instrumental in their achieving greater equality and more decision-making authority, in addition to some domestic help from their husbands, particularly grocery shopping and child care. The extent to which the husband is involved in running the household and raising the children depends on his levels of acculturation and education and, perhaps, on his own upbringing. If he grew up in a home where the father was involved in cooking, cleaning, shopping, and child care, he may have an expanded view of the male role. But this will not likely be the case if he was always catered to by the women in his childhood home. The more traditional husband may help his wife with household chores during her years of work, but it may return to a less egalitarian and cooperative marriage once husband and wife have both retired.

Despite the lack of employment for Cuban men when they first arrived in the United States, their work situation has since improved. Their rate of labor-force participation (73.3%) is almost identical to that of White non-Hispanic men (73.9%), and they now have lower rates of unemployment (5.2%) than Cuban American women (8%) (U.S. Bureau of the Census, 1991).

Cuban American men and women still experience some occupational differences, however. Cuban American women are less likely to work in managerial or professional jobs (20%) than in specialty and technical sales and administrative jobs (50%); Cuban American men are as likely to work in the former (21.6%) as in the latter (21.9%). Cuban American men are more likely to work in precision production, craft, and repair (22.6%) and as operators, fabricators, and laborers (20.6%) than are Cuban American women (2.6% and 11.7%, respectively). The remaining men (11.7%) and women (16.5%) work in service occupations (U.S. Bureau of the Census, 1991).

The average annual income of Cuban American families, at $39,455, is lower than that of White non-Hispanic families, at $40,987, but higher than that of other Hispanic groups (U.S. Bureau of the Census, 1990). This relative advantage over other Hispanic groups is due to the older age structure of the

Cuban American population—more people are in the labor force. Another reason is the number of multiple-earner families; in 1990, more than 50% of Cuban American families had two or more earners (U.S. Bureau of the Census, 1991).

Life-Cycle Transitions

Although the majority of Cuban Americans live in households headed by a married couple, this group experienced increased marital instability between 1960 and 1980 (an increase of 5.1%) as women began to assert themselves at home and in the workplace (Bean & Tienda, 1988; "For Cuban Americans," 1988). The stress of social change has resulted in a corresponding increase in the rate of divorce; while only 5.2% of Cuban Americans age 15 and older reported being divorced in 1980, 8.3% did so in 1990 (Bean & Tienda, 1988; U.S. Bureau of the Census, 1992). This trend has also resulted in an increase in the percentage of female-headed households (16.4%) over the last decade. Because of the accelerated rate of divorce in the Cuban American community in recent years, marital dissolution no longer carries the stigma it once had.

Because the Cuban American population tends to be older than other Hispanic groups, there is naturally a greater proportion of elderly members. Although living in exile is difficult for all Cuban Americans, it has been especially challenging for the elderly. Their mental health is seriously threatened, not only by the usual predicaments confronting the aged, but by many other complications associated with their special status as immigrants and members of a minority group (Szapocznik, 1980). Social isolation and loneliness, loss of country and of a way of life, loss of status, and the effects of transplantation—these are some of the conditions that would not have been experienced by these elders had they remained in their native country. Moreover, their inability to speak English and their lack of knowledge of American ways prevents them from assimilating and from participating in the social programs routinely available to American elders. For the most part, they are incapable of negotiating the social services delivery system.

Cuban American older adults are more likely to depend on the federal government for their support than on their children and extended families. Economically, they are primarily dependent on Supplemental Security Income (if they never worked in the United States or if their Social Security benefits are very low), Social Security, Medicare, Medicaid, and food stamps. This dependency on public monies for their basic subsistence and health care may explain why elderly Cuban Americans have experienced problems using the health-care system. In one study, elderly Cuban Americans were less likely to see a doctor than were younger Cuban Americans (Schur, Bernstein, & Berk, 1987).

Placing the elderly in nursing homes is not a common practice in Cuba because they are cared for by their extended families. But in the United States, the changes in the Cuban American family have resulted in an increasing need for such facilities. Because of language and cultural differences, these nursing homes have been developed by Hispanic social service providers for the special needs of this population. Casa Central, a Hispanic multiservice agency in Chicago, saw the need not only for a nursing home for the Hispanic elderly, but also for homes for independent living where older adults could participate in day programs offered by the agency. While this is not to suggest that the majority of the Cuban American elderly are now placed in nursing homes, it does imply that because of migration, the traditional methods of caring for this population are also beginning to change.

Family Strengths and Challenges

Despite an increased divorce rate, familial differences resulting from migration, and the long-standing Cuban tendency toward the nuclear family, the extended family remains a source of strength and support for Cuban Americans. According to some researchers, the extended family can still be expected to come together and offer support during times of crisis (Gil, 1968; Queralt, 1984).

Parents will rally to help their children—of all ages—with emotional and task-oriented support. This strong family bond stimulates parents to better accept their children's emancipation and new lifestyles in the United States. Although divorce is still frowned upon, it would not be unlikely for a daughter who is going through a divorce to stay indefinitely at her parents' home. Extended family members will also come to the aid of other family members, in spite of great geographic distances. For example, if a family member is ill in Miami, a family member from New Jersey may take time off to go help out.

Another strength of the Cuban American family is the capacity to adapt to new environments, new roles, and new situations. The challenges of migration propelled families and individuals to grow far beyond their comfort zones. Although the pain of migration has eased, the adaptational skills remain and can be used for coping with the rapid changes currently taking place in American society. For example, the loss of a job, though worrisome, may not be catastrophic for a Cuban American family because they have survived worse, having lost everything as a result of the revolution. The suffering they have already endured has strengthened them, leaving them with the feeling that they can transcend just about any situation in life.

Religion and spirituality lend strength to the Cuban American family. A strong belief in God and in the saints of the Catholic Church has also given them the courage to overcome economic, emotional, and political hardships.

When all else was lost, faith in a higher power prevented them from despairing. Cubans are also able to turn to the church community in times of need. Religious leaders may serve as sources of counsel and solace.

The sense of pride Cubans have for their heritage, at times perceived by outsiders as overbearing, is also a significant strength. Because of their pride in themselves, Cuban Americans have not succumbed to the negativity that most ethnic groups are generally exposed to in the United States. The messages of inferiority and inadequacy broadcast by mainstream society are virtually ignored. Because of their feelings of self-confidence and pride, Cuban Americans can dismiss the script that society has written for them as "minority" group members.

The extreme stress of migration has stimulated changes in both the family and individuals (Grant, 1983). Whether voluntary or involuntary, the effects of migration have been linked to psychological stress and to a range of mental, physical, and social disorders (David, 1970). Despite the apparently successful adjustment of Cuban Americans as a whole, segments of the population have adjusted poorly, resulting in various problems such as depression and family conflict.

For Cubans, adapting to the United States has meant embracing a lifestyle that is faster, more impersonal, and more individualistic than what they are used to (Szapocznik, Santisteban, Hervis, Spencer, & Kurtines, 1981). It has also meant working harder in order to achieve and acquire material things: "In Cuba, they say, we worked to live. In Miami, we live to work" ("Mariel Generation," 1988, p. 22a).

The rapid rate of change has caused dislocations for those who have adapted too quickly. For example, the young, who are in a greater rush to assimilate, cut themselves off from their roots and cultural heritage (Szapocznik, Scopetta, & Kurtines, 1978). Yet people living in a bicultural environment will have a tendency to become maladjusted if they remain or become monocultural (Santisteban, Szapocznik, & Rio, 1981).

Although it has advantages, growing up biculturally can also be a liability (Boswell & Curtis, 1984). For some Cuban American youths, or adults who grew up in the United States, this has led to an identity crisis—they feel neither completely Cuban nor completely American. While being a part of both worlds, they also feel estranged from both. Value conflicts result because of the clash between the mainstream culture's emphasis on individualism and the traditional Cuban culture's tendency toward familialism.

The capacity to live biculturally is threatened by mainstream society's discomfort with difference and diversity. For example, Cuban Americans in Miami are perceived as clannish because of their effort to maintain ties to their culture of origin. Many English-speaking residents resent the pervasiveness of the Spanish language. In the 1980 U.S. census, 94% of Cuban Americans reported Spanish as their household language (Bean & Tienda, 1988). This resentment led to the 1980 repeal of a law passed in 1973 declaring Dade County, Florida, a bilingual jurisdiction, which made Spanish the second official language for such things as election ballots, public signs, and local directories (Moore & Pachon, 1985). Actions such as this one would, of course, hinder recent immigrants or those not speaking English from becoming more integrated into American society.

Although Cuban Americans may hold on to their language and other cultural ways, their higher rates of **out-marriage** may eventually threaten the maintenance of their traditions. Cuban Americans are more likely to marry non-Cubans than are Mexican Americans and Puerto Ricans (Boswell & Curtis, 1984). Although in 1970, 17% of Cuban-descent women had married non-Cubans, 46% of second-generation Cuban American women had married non-Cuban men by 1980. This compares with 33% and 16% for Puerto Rican and Mexican American women, respectively.

Because the Cuban migration has been characterized by waves, the "old" immigrant community has been fed at different points in time by "new" immigrants. This means that Cuban American extended families will always have members at varying degrees of acculturation. In order to prevent further familial dislocation, they must try to maintain a bicultural orientation—to "navigate" mainstream society while remaining embedded within the extended family and the Cuban American community. As long as mainstream society feels threatened by diversity and continues to make it difficult for immigrants to adjust by insisting on conformity to a monocultural Western ideal, younger members of Cuban American society will be discouraged from accepting the culture of their ancestors.

Misconceptions and Stereotypes

One characteristic that has been considered typically Cuban and that has been misunderstood by outsiders is, according to Bernal, "a sense of specialness that many Cubans have about themselves and their culture" (1982, p.195). Bernal speculates that this sense of specialness may stem from the fusion of European, African, and indigenous cultures. It may also stem from the geopolitical importance the island of Cuba has had in relation to powerful nations. Because of its strategic location, over hundreds of years it has attracted Spain, the United States, and the former Soviet Union (Jimenez-Vasquez, 1995).

While Cubans' sense of specialness may have contributed to their ability to adapt and their relative success in America, some perceive it as arrogance and grandiosity (Bernal, 1982). Because of their love of their culture and their efforts to preserve it, Cuban Americans are often considered to be clannish. This may lead to a defensive treatment of Cuban Americans by others, in response to their perceived arrogance and superiority.

Another cultural characteristic of Cuban Americans that may be misunderstood is *choteo*, or humor. *Choteo* is a "typical Cuban phenomenon and a type of humor that has been defined as ridiculing or making fun of people, situations and/or things, [which once] served as a defensive function in the social reality of Cubans" (Bernal, 1982, p. 195). Characterized by exaggeration, this type of humor is a way of making light of serious situations through jokes. People from other ethnic groups and Hispanic subgroups may perceive such behavior to be inappropriate.

Personal Interview

Martha (not her real name) is a 34-year-old single Cuban American graduate student in social work. She migrated to the United States with her family in the early 1960s as part of the first wave of immigrants. Martha's family settled in Los Angeles, California.

What challenges did you face in adjusting to life in the United States?

Martha: All along, I have had challenges that I didn't even realize and that I did not attribute to cultural factors. I feel stifled in expressing myself. I just feel that in American culture you greet somebody and you ask, "How are you?" And you have to say, "I am doing fine"; you can't really say, "Oh, I have a headache," or "I saw a great movie last night." You can't just express your feelings without getting strange looks.

So this is one of the major challenges you've had. Did you find that people reacted to you in a certain way either positively or negatively because of your being Cuban?

Martha: I think that growing up in Los Angeles, in a mostly Hispanic neighborhood, it was on a different level. It was more like being un-

der a microscope. The dominant culture was Mexican, so Cubans kind of stuck out and I felt like a minority within a minority. And Cubans and Mexicans have some very distinct differences that can spark some problems. It just seems like night and day. Cubans joke [*el choteo*] a lot, and it is not considered that you are hurting people. But I had to restrict myself in the Mexican community because that is taken the wrong way. And we had Mexican gangs in the neighborhood so you really had to be careful.

In Michigan I feel less restricted now because I think that people consider my heritage as being kind of exotic, so they actually want to know about what it is like being Cuban. It's great. I think that as long as it is looked at as being something novel, then I feel free to express my Cubanness—more so in some ways than being in L.A.

In L.A. you had to try to fit into the dominant Hispanic group, which in this case was Mexicans?

Martha: Exactly. But as far as challenges, I miss the warmth, and being accepted. I feel accepted in the Cuban community, not just because I am Cuban but even when Americans come to visit, they are treated the same way, they are given the hugs and kisses and food and offered to dance—"Come on in." They have the *"quince"* for the girls ["sweet fifteen" parties]. I love those parties because to me they are very inclusive. We used to have Colombians, Peruvians, Mexicans in those parties too, and some Americans.

What helped you in the Cuban culture to adjust to these challenges?

Martha: What helped was all the dry stuff on ethnicity that I read that said here are the differences between the cultures, here are the stats, and here's what they do. And I would read this and I would say, yeah there are some things that are pretty right and others that are different from my experience. Gaining that cognitive knowledge of who I am and where I fit into the mosaic here in the United States helped me to identify myself. I just needed to have a framework and a label, like Cuban American or Latina.

But what helped you before you got this knowledge? What were the strengths within the Cuban culture that might have helped you face the challenges that are inherent in being a minority?

Martha: You know, I haven't thought about that much. There was a little bit of racial self-hatred that was almost a necessity to forge ahead because I had to try to be both, to try to be bicultural. I think that there is where I went full circle because at first I was very Cuban, then I got a little bit older in school and thought, "Oh, I am sticking out like a sore thumb so I better adjust," and I became a little bit more American. I watched people to learn how to restrict my affect or emotions and after

I did that for a while, it didn't feel right. Now I say, I am an American, but I am Cuban too, and it's okay.

When you were going through those struggles about identity, where did you turn?

Martha: Different Cuban people who were going through the same thing and who were going to the *Cofradia*, a fraternal order in the neighborhood for Cubans. To be hooked into that helped me stay Cuban, but then I almost had to separate the two lives for a while until I got it straight in my head. So I got support from the Cuban community. I tried to shy away from Americans who did not accept the cultural differences. I made friends with people who saw my Cubanness as an asset.

When you did go to the Cuban community, were you able to articulate that you were having this struggle, or were you just turning to them because they were Cuban?

Martha: It wasn't verbalized. It's funny because as Cubans, we talk a lot, we are verbal, but at the same time, we are not. We are experiential people, we like experience, we like events, people. And if you have a problem, you just get into an environment that addresses them. When you have the stereo blasting in the middle of the street and there is a block party, you are in the environment, you are within the events that are taking place, and you subconsciously are getting your needs met without telling people.

You spoke earlier about having self-hatred and said that it helped you. Can you tell me more about that?

Martha: I grew up in a lower-middle-class neighborhood that, although it had a Hispanic flavor, also had quite a few Caucasians.

I could sense a hierarchy of social status that was tied in with culture and money. And see, as a poverty-stricken Cuban I didn't fit in; most of the Cubans in the neighborhood were better off, so that was another adjustment. I had to say, I am going to reject this mentality that because I am a minority I am going to be low-income. It's almost like I had to create my own vision and say, "What do I want? This is how I want to live, I want to get out of here." It seemed at the time that the only way to do that was to say, "I can't be Cuban then." I've got to have American values, I have to look American, I have to talk American and I can be accepted to these levels and work my way up. And then maybe, after I get there, I can say, "Okay guys, I am Cuban." Now I am kind of upset that I was almost ashamed of being Cuban back then.

I guess it's just part of the process of finding yourself.

Martha: I remember American kids would taunt me by pretending that their pencils were cigars. They knew because my name was Spanish. And then I got it from the Cubans, too. Cubans who came later would taunt that I was denying my Cubanness. Since they left Cuba when they were teenagers, they identified much more with Cuban culture and they spoke with an accent, and they chose not to speak in English. They would speak back to the teacher in Spanish even though they understood English. They had a chip on their shoulder. That was another thing that fueled my racial self-hatred. I didn't want to be like that. I wanted to be open-minded.

It sounds like at some point you felt displaced from different waves in the Cuban community.

Martha: Yeah. I felt a little trapped because Cubans know each other; they are very intuitive people and they can read a situation easily, or at least this is what I have observed. I never even knew some of these people, so how did they know that I wasn't really proud of being Cuban? And so now, being Cuban is special to me because I like all that stuff. I like the expressiveness, I like the intuition, I like being a family, knowing that if you are Cuban, you are expected to be close to other Cubans, but at the same time it was kind of a trap then when I was trying to be American.

How would you like Cubans to be viewed by outsiders?

Martha: I would like Cubans to have the reputation of being well-balanced. I think that we have a good mix of being businesslike and yet being real and of having hope. I think we have a lot of hope. Here's little Cuba who has stood up to the United States. That's how we are, we are very proud, we can do it against the odds. But think about it, how could that little country have kept the United States scared in 1961? I think that it's all healthy stuff—having guts, being proud of yourself, taking personal responsibility, but at the same time being caring and helping others. Even though you might expect people to pick themselves up by their bootstraps, if they can't, you are there to help them out. Another thing: You know how they say that Hispanics are very sexist—well, in Hispanic culture we get to carry our mother's name and our father's. Women get to keep their identity that way, and the children feel like they are a part of their mom and their dad.

Questions for Discussion

1. How are Cuban Americans similar to other Hispanic groups? How are they different?

2. What values are characteristic of Cuban culture? How might some of these values clash with those of American culture?

3. Discuss the concept of "waves" in the Cuban migration. Why is it important to understand these waves of immigration?

4. Why has Cuban migration to the United States become so controversial? How does this compare to the controversy over Mexican immigration?

5. Identify the problems and tensions that have developed in Cuban families (both nuclear and extended) as a result of migration. Why have these problems been especially challenging for elderly Cubans?

6. What strengths of Cuban families have helped them deal with the challenges of migration?

7. What factors have contributed to the changing roles of Cuban American women?

8. How has the adjustment to the United States been different for Cubans than Mexicans and Puerto Ricans? What accounts for these differences? How has the adjustment experience been similar?

9. If you were Cuban, what would be the advantages of coming to live in the United States? What would be the disadvantages? What factor would influence you the most in deciding whether or not to come?

10. What similarities exist between the Mexican American, Cuban American, and Puerto Rican interviewees? What similarities can you find between their life and your own life?

Suggested Resources

Readings

Behar, R., & Leon, J. (Eds.). (1994, Spring). Bridges to Cuba: Puentes a Cuba. *Michigan Quarterly Review, 32,* 3.

Fernandez, R. G. (1988). *Raining backwards.* Houston, TX: Arte Publico Press.

Garcia, C. (1992). *Dreaming in Cuban.* New York: Knopf.

Videos

Films for the Humanities (Producers). (1989). *The Cubans*. (Available from Films for the Humanities, P.O. Box 2053, Princeton, NJ 08543)

Films for the Humanities (Producers). (1993). *Latina women*. (Available from Films for the Humanities, P.O. Box 2053, Princeton, NJ 08543)

Pena, E. (Producer), & Ichaso, L. (Director). (1990). *El super*. (Available from New Yorker Films Video, 16 West 61st Street, New York, NY 10023)

References

Bach, R. L., Bach, J. B., & Triplett, R. (1981). The flotilla "entrants." The latest and most controversial. *Cuban Studies / Estudios Cubanos, 11–12*.

Bean, F., & Tienda, M. (1988). *The Hispanic population of the United States in the 1980s*. New York: Russell Sage Foundation.

Bernal, G. (1982). Cuban families. In M. McGoldrick, J. K. Pearce, & J. Giordano (Eds.), *Ethnicity and family therapy* (pp. 186–207). New York: Guilford Press.

Boswell, T. D., & Curtis, J. R. (1984). *The Cuban American experience: Culture, images, perspectives*. Totowa, NJ: Rowman & Allanheld.

Chavira-Prado, A. (1994). Latina experience and Latina identity. In T. Weaver (Ed.), *Handbook of Hispanic cultures in the United States: Anthropology* (pp. 245–266). Houston, TX: Arte Publico Press.

David, H. P. (1970). Involuntary international migration: Adaptation of refugees. In E. B. Brody (Ed.), *Behavior in new environments: Adaptation of migration populations*. Beverly Hills, CA: Sage.

Fields, S. (1976). Storefront psychotherapy through seance. *Innovations, 3*(1), 3–11.

For Cuban-Americans, an era of change. (1988, April 13). *The New York Times*.

Fradd, S. (1983). Cubans to Americans: Assimilation in the United States. *Migration Today, 11*(4–5), 34–41.

Garrison, V. (1977). Doctor, espiritista or psychiatrist?: Health-seeking behavior in a Puerto Rican neighborhood of New York City. *Medical Anthropology, 1*(2), 165–191.

Gil, R. M. (1968). *The assimilation and problems of adjustment to the American culture of one hundred Cuban adolescents*. Unpublished master's thesis, Fordham University, Bronx, NY.

Gil, R. M. (1983). Issues in the delivery of mental health services to Cuban entrants. *Migration Today, 11*, 43–48.

Grant, G. (1983). Impact of immigration on the family and children. In

M. Frank (Ed.), *Newcomers to the United States* (pp. 26–37). New York: Haworth.

Hernandez, A. R. (1974). *The Cuban minority in the U.S.: Final report on the need identification and program evaluation.* Washington, DC: Cuban National Planning Council.

Jimenez-Vasquez, R. (1995). Hispanics: Cubans. *Encyclopedia of social work* (19th ed.). Washington, DC: National Association of Social Work Press.

Mariel generation feels separate from fellow exiles. (1988, December 27). *The Miami Herald.*

Moore, J., & Pachon, H. (1985). *Hispanics in the United States.* Englewood Cliffs, NJ: Prentice-Hall.

Papajohn, J. C., & Spiegel, J. P. (1971). The relationships of culture value orientation change and Rorschach indices to psychological development. *Journal of Cross-Cultural Psychology, 2,* 257–272.

Pedraza-Bailey, S. (1980). *Political and economic migrants in America: Cubans and Mexican Americans.* Unpublished doctoral dissertation, University of Chicago.

Portes, A. (1969). Dilemmas of a golden exile: Integration of Cuban refugee families in Milwaukee. *American Sociological Review, 34,* 505–518.

Queralt, M. (1984). Understanding Cuban immigrants: A cultural perspective. *Social Work, 29,* 115–121.

Rodriguez, A., & Vila, M. E. (1982). Emerging Cuban women in Florida's Dade County. In R. E. Zambrana (Ed.), *Work, family, and health: Latino women in transition* (pp. 55–67). New York: Fordham University Hispanic Research Center.

Rogg, E. M., & Cooney, R. M. (1980). *Adaptation and adjustment of Cubans: West New York, New Jersey.* New York: Fordham University Hispanic Research Center.

Sandoval, M. C. (1979). Santería as a mental health care system: An historical overview. *Social Science and Medicine, 13B,* 137–151.

Santisteban, D., Szapocznik, J., Rio, A. T. (1981, June). *Acculturation/biculturalism: Implications for a mental health intervention strategy.* Paper presented at the XVIII Interamerican Society of Psychology, Santo Domingo, Dominican Republic.

Schur, C. L., Bernstein, A. B., & Berk, M. L. (1987). The importance of distinguishing Hispanic subpopulations in the use of medical care. *Medical Care, 25,* 627–641.

Szapocznik, J. (1980). *A programmatic mental health approach to enhancing the meaning of life of the Cuban elderly.* Washington, DC: COSSMHO.

Szapocznik, J., & Hernandez, R. (1990). The Cuban family. In C. Mindel & R. W. Habenstein (Eds.), *Ethnic families in America: Patterns and variations* (pp. 160–172). New York: Elsevier.

Szapocznik, J., Santisteban, D., Hervis, O., Spencer, F., & Kurtines, W. (1981). Treatment of depression among Cuban American elders: Some validation evidence for a life enhancement counseling approach. *Journal of Counseling and Clinical Psychology, 49*(5), 752–754.

Szapocznik, J., Scopetta, M., Arnalde, M., & Kurtiness, W. (1978). Cuban value structure: Treatment implications. *Journal of Consulting and Clinical Psychology, 46*(5), 961–970.

Szapocznik, J., Scopetta, M. A., & Kurtines, W. (1978). Theory and measurement of acculturation. *Interamerican Journal of Psychology, 12*, 113–130.

U.S. Bureau of the Census. (1990). *Statistical abstract of the United States, 1990*. Washington, DC: U.S. Government Printing Office.

U.S. Bureau of the Census. (1991). *Current population reports: The Hispanic population of the United States, March 1991*. Washington, DC: U.S. Government Printing Office.

U.S. Bureau of the Census. (1992). *Statistical abstract of the United States, 1992*. Washington, DC: U.S. Government Printing Office.

Wenk, M. G. (1968). Adjustment and assimilation: The Cuban experience. *International Migration Review, 3*, 38–49.

Barbara C. Aswad

11

Arab American Families

Historical and Cultural Background

The Arab American community originates in several Arabic-speaking countries in the Middle East. It encompasses a variety of family types, which reflect differing historical periods of migration, diverse socioeconomic levels, and varying religious beliefs, in addition to individual histories and experiences. Thus, there is not one family type, but many. Arab Americans do share, however, certain cultural, historical, linguistic, and social features that permit a discussion of the family in its role as a central social unit. It is ideally large, patrilineally organized, and based on intimate reciprocal relationships. It has been an important ingredient in migration and in the adaptation of Arabs to American society.

During the late nineteenth and early twentieth centuries, early immigrants came from the Lebanese Mountains in an area that was then part of the Syrian Province of the Ottoman Empire. The vast majority of the migrants were Christians, although a few were Muslim Lebanese. A second wave of immigrants, who entered the United States after World War II, came from more diverse economic backgrounds and from different regions, such as Syria, Iraq, Egypt, Palestine, Jordan, Yemen, and, less frequently, Saudi Arabia and Kuwait. Many were highly educated. Meanwhile, immigration continued from Lebanon; consequently, Lebanese constitute by far the largest subgroup of Arabs in the United States (U.S. Bureau of Census, 1990). There have been very few migrants from North African countries other than Egypt.

Religion plays a key role in Middle Eastern culture and serves as an important social boundary, across which marriage is difficult. Skin color and even language are not as strong determining factors as religious affiliation. As a result, the churches and mosques established by Arab American communities remain major centers of organization and socialization, both for the early, predominantly Christian, immigrant population and for the more recent, and heavily Muslim, groups of migrants.

Social values other than religion that organize Arabs include the ideology of the extended patrilineal family, the village, and national or regional affiliation. Identification with **patrilineality**, the father's line of descent, is a basic ascribed relationship for both sons and daughters, and even though daughters may move to their husbands' families when they marry, they are still regarded as members of their fathers' line and known by their fathers' names.

Kinship and marriage are of primary importance in the system of **chain migration**, whereby one son in a family immigrates to the United States and establishes himself, then brings other members of the family, and so on, until many relatives have settled together. Relatives often provide the economic basis for an enterprise such as operating a store. The honor of these lineages and families is a strong factor in the everyday lives of Arabs in America.

In addition to grouping themselves around members of the extended family, Arab Americans tend to create communities centered on village affiliation, provided such groupings do not cross religious boundaries. The settlement patterns of early groups in Detroit, Michigan, illustrate this concept. The early Lebanese Catholic Christians, for example, settled first near the center of the city; subsequently, they moved nearer the Chrysler Corporation on the east side; and later still, they left their automotive jobs and migrated to the eastern suburbs. The Lebanese Muslims, on the other hand, originally worked at and settled near the Ford Motor Company plant in the north-central region; they moved to the city of Dearborn west of Detroit, when Ford moved there, and subsequently have migrated to the western suburbs. The Lebanese Greek Orthodox Christians originally settled with the Muslims near the Ford Motor Company; later, however, they did not move to Dearborn but migrated to the northern suburbs (Abraham & Abraham, 1983; Aswad, 1974).

Although it included many chain migrants like those in the first wave, the second wave of immigrants also brought a large number of students who came to the United States for educational opportunities but who stayed and settled without large kin networks. They often intermarried with Americans; thus, their family arrangements are unique, featuring a great deal of interaction with non-Arabs, especially in the second generation (Abu-Laban, 1993; Elkholy, 1988). For some in the upper classes, however, especially those with Arab spouses, large Arab friendship groups, much like **fictive kin**, are established, and a great deal of socializing continues. Marriages take place within these groups so often that many of the members eventually become relatives.

It is important to note that migration from Arabic-speaking countries has never stopped. Although it slowed during the Great Depression, it increased after World War II and continues today. Continuous immigration is due in part to the social upheavals that have occurred in the Middle East and to a relaxation of certain immigration regulations. Consequently, family structures have changed through the generations along with economic changes, but there has also been a constant infusion of Middle Eastern values. Occasionally these changes have produced tensions between different groups and generations of immigrants over family values. The cultures of the Middle East have also changed during these years, and some members of the new immigrant groups feel that American Arab cultures have not changed as much as have those in the homelands.

Thus, cultural ideologies and feelings of belonging for Arab immigrants and their descendants in America are influenced by forces in the Middle East, especially the currently reemerging forces of Islam. The American political climate has at times presented extremely negative stereotypes of Arab culture and Islam (Shaheen, 1984; Suleiman, 1988). Many Arabs share feelings of being discriminated against or marginalized as members of the Third World, as members of the Islamic religion, or as people of color. Although there is disagreement on the issue of Arab Americans being recognized as an official minority (they currently are not), many feel they should have the same advantages as other Asian Americans.

Intergroup relations are affected by the stereotypical images minority and dominant groups have about each other. As Elkholy (1988) states, "The stereotype, which creates social distance, is extended to the members of a given group, and thus the interaction becomes biased" (p. 443). The negatively stereotyped group also develops stereotypes regarding the dominant group, and these attitudes may affect rates of intermarriage and interaction.

The Immigration Experience

The Arab immigration experience can be divided into two major historical periods: the first commencing around the end of the nineteenth century; the second beginning after World War II and continuing today. Migrants initially entered the United States on the East Coast or from Mexico. Some then traveled to states such as West Virginia, Texas, and South Dakota, and later to Michigan and California. Today the major areas of Arab American settlement are in the census regions of the Mid-Atlantic, the Eastern North-Central Midwest, the Pacific, and the South Atlantic. Although census data reflect a smaller number of Arabs in the United States, some experts estimate the Arab American population at 2–3 million (Zogby, 1990). The states with the largest populations are, in descending order: California, New York, and Michigan. The vast majority are urban, and approximately two-thirds speak Arabic at home (U.S. Bureau of the Census, 1990).

The early immigrants were primarily peasants from small villages. Because their occupations were primarily agricultural, they had few skills that were marketable in an industrial society, and they brought little capital with them. They became peddlers, owners of small stores, or unskilled laborers in factories. Many Lebanese migrated to the United States in this early wave because their country had become a dependent cash-crop area for French silk production, and its economy had suffered from silk-worm diseases, the introduction of rayon, and the increasing amount of Japanese silk in the world market.

Other factors promoting emigration from the Middle East included the increasing brutality of the collapsing Ottoman Empire and its policy of forcing Christians to serve in the army, and the efforts of steamship entrepreneurs to enlist workers by paying for their voyages to America. The "gold in the streets" stories encouraged others to follow. Thus, these immigrants, like most others, experienced both a "push" to leave their homes and a "pull" to move to America (Aswad & Bilge, 1996; Naff, 1985).

Christian immigrants had an advantage in adapting to a primarily Christian country and emphasized their religious ties to the dominant culture, while Muslims were concerned about the dilution or disappearance of their religion (Haddad & Lummis, 1987). Christians could join other Christian churches until their own were built; they often sent their children to Christian schools, thus encouraging aspects of **acculturation**. Muslims met for religious purposes in their homes until they could build mosques. Although a few sent their children to Christian schools because they were strict, most Muslim children attended public schools (Aswad, 1974).

During the first part of the twentieth century, the United States stressed **assimilation** into the dominant culture, and Arab immigrants often gave their children Anglo names for public use while using Arab names at home. **Outmarriage** did occur, especially by Arab Muslims because there were few Muslims in the United States, and by Catholic Arabs who might marry non-Arabs within the Catholic Church. However, many Arab Americans returned home to bring brides to the United States. They also sent for other family members, and before long, kin and village groups emerged.

By World War II, the Arab population in the United States was small and essentially ignored as an ethnic group. Arab immigrants who came after World War II were more diverse in nationality, socioeconomic status, and religion than the earlier wave. Again, events in the Middle East as well as those in America affected the nature of migration. The war in Palestine and the establishment of the Israeli state in 1948 created many Palestinian refugees, and the uncertainties accompanying the war sent many Palestinians to the United States.

The 1965 U.S. Immigration Act allowed the entrance of more immigrants from Third World countries that had been restricted since the 1920s. Among those groups whose numbers increased were Yemeni Muslim immigrants from southern Arabia. Most Yemeni were men who were single or who left their wives and children behind. They came from villages or from the port city of Aden, and some had little education. They were "recurrent migrants," working in factories in such cities as Detroit and Buffalo (New York) or picking fruit in California for several years, then returning to Yemen for several years. Since the late 1970s, many have brought their families with them.

One of the largest groups of Arabs to immigrate after World War II were students and professionals, primarily males, from many parts of the Arab world. They became known as the "Brain Drain" group, in reference to the loss of their skills by their countries of origin. Although they came primarily for education, many stayed here because of disruptions in their homeland and the high salaries in the United States. A significant number of this student group married Americans. They did not have the language problems or lack of skills of earlier immigrants. They typically lived in communities without large Arab populations, and their children often had more American than Arab relatives and friends (Abu-Laban, 1993).

Other professionals and upper-income Arab people have continued to immigrate, escaping upheavals abroad. Most have brought their spouses or have married within their culture. They form groups and networks with other upper-income immigrant Arabs and encourage their children to marry within the culture.

Conflicts in Lebanon during 1976–1990 sent waves of refugees to the United States and Canada. Hundreds of thousands of Lebanese and Palestinians were killed or wounded in religious and class conflicts by massive Israeli bombings and by the military regime set up by Syria. The wars have affected Lebanese communities in the United States, causing their populations to swell. For example, the Dearborn Muslim Arab community expanded from 5000 to 18,000 during this period. Tensions sometimes arose between second- and third-generation Lebanese and the new immigrants, and between those who hoped to return to Lebanon and others who wished to remain in the United States.

Numerous Egyptian Coptic Christians have also migrated recently. A minority group in Egypt, they have felt threatened by the resurgence of Islam. Many in this community are well educated. In 1995 another group of immigrants arrived from southern Iraq, where they had been part of the unsuccessful American-supported Shiite Muslim rebellion against Saddam Hussein in 1991. They had lived in camps in Saudi Arabia; most were poor. They comprise the only primarily Arabic-speaking group to have been granted official refugee status by the United States, although the Lebanese were given temporary work permits during their war. Iraqi Chaldeans, who speak a Semitic language related to Arabic, and many of whom also speak Arabic, had refugee status from the 1960s, when they began to emigrate in large numbers, until the early 1990s.

Refugee status traditionally meant that new immigrants could receive welfare and other forms of assistance. Most Iraqi Shiites were originally scattered throughout the United States, but they have migrated to live near the primarily Shiite Muslim community in Dearborn, Michigan.

Thus, political conflict in the Middle East has influenced the settlement patterns, identity, and family structure of Arab Americans. The circumstances of immigration also affect a family's situation. Early Lebanese chain migration led to the establishment of large families and villages, which in turn protected subsequent immigrants and also led to the maintenance of the traditional culture. This was particularly true in lower-income communities, where people lived close to each other and shared community facilities such as coffee houses, restaurants, bakeries, and religious institutions. Of course, they also shared their neighborhood with people of various immigrant nationalities (Aswad, 1974).

America itself changed after the 1960s, as ethnic pride revived cultural identity and emphasized nationwide diversity, or **pluralism**. American culture also changed in ways that affected Arab American families, such as increased sexual liberalization and the feminist revolution. These movements put strains on the traditional patrilineal family ideals, which restrict or forbid dating and which honor parental authority.

Traditional and Emerging Family Systems

Understanding the Arab family as the basic unit of social organization is crucial to understanding the values of Arab Americans. As a vehicle for migration and socialization, the family cushions the economic and emotional difficulties of adjustment to a new country. The family's reputation is dominant in the training of the individual, who thinks of the family first and then of himself or herself. In return, the family provides protection, emotional and economic support, and identity. Ideally the family is large and extended, with grandparents, aunts, uncles, and cousins living close enough that they can visit often and provide assistance. However, among both the early and the recent waves of Arab immigrants to the United States, the family was often broken up.

The North American context requires a multivariate analysis. Studies demonstrating variation among different immigrant groups, depending on when they migrated and matured, have been done by Abu-Laban (1993) of Muslim Arabs in Canada and Cainkar (1991) of Palestinians in Chicago. Another study of Muslims, many of them Arabs, was conducted by Haddad and Lummis (1987) regarding aspects of marriage and the family in a large national sample.

Household Size and Composition

A smaller percentage of Arab American households have one or two people than any other group, and some have five or more people. Large families are only slightly more prevalent among those born in the Middle East than among American-born Arabs (Zogby, 1990).

The 1980 and 1990 U.S. censuses reflect the influx of a new wave of immigrants. This new community is younger, more likely to be foreign-born, and less likely to be assimilated in terms of marriage and language. Some 47% of Arab Americans are under age 25, while only 5.9% are 65 and older. The concentration is in the 20–40 age range (U.S. Bureau of the Census, 1990). In one study, Arab Americans were generally younger than other ethnic groups selected for comparison: Italians, Irish, and Asian/Pacific Islanders (Zogby, 1990).

Large families are desired in the Middle East, and people without children or with only a single child are often viewed with concern. In a study of the working-class community in Dearborn, Aswad (1994) found that among Arab American women, of whom 48% were still young (ages 20–29) and thus could have more children, 38% had five or more children. However, that number declines among people in higher socioeconomic levels.

Household composition may be extended or nuclear. However, even if a household is nuclear, extended family relationships continue to be significant. When they marry, young men and their wives may try to live near or sometimes in the residences of their fathers and their brothers, especially in new immigrant communities. Women often want to live near their male patrilineal relatives (which typically include father and/or brothers), who serve as a deterrent against potential mistreatment by their husbands. Women also want to live near their mothers for advice and assistance in raising children. Daughters as well as sons do not really leave their patriline for good, as they do in other patrilineal cultures, such as the traditional Chinese. Women become part of their husbands' family through the birth of children, particularly sons, but always maintain ties to their patriline. Since there is also a tradition of first- and second-cousin marriage within the patriline in the Middle East, both spouses often live near their relatives.

Haddad and Lummis (1987) found that 50% of the Muslims they surveyed had favorable or mixed attitudes toward cousin marriage, while 50% disapproved of such matches. Although Christian Arabs observe more restrictions on first-cousin marriage, it is found among these communities as well. Among

Christians from Ramallah, Palestine, Saba and Swan (1974) found that about 33% favored cousin marriage. Since marriage to cousins is sometimes related to migration, its occurrence may be higher in the migrant groups than abroad.

The migration experience, however, may separate brothers and men of the patrilineage. For example, in a survey of 55 Arab Americans on welfare in Dearborn in 1991, Aswad (1991) found that 80% of both men and women said they had relatives living near them; however, 33% of the women and only 15% of the men lived close to their fathers. Fifty percent of the women lived close to their mothers, and only 16% of the men did so. The discrepancy among women who lived closer to their mothers than their fathers is a result of some mothers' being widowed. Forty-six percent of the women and 33% of the men said they lived close to their brothers. Thus, in that group, which may be an unusual sample because of its extremely low income, women in fact lived closer to their relatives than did men.

Structurally, **conjugal relationships**, or relationships through marriage, are not as close as **consanguineal relationships** (through blood), and sometimes they are considered contractual arrangements. As mentioned above, however, due to the occurrence of cousin marriage within the patriline, husband and wife may be in the same kin group.

Children help connect in-laws. Children must be respectful to relatives on both their father's and their mother's sides, but particularly their father's because of patrilineal authority. Their relationships with their mother's relatives can be more relaxed and informal, and can serve as sources of friendship. When migration separates a family, the mother's family may become more important than the father's.

Socialization into large family networks may be understood by many mainstream Americans who come from such a tradition, such as Italian Americans and African Americans. However, for those who were raised in nuclear families, the extended family lifestyle may be difficult to understand. In marrying, one becomes deeply involved with the family of one's spouse, and because families are extensive and relationships intensive, much of a couple's time, emotion, energy, and even money is expected to be spent on the family. In nuclear families, the most important relationship is the husband and wife, and the independence of this nuclear unit is expected. But large families view the husband-wife unit as competing with other relationships and see the nuclear family as less independent. Many cross-cultural marriages do not survive the different role expectations.

If Arab Americans marry outside the culture or increase their wealth, they may move away, and family ties may weaken. Family ties are seldom cut, however, except for Arabs who have few relatives in the United States, or in cases in which there is major conflict within a family. Because members of merchant families have numerous business dealings with each other, there is always the potential for conflict. And while other relatives may try to mediate in conflicts, wives often get caught between their husbands' interests and those of their fathers or brothers.

Settlement sometimes presents a problem for large and extended families. This is particularly true for poor families who have to crowd into a small house or apartment, or for those in the suburbs where nearby houses may not be available. In primary ethnic communities such as Dearborn, the pejorative label "porch monkeys" is sometimes applied to Arab Americans who use their porches and yards as extensions of their houses for neighborhood activities. Family loyalty extends to village and sectarian groups, promoting what mainstream Americans term *clannishness*.

The Socialization of Children

In Arab American families, children are valued and given a great deal of attention. But they are expected to respect their parents. As young children, they are allowed quite a bit of freedom and are cared for by many members of the extended family, who have the authority to both praise and discipline them. If children misbehave, they are shamed or pinched; occasionally they may be hit, but excessive physical punishment is usually stopped by other adults.

Boys are considered to be more of a blessing than girls, and this attitude is verbalized. A son's education is often given more emphasis than a daughter's, although in the second and third generations of immigrants, this double standard may be significantly eased.

Appropriate behavior for young women is modesty in public and helping around the home. Many traditional parents prefer that their daughters not work directly with men. For example, among the Muslim population in Dearborn, women seldom are allowed to work at the Ford Motor Company, but jobs as clerks, secretaries, teachers, or pharmacists are considered suitable (Aswad, 1994).

Boys are expected to help their fathers in the family business if their fathers are small shopkeepers, but in general they are allowed more latitude in areas of occupation than are girls. In contrast to females, males are allowed to appear self-assured in public and even to show off.

The traditional lines of authority in the Arab American family are **patriarchal**, favoring males over females and parents over children. However, not every family today follows this tradition; patriarchy does not always play a critical role in determining the status of family members. In many Arab American families, women dominate or children get their way. However, the ideas of the "democratic" family and parents as friends to their children are strange concepts to most Arab Americans, and sometimes result in tension between first and second generations. As stated by Elkholy (1988):

The tradition-oriented first-wave Arab in America was puzzled by the independence and disobedience of his children. He often expressed his disappointment about the new pattern of family relations by saying, "We lost our children in America," for they still dream of the patriarchal pattern, which they imagine (incorrectly) to be unchanged in the old country. (p. 448)

Arab American second-generation children may resent the pressure their parents use to make them conform to their standards. Thus, the generation gap is often wider in the United States than in the Middle East, and family stress results. If the parents do not speak English, the gap may be widened to such an extent that a role reversal occurs, in which case the children begin to dominate the parents.

The concept of leisure also differs between parents and children. Arab parents born abroad spend much time with friends and relatives. However, second-generation Arab American teenagers may want to go to movies and athletic activities in addition to, or instead of, visiting with relatives or attending cultural or religious events. And many of their friends are not of Arab heritage, further compounding the generational differences.

Socioeconomic and residential factors also affect the potential for generational conflict. Upper-class Arab Americans experience the pressure of conforming to mainstream customs because they usually do not live or work in primary ethnic communities. However, they often go to great lengths and spend much time inviting Arab friends and relatives to form groups that will maintain their cultural values. Religious institutions and other clubs provide activities to keep children in the group and to educate them regarding cultural values, history, traditions, and language.

Intimate Relationships

Marriage in the Arab American community is highly **endogamous**, favoring marriage between cousins and between people within the same religious, village, or national community. Marriages are often arranged, or pressure to choose certain mates is exerted by controlling group activities and regulating dating practices.

Because contemporary American dating habits threaten several requirements of the patrilineal family and Arab society, dating has become a major area of concern for the Arab American family. There is a double standard for sons and daughters. Boys are given more privileges, such as staying out late. One study of Muslims found that males dated more than females, with only 37% of males never having dated, while 80% of females never did, and another 10% of females "hardly ever" dated (Ba-Yunis, 1991).

The behavior of girls is more closely monitored because they are expected to be virgins at marriage. Fathers, mothers, and brothers traditionally monitor the behavior of their unwed teenage daughters and sisters, and even punish them if they dishonor the family's reputation. This is often a source of stress for immigrant girls, especially those raised outside a primary Arab community. A girl may be cut off from the family, harshly beaten, or even killed for dishonoring her family if she has sexual relations with a man. Some girls hide the fact that they are dating, particularly if they date members of other ethnic groups. Some more liberal families do allow their daughters to date, but it is usually a cause of tension. Dating in a group of friends, especially friends who are children of their parents' friends, is preferred.

Restrictions on female sexuality, both before and after marriage, are related to the principle of patrilineality. It is important that children are legitimate, in order to carry on the patriline. In **matrilineal** families, where identity, power, and resources are traced through the mother, there is not the same need for the biological assurance of the mother.

In the Middle East, dating is necessarily restricted for males because females are restricted. But in the United States, a country with vastly different mores regarding premarital courtship, young men often feel free to date American girls if they cannot date Arab girls. Cainkar (1991) writes:

> The implicitly understood rule is that male social and sexual freedom is permissible as long as it is exercised with non-Arab females. Since they are "outsiders," they are not perceived as a threat to the traditional Arab way of life. However, should Palestinian females engage in such behavior, it would be viewed as an act of rebellion. "Outside" females cannot threaten the system, but "outside" males can. American born / raised Palestinian Muslim females live on the margins of two societies, while the males traverse them at will. (p. 294)

Males may also date outside their ethnic group to avoid dishonoring Arab girls or being penalized by their families; while such behavior may not be welcomed, it is tolerated. If a young man becomes serious about a non-Arab woman, strong pressure will probably be placed on him not to marry her. Out-marriage is desired by neither the Muslim Arab nor the Christian Arab community, but it is more strongly resisted by Muslims. Even if the outside female spouse is brought into the community, she is viewed as having taken away a potential mate for Arab women who are already restricted from outside marriages (Elkholy, 1996).

The family is usually involved to some extent in the marriage. At one extreme, family involvement can entail selection of the mate, or sending a son or daughter back to the country of origin to marry a cousin. At the other extreme, the family may permit choice and even out-marriage, especially for males. In most cases, family involvement falls between these two extremes. The family may dictate a certain degree of **endogamy**, such as marriage within the village or ethnic group, within the national group, within the religion, or to a relative. The mother is often a crucial person in selecting her daughter-in-law; this function adds to her importance in the family (Quereshi, 1991).

Variations are demonstrated in a comparison of Yemeni and Lebanese immigrant women, in which Aswad (1991) found that 75% of Yemeni had marriages arranged by their parents, while only 28% of the Lebanese did. Haddad and Lummis (1987) found that only 35% of the Muslims they surveyed across the United States disapproved of arranged marriages. On the other hand, Cainkar (1991) found that among Palestinians in Chicago, arranged marriages have all but disappeared.

Arab Americans tend to marry younger than many other Americans, although it depends on their education and their generation. The man's family initiates the marriage and is responsible for the wedding arrangements; the woman's side must wait for a proposal. The marriage is contracted and witnessed by men. Among Muslim families, a sum of money is paid by the groom's family to the family of the bride. Most of this money accrues to the bride herself. In some cases it is paid before the marriage; alternatively, a portion can be paid at the time of marriage, and the rest set aside as a trust in case of divorce. Some women's fathers may keep part of the money in order to pay for their own sons' marriages. Women retain rights to their property and inheritances after marriage; they need not give it to their husbands, although some are pressured into doing so.

Weddings take different forms among Muslims and Christians, but all are occasions for festivity and socializing. Muslims have a home ceremony in which the legal marriage is performed by a religious functionary before the family members. This is followed by a large reception with dancing, music, and gift giving. Christian weddings are performed in churches and also are followed by large receptions. The size of the reception reflects the status of the couple and their families. Among some upper-class Arabs, receptions may cost as much as $25,000.

We have discussed the double standards regarding men's and women's sexuality before marriage, and how a bad reputation may delay or narrow a girl's marriage choices. The double standard also applies after marriage. Although men are allowed some latitude in extramarital affairs, they are frowned upon, particularly if they are conducted in a manner that brings disgrace to the family.

There has been very little written about the sexual behavior of Arab immigrants in the United States. We do know that there is dating among some immigrants and members of younger generations. Generally, Arab American girls resist having sexual intercourse before marriage. The pressure to resist is so great that teenage pregnancies are a rare occurrence among unmarried girls. If a girl does become pregnant, she may be expelled from the community, pressured to have an abortion, or quickly married to the boy.

Sexuality is perceived as a private matter, and couples are discouraged from being demonstrative in public. In the home there is more liberty; however, as open displays of sexuality strain the larger family relationships, there is decidedly less tolerance for such behavior than the mainstream American family allows. The lack of privacy may also limit the degree of affection a couple can demonstrate, especially in the crowded housing conditions in which many immigrants live.

Arab Americans have varying attitudes regarding birth control. Catholic communities generally oppose it, and most Arabs, whether Christian or Muslim, favor large families. But more highly educated couples and members of younger generations undoubtedly use contraceptives, as evidenced by their smaller families. Abortion is generally discouraged in both religious groups. Haddad and Lummis (1987) found that 50% of Arab Americans feel abortion is not permissible for Muslims within the first 40 days of a pregnancy, while only 22% feel that is acceptable.

Cainkar (1996) examined Palestinian American women's evaluation of their own position compared to that of American women. She found that the vast majority of Palestinian women felt their lives were better than those of other American women. Haddad and Lummis (1987) reported that 47% of Muslim women felt they were treated as well as or better than the average American; however, among those born in the United States, only 33% expressed a similar view.

Cainkar (1991) points out that both traditional and liberal Palestinian men prefer to marry Arab women from their homelands rather than those born in the United States because they fear that Palestinian American women are "too American." This adds to the pressures restricting women's out-marriage and further depletes their pool of eligible mates. In addition, if a woman waits too long to marry, her "value" goes down. Cainkar (1991) finds that teenage Palestinian American born girls live lives of isolation and marginality.

Work Relationships and the Family

The family has been a critical economic unit for many Arab American immigrants. During the early wave of immigration, many stores were created and run by the labor of entire families (Naff, 1985). Women and children played an important role in this enterprise. Women also helped augment the family income by peddling and by working in the clothing factories of northeastern U.S. cities.

An example of an economic niche that successfully employs Arab American relatives is the Iraqi Christian Chaldeans' monopoly on "Mom and Pop" stores in the Detroit area (Sengstock, 1974). In a similar fashion, Lebanese, Palestinians, and Yemenis are beginning to dominate the gas stations in the region. Within these kin and village units, money is loaned and economic connections are developed. The Chaldeans' economic niche extends from storefronts to large wholesale activities (Sengstock, 1974). Family members are expected to work without pay, to reduce overhead. As these economic niches eventually close, members of younger generations enter other occupations.

A high percentage of Arab Americans are employed in entrepreneurial occupations. Zogby (1990), citing the U.S. census, points out that Arab Americans are more likely to be self-employed, less likely to work for the local government, and much more likely to be in managerial and professional specialty occupations than are other ethnic groups. About 24.9% are involved in the retail trade, substantially more than the 16.1% for the entire U.S. population. Many Arab American women are self-employed as dress designers, bakers, or home-based salespersons.

The unemployment rate for Arab Americans born abroad is higher than the U.S. average, but lower than the national average for U.S.-born Arab Americans (Zogby, 1990). The poverty rate for Arab Americans is higher than the national average, at 10.5% versus 9.6%. However, Arab Americans' educational level is higher than the average for the general U.S. population (Zogby, 1990). These educational levels and unemployment rates reflect the diverse socioeconomic levels of Arab American immigrants; some may have few skills (especially in terms of language), and others may be in the upper professional classes and have numerous graduate degrees.

Life-Cycle Transitions

Among Arab Americans, divorce is discouraged because it carries a stigma and casts shame on a family. However, it is more common and more nearly accepted among Yemeni populations than among Lebanese and Syrians or in Catholic communities (Aswad, 1991). When they see divorce threatening, members of the family and community usually try to intervene.

In a recent study, Aswad (1994) found that lower-class women feel that welfare provides a safety net that would help them in the event of divorce. Hogben (1991) reports a low divorce rate in the Muslim population in Canada: 2.2% for males and 3.1% for females. By contrast, Haddad and Lummis (1987) found that 54% of Arab Americans surveyed disagreed with a statement indicating that couples should live together if they are unhappy. Among the women the author interviewed who were on welfare, 16% were divorced.

Following a divorce, it is generally easier for a man to remarry than for a woman. In the United States, a divorced Arab American woman may marry out of the community, but she still risks losing the backing of the community and her ties to it. A man does not bear as great a risk, although he too may be somewhat ostracized.

Traditionally, divorce leaves the woman at a disadvantage, since the children ultimately belong to the father's family. But attitudes toward child custody are changing. According to Haddad and Lummis (1987), 45% of Arab Americans agree that women should be granted custody of their children until the children turn 18.

The divorce rate is generally low among Arab Americans because of the emphasis on family relationships and family honor. However, given the relative ease of obtaining a divorce in America, and considering that more women are securing employment, welfare, and child custody, one might expect an increase in the number of divorces initiated by women for reasons of infidelity, abuse, or poverty (Aswad, 1994). Although the divorce rate is lower for Arab-born than for U.S.-born Arab Americans, the overall figure is still low compared with that of the dominant culture (Zogby, 1990).

Single parenthood is considered abnormal by Arab Americans, unless the parent is a widow or widower. Zogby (1990) found that Arab American women born abroad had twice the incidence of widowhood (13%) as Arab American women born in the United States (6.4%). For men, the rates were considerably lower: 1.2% for Arab American men born abroad, and 1.1% for U.S.-born Arab American men (Zogby, 1990).

Girls often marry earlier than boys, posing a dilemma for young women who aspire to higher education. However, according to the 1980 U.S. census, U.S.-born Arab American women are twice as likely to be single beyond age 15 as are Arab-born women (36.2% and 17.8%, respectively). A much larger percentage of Arab American males remain single, particularly those born abroad: 42% of Arab-born men 15 and older are single. Among Arab Americans born in the United States, men and women remain single over 15 years of age at almost equal rates (40.3% for men; 36.2% for women) (Zogby, 1990).

Sengstock (1996) studies the needs of elderly Muslims. She found a disparity between the subjects' perceptions of their own needs and the perceptions of the (generally non-Arab) interviewers. This discrepancy is attributable to the dependency of the elderly on their kin groups, who ease some of the burdens experienced by older adults in the dominant culture. Naturally, if the elderly have little access to resources or do not speak English, they may indeed have certain needs, such as assistance with shopping and transportation. But in areas such as finances and medical care, elderly Arab Americans expressed less need than the interviewers felt they exhibited. In the area of mental health, however, the interviewers perceived the needs to be less than the elderly themselves did (Sengstock, 1996). Perhaps the non-Arab interviewers saw only the presence of the family and not the strains within the family.

Family Strengths and Challenges

The major strength of the Arab American family is its expansive and intensive network, and the general involvement of its members in reciprocal relationships. Ideally, members protect each other and are made to feel welcome. Although there is less alienation of the individual than often occurs in Western industrial capitalistic societies, this pattern changes when migration puts strains on families by disrupting them and separating their members. Changing gender-role expectations also put a strain on the traditional Arab American family; most women want to retain family support, but would like to see some flexibility in the patriarchal system.

Forms of familial reciprocity include the protection and indulgence of children; the planning of marriages, with an eye to the behavior and economic status of potential in-laws; and care in later years as family members age. The norms governing honorable behavior are strong, but there is also tolerance for individualism within the family. Much emphasis is placed on promoting individuals through both education and assistance in migration issues and business enterprises. Arab American family members also help each other during periods of illness, through the grieving process following a death or other catastrophe, and in other times of crisis. The intimate nature of familial relationships pulls the individual into the group, making it very difficult to abandon the group or fail to reciprocate.

Certainly these strong family ties have been vital during times of conflict and upheaval in the Middle East, which have resulted in the migration of many Arabs to the United States. Adaptation to a new environment is difficult, and those who migrate from the hot climates of the Middle East to northern countries find visiting with the family to be a major form of entertainment during long periods of indoor living.

The closeness of the family influences both the decision to emigrate and the decision about where to settle. In a survey by Aswad (1974) of an Arab primary ethnic community, the most significant factor determining residence was kin ties. Of those surveyed, 65% said they came to the region because of kin, and 41% said relatives helped them obtain their first job (Aswad, 1974). Assistance is also given to relatives abroad. Among Arab Americans in Canada, Abu-Laban (1993) reports that 50% of the foreign-born sent money to relatives, and of the Canadian-born, 22% had sent money abroad to relatives.

But customs change, and children may move away or families may be split apart through migration. Visits and telephone calls are a major source of keeping in touch, and much time and money are spent on these forms of maintaining contact. Family visits are not for just two weeks, about the norm in the dominant culture; instead, they may last a month or more.

Health problems, both physical and psychological, are also tended to by family members, who make every effort to provide needed services. Visiting is a constant source of relief for the sick and elderly. In fact, hospital staff members may complain about numerous Arab American family members crowding into hospital rooms, and tending to be noisy by mainstream American standards. And the elderly are not excluded from parties and visits; at a party, one usually sees family members ranging in age from babies to elderly. This inclusiveness reinforces a concern for and flexibility toward human nature, and promotes an understanding of the problems of family members of different generations.

Although comparative statistics are not available, domestic neglect and abuse are probably as prevalent in Arab American families as in other American homes. However, the amount of time spent in large social groups may tend to diffuse one-on-one interaction, and therefore any potential abuse. Also, neighbors often feel obligated to try to mediate disputes. The abuse of children among mainstream Americans is surprising to most Arab Americans.

Psychological problems are tolerated until they become disruptive; then several members of the family might take action. Arab Americans tend to try to "solve it in the family," rather than talk to counselors or therapists. However, there is a growing willingness among Arab Americans, especially women, to discuss family problems with Arabic-speaking family counselors (Aswad & Gray, 1996).

Although the family has provided a cushion for Arab Americans in their adjustment to life in the United States, it also presents challenges. The emphasis on community rather than individualism is a major difference from the dominant culture. Time spent in family matters leaves less time for friends or educational activities. Particularly for teenagers, this may be a problem.

If marriage within the group is planned or assisted by parents, the alternative concept of free choice in mate selection may create conflict between young people and their parents. Restrictions on dating and the insistence on female virginity before marriage are obviously in conflict with the dating patterns of mainstream America. In general, the discrepancy between individualism and parental authority is strongest among adolescents in schools where there is a strong influence of non-Arab Americans.

Other differences appear in gender roles. For example, Arab American women, influenced by the push for equality through women's movements in

America and the Middle East, are causing strain in some families. The availability of welfare for poor women who might leave difficult marriages provides an alternative to traditional patriarchal authority (Aswad, 1994).

The challenges are greatest among immigrant families who are raising their children in the United States or who migrate with pre-teenage children. As Cainkar (1991) reports, American-born teenage girls have specific problems of isolation and marginality. Lack of adjustment is greatest among those who migrate in old age, although Sengstock (1996) indicates that because of their family connections, elderly Arab American immigrants do not feel alienated. Adjustment difficulties also occur among immigrants who interact with mainstream Americans regularly in their jobs or their residences, and who live far from relatives or Arab friends.

Some families are forced to split apart because of migration. Family stress may become serious if there are political conflicts between the United States and the country of origin (Aswad, 1991). For example, during the Persian Gulf War in 1991, the Iraqi community was extremely fearful for its safety in America. Pressures placed by Zionists on Palestinians, and negative stereotypes of Islam, are other examples of how politics can cause stress and fear within Arab American families and communities.

In cases of intermarriage, problems arise if the spouse from outside the group does not join the Arab family in most of its activities. The non-Arab spouse may feel that his or her personal time is diminished by the time and energy required by family activities and obligations. And problems may arise over religion; for example, both Muslim and Catholic traditions pressure spouses to convert. Because the children are viewed as members of the man's family, there is more pressure on outsider males to convert than on outsider females. However, non-Arab women often do not understand why their children are considered more a part of their husband's family than their own; in the event of divorce, this problem becomes more acute. Marriage to women outside the group is even more threatening in the United States because custody is usually awarded to the mother, and the traditional Arab American family feels it will lose control of the children to outsiders.

In contrast, the benefits of merging two cultures or two religious traditions are substantial. Children benefit from the security of the Arab family and simultaneously gain from the more liberal structure of the American family.

Arab American families have changed—as a result of time, especially after two or three generations, and as a result of out-marriage with members of other ethnic groups. As some family members rebel or blend different cultures and create new patterns, others may be alienated from their roots, while still others introduce patterns from the Middle East. However, the strong values of extensive reciprocal family relationships remain, especially when they are revived by the continuing immigration of relatives and friends.

Misconceptions and Stereotypes

Perhaps the most common misconception about Arab American families is the nature of patrilineality. Although patrilineality may include patriarchy, it entails a wider set of duties and obligations. Patrilineal rules give older generations power over younger, and men privileges over women. Yet it is necessary to mention that women have more power than Westerners conceive. Their power lies within their patrilineage, in their roles as mothers and sisters, and in their ability to influence relationships. It also lies in their potential to disrupt the social system by noncompliance with patriarchy. Patriarchy is not confined to homes that are patrilineal. Many Americans do not understand why men may take their children from their wives; but when one understands that the individual eventually belongs to his father's line, the practice is better understood as a cultural custom, not a mean-spirited characteristic of Arab males.

Arab Americans grow up, live, and work in a society of primary group relationships. In general, they prefer being and working in groups, rather than independently (Barakat, 1993). By contrast, the mainstream American norm, which encourages independence and individual initiative, may be considered as aloofness and selfishness to Arab Americans. Arabs are often friendly and hospitable to outsiders they trust or with whom they want to make contact, welcoming them into groups and families to share food and conversation. If these overtures are not reciprocated, they do not understand. On the other hand, if Arabs do not trust another group, they often appear reserved and especially may restrict contact with the women in their families.

The customs of having a big family, of expressing loyalty to the group rather than to the individual, and of promoting solidarity and friendship among relatives may be perceived as strange or even alienating by mainstream Americans. Arab Americans may seem aggressive and boisterous in their exclusive groups. Many Americans from diminished families have difficulty understanding how Arabs can have so much fun with their relatives. But sometimes Americans idealize the group spirit and minimize the fact that there can be conflicts and problems with dominance, control, and abuse among Arab American family members.

Language is often a barrier between members of different cultures. For example, in a store, non-Arab customers may feel they are being discussed by the Arab-speaking owners, when in fact the owners are just discussing business.

The depth of ethnic pride in Arab culture is sometimes underestimated by Americans. Although they appear to be assimilating, Arab Americans still maintain their roots and traditions.

Personal Interview

Mrs. Hassan is a 72-year-old Lebanese Muslim widow who came to the United States at the age of 2. She married a Palestinian Muslim who owned a small clothing shop. She has two sons and now lives in a retirement center in Michigan. Her story tells of the life of her immigrant parents, her own life, and her children's lives. Generational differences, and her own occasionally divided sentiments, are apparent in her responses.

What do you remember about your early childhood here?

Mrs. H.: My father, who was a peasant, came from Lebanon about 1910 at age 15 with his cousin who was 13. They went to West Virginia to join his brother and sold linens and tapestries to men who worked in the coal mines. He served in World War I, then went to Lebanon, where he built a house and got married to my mother, a first cousin who was trying to manage her family's property because her brothers had gone to America. But conditions were very hard in Lebanon, and he came back via Cuba, where he had another brother. It was a hard choice, he used to say, but they were poor. He would say that when people ate oranges in Lebanon, they said, "Don't let the peel hit the ground because someone can survive on it." Now I know how the Palestinians feel. He later worked for his mother's brother. The Lebanese Christians were not as restricted as we were; they were very Americanized and well-off financially. There were no Muslim mosques, and we went to Baptist churches for our spirituality.

Then we heard of Detroit and wanted to be near an Arab community. Virginia was a beautiful area with mountains more like Lebanon, but there were few Arabs there, and Southerners aren't really friendly to foreigners, Jews, or Blacks. When we got to Dearborn, it was like a privilege to be a foreigner. People ate Arabic food, spoke Arabic, and there was a mosque. I later joined the clubs there, and my father worked hard for the mosque. I lived there 42 years, and all my relatives lived close by. It was primarily an Italian and Polish Catholic community with a few Arabs, but we felt welcome. Now the community is almost all Arab.

How was it growing up as an Arab girl?

Mrs. H.: It is different today. A girl of 5 might as well have been a woman then. My mother put the dishpan on the chair, and I washed the dishes. My Dad was definitely the boss. My mother would say, "Don't you know, God is first and your husband second." He disciplined us with a belt. Now they would call it abuse. But today there are too many problems. Once my father beat me when I was 30. Kids wouldn't have the problems they have today if their fathers were more strict. He didn't hit my mother though, and I don't know any wife who is beaten, but there probably are some. I had two sisters and a brother. [My brother] was spoiled, and even though he was 3 years younger than me, he could boss me around. He told me how to act. Girls always have it harder. Although I would have loved to have a girl, I am glad I had boys—they are easier. It is hard to be a girl. Men have it better when they are young, in the middle years, and when they are older.

How have things changed over the last generation in the area you live in?

Mrs. H.: In the 1950s and 1960s, Arab boys and girls here could date, and not just in groups. The boys may have started dating American girls, but then the girls followed suit, dating Arabs and sometimes non-Arabs. Their parents trusted them and wanted them to marry Arabs. They didn't get pregnant. None wore scarves, and many girls wore shorts; my sister still does at 60 years of age. Now with the immigrants from the Middle East, there is much less going out by the girls. Also, there was more marriage to non-Arabs before; there were not as many Muslims here as there are now. The community is more strict and the girls, often at a very early age, are covered up. I saw a Yemeni girl of 5 almost totally covered except her face. She said she wanted it that way like her sisters. My mother's brother said that now you are in America, you don't cover up, and that was over 70 years ago. But why should Arabs be criticized when Indians also cover up and they are not criticized? But sometimes I see the young people feeling guilty that they don't know Arabic in the mosques. I don't like them to feel bad.

Should marriages be arranged? Was yours, and did you arrange your sons' marriages?

Mrs. H.: My husband was 20 years older than I was, and it was arranged by the Imam [religious leader]. My sons went to college and married non-Arabs. What could I say? They said, "What if you like her and I don't?" At first I was disappointed, but they have nice wives and children, are successful financially, and now I've changed my thinking about culture, about what is good and bad. It bothered me that they left Islam and the community, especially when I see a group of young Arab men together. But my kids live in a culture different than that of their parents. We don't live in Lebanon, we live here. They are yuppies. One of my sons is a Baptist and the other doesn't go to any religious center. That bothers me. He worries a lot about his daughter—her shorts and her dating. As for arranged marriages generally, I still think parents know better who their children should marry than their 19-year-old children.

What about divorce?

Mrs. H.: Now there is more of it everywhere. It is increasing, even in Arab culture. Some may get on welfare; if the money wasn't there, they might not get divorced.

Did you feel discriminated against as an Arab?

Mrs. H.: I did sometimes. When sports teams played our school, they would say we need to have the police there. One hears "Arab lovers" or nowadays "ragheads." Our kids gave them bad names back. Nationally I am a Democrat, but feel the Zionists have a lot of power in Washington. The Jewish people are wonderful people, very generous and socially conscious, but it's overdone on Israel.

Do you like living in a retirement apartment?

Mrs. H.: Very much, I like my independence. I volunteer in the mornings at the Arab community center and keep busy, but my time is my own.

Questions for Discussion

1. What are some stereotypes about the Arab American family? What is their basis, and what is the reality? How do people of Arab background perceive the American nuclear family? Why?

2. How does the principle of patrilineality affect social roles in the Arab American family? Name people who would be in your patriline (like your father's brother) to see if you understand the model. How does this compare to the American Indian family, the Mexican American family, and the Chinese American family?

3. Discuss the cultural and economic conditions of the different periods of Arab American migration. How do the conditions, region, and period of entrance affect their experience in America?

4. What is similar about the immigration experiences of Arab Americans and Asian Indian Americans? How has this shaped their experience in the United States?

5. How do different conditions such as occupation, language, religion, and life cycle affect Arab American family adjustment in the United States?

6. What is the effect of American politics in the Middle East on Arab Americans—the family, marriages, and the community?

7. Compare the role of religion in the Arab American family to that in the Mormon and Cuban American families. How are they similar and different?

8. Arranged marriages are common in many of the ethnic groups discussed in this book. What are the advantages of an arranged marriage? What are the disadvantages? How does the system of arranged marriage compare with your system of dating?

Suggested Resources

Readings

Abu-Jaber, D. (1993). *Arabian jazz*. New York: Harcourt Brace.

Aswad, B. C., & Bilge, B. (1996). eds. *Family and gender among American Muslims: Issues facing Middle Eastern immigrants and their descendants*. Philadelphia: Temple University Press.

Haddad, Y. Y., & Lummis, A. (1987). *Islamic values in the United States*. New York: Oxford.

Harik, I. (1987). *The Lebanese in America*. Minneapolis, MN: Lerner.

Kadi, J. (1994). *Food for our grandmothers: Writings by Arab-American and Arab-Canadian feminists*. Boston: Southend Press.

Videos

ACCESS and Olive Branch Productions (Producers), & Mandell, J. (Director). (1995). *Tales from Arab Detroit*. (Available from ACCESS, 2651 Saulino Court, Dearborn, MI 48120)

Miller, L. (Producer), & Wilson, D. (Director). (1992). *Islam in America*. (Available from Christian Science Monitor, 1 Norway Street, Boston, MA 02115)

Schlessinger, A. (Producer), & Fabrav, R., & Baker, J. (Directors). (1993). *Arab Americans*. (Available from Schlessinger Video, P.O. Box 1110, Balacynwyd, PA 19004)

References

Abraham, S., & Abraham, N. (Eds.). (1983). *Arabs in the New World: Studies on Arab-American communities*. Detroit: Wayne State University, Center for Urban Studies.

Abu-Laban, B. (1993). *An olive branch on the family tree: The Arabs in Canada*. Toronto: McClelland & Stewart.

Aswad, B. (Ed.). (1974). *Arabic-speaking communities in American cities*. New York: Center for Migration Studies.

Aswad, B. (1991). Yemeni and Lebanese Muslim immigrant women in southeast Dearborn, Michigan. In E. Waugh, S. McIrvin Abu-Laban, & R. Qurashi (Eds.), *Muslim families in North America* (pp. 256–281). Alberta, Canada: University of Alberta Press.

Aswad, B. (1993). Arab Americans: Those who followed Columbus. *Middle East Studies Association Bulletin, 27*, 1.

Aswad, B. (1994). Attitudes of immigrant women and men in the Dearborn area toward women's employment and welfare. In Y. Haddad & J. Smith (Eds.), *Muslim communities in North America* (pp. 501–520). Albany: State University of New York Press.

Aswad, B., & Bilge, B. (Eds.). (1996). *Family and gender among American Muslims: Issues facing Middle Eastern immigrants and their descendants*. Philadelphia: Temple University Press.

Aswad, B., & Gray, N. (1996). Challenges to the Arab American family and ACCESS, a local community center. In B. Aswad & B. Bilge (Eds.), *Family and gender among American Muslims: Issues facing Middle Eastern immigrants and their descendants* (pp. 223–240). Philadelphia: Temple University Press.

Ba-Yunis, I. (1991). Muslims in North America: Mate selection as an indicator of change. In E. Waugh, S. McIrvin Abu-Laban, & R. Qurashi (Eds.), *Muslim families in North America* (pp. 232–249). Alberta, Canada: University of Alberta Press.

Cainkar, L. (1991). Palestinian-American Muslim women: Living on the margins of two worlds. In E. Waugh, S. McIrvin Abu-Laban, & R. Qurashi (Eds.), *Muslim families in North America* (pp. 282–308). Alberta, Canada: University of Alberta Press.

Cainkar, L. (1996). Immigrant Palestinian women evaluate their lives. In B. Aswad & B. Bilge (Eds.), *Family and gender among American Muslims: Issues facing Middle Eastern immigrants and their descendants* (pp. 41–58). Philadelphia: Temple University Press.

Elkholy, A. (1988). The Arab American family. In C. Mindel, R. Haberstein, & R. Wright (Eds.), *Ethnic families in America. Patterns and variations* (pp. 438–455). New York: Elsevier.

Elkholy, A. (1996). *The Arab Moslems in the United States*. New Haven, CT: College and University Press.

Haddad, Y., & Lummis, A. (1987). *Islamic values in the United States*. New York: Oxford University Press.

Hogben, W. (1991). Marriage and divorce among Muslims in Canada. In E. Waugh, S. McIrvin Abu-Laban, & R. Qurashi (Eds.), *Muslim families in North America* (pp. 154–184). Alberta, Canada: University of Alberta Press.

Naff, A. (1985). *Becoming American: The early Arab immigrant experience*. Carbondale: Southern Illinois University Press.

Quereshi, R. (1991). Marriage strategies among Muslims from South Asia. In E. Waugh, S. McIrvin Abu-Laban, & R. Qurashi (Eds.), *Muslim families in North America* (pp. 185–212). Alberta, Canada: University of Alberta Press.

Saba, L., & Swan, C. (1974). The migration of a minority. In B. Aswad (Ed.), *Arabic speaking communities in American cities* (pp. 85–110). New York: Center for Migration Studies.

Sengstock, M. (1974). Iraqi Christians in Detroit: An analysis of an ethnic occupation. In B. Aswad (Ed.), *Arabic speaking communities in American cities* (pp. 21–38). New York: Center for Migration Studies.

Sengstock, M. (1996). Care of the elderly among Muslim families. In B. Aswad & B. Bilge (Eds.), *Family and gender among American Muslims: Issues facing Middle Eastern immigrants and their descendants* (pp. 271–297). Philadelphia: Temple University Press.

Shaheen, J. (1984). *The TV Arab*. Bowling Green, OH: Bowling Green State University Popular Press.

Suleiman, M. (1988). *The Arabs in the mind of America*. Brattleboro, VT: Amana Press.

U.S. Bureau of the Census. (1990). *Statistical abstract of the United States, 1990*. Washington, DC: U.S. Government Printing Office.

Zogby, J. (1990). *Arab Americans: A demographic profile of Arab Americans*. Washington, DC: Arab American Institute.

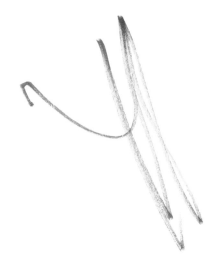

12

Hamilton I. McCubbin

Laurie D. McCubbin

Hawaiian American Families

Historical and Cultural Background

The Native or Aboriginal Hawaiian American family is best understood when placed in a historical context. Embedded in the history of the Hawaiian Islands are values, beliefs, and practices that help define and characterize the Native Hawaiian family today. People first came to the Hawaiian Islands around A.D. 700. Coming in search of land and a new home, they brought with them pigs, dogs, fowl, and various plants such as the taro and coconut. These people were called Polynesians by the early European explorers, meaning "people of the many islands." They were also called by the Hawaiians the *Ka poe kahiko*, meaning "people of the past," the Polynesian ancestors of the Hawaiian people. These early travelers gave Hawaiians the foundation of their culture and their religion.

According to folklore, Hawaiians descended from *Papahanaumoku*, Earth Mother, and *Wakea*, Sky Father. Hawaiian **genealogy** is from the land; therefore, their relationship to the land is familial—they are children of Mother Earth. To Hawaiians, nature, family, and spirituality are interdependent and interconnected (Marsella, Oliveira, Plummer, & Crabbe, 1995; Trask, 1993, 1995). One is united with natural and spiritual forces of the world. The spiritual essence of this unity is *mana*. **Mana** is the spiritual force and power shared by all living things. This quality was embodied by the chiefs, or *ali'i*, who were the representatives of the gods and ruled the land. A leader knew and understood the link between Hawaiians and the land. The *ali'i* maintained the *pono*, the balance between people, land, and the cosmos with *mana*.

The overarching value system of the Hawaiian family, the *'ohana*, is based on *aloha, kokua,* and *aloha aina*. **Aloha** is affection ranging from extending a greeting to a new person to embracing a loved one. **Kokua**, which means help or aid, is the foundation of Hawaiian civilization. It is aid given freely, without any thought of reward or an expectation of the return of the favor. ***Aloha aina*** is the value of ensuring the preservation of the balance between life, land, and sea.

The evidence of these relational dynamics between the family and the land, agriculture and the community, focuses on the *taro* plant; "the food plant that was the Hawaiian staple of life." This is implicit in the use of the terms *aina* and *'ohana*. *Ai* may designate food or eating in general, but specifically refers to the paste termed *poi* made from the corm (the starch filled base of the taro). The Hawaiian diet was built around *poi*. Now the *taro* differs from all other food plants in Hawaii in propagating itself by means of *oha* or sprouts from the sides or base of the main corm. This base is often termed *makua*, meaning parent or father. To expand his *taro* patch, the *taro* planter literally breaks off and transplants the *oha*. As the *oha* or sprouts from the parent *taro* or *makua* serve to propagate the *taro* and produce the staple of life, *oiai* on the land (*aina*) cultivated through generations by a given family, so the family or *'ohana* is identified physically and psychically with the home-land (*aina*) whose soil has produced the staple of life (*ai*, food made from *taro*) that nourishes the dispersed family (*'oha-na*).

The Hawaiians' initial contact with the Western world was on January 18, 1778, when Captain James Cook, a British sea captain, arrived at the Hawaiian Islands with his crew and two ships. At first the Hawaiians thought Captain Cook was *Lono*, the God of Agriculture, and he was given a grand *aloha* welcome with gifts and offerings. But within a year it became clear that he and his crew were beginning to use up the islands' resources without replenishing them. The crew members were having sexual relationships with the native women, which caused the chiefs to establish a *kapu*, a taboo or law, to keep the women from visiting the ships. The foreigners' presence began to be an imposition, and conflicts between the cultures began to arise. One of these conflicts led to the death of Captain Cook on February 14, 1779.

More foreigners visited Hawaii to see the islands and their abundant resources. In response, a leader emerged to help form a Hawaiian nation and protect the Hawaiian culture. This ruler was King Kamehameha the Great—a warrior who represented *mana* and all its power. He unified the eight Hawaiian Islands and brought peace. During the period of his rule, 1796–1819, Hawaii evolved into a nation that established relationships with foreigners and implemented foreign trade. He also formed a monarchy with his son, Kamehameha II, as the heir to the throne. The monarchy he established was to keep Hawaii a separate nation despite foreign economic and cultural influences.

Other kings followed in his footsteps and took measures to help and protect Hawaiians from the ways of the Western world. The Hawaiian economy was based on the value *kokua*, generosity and giving without expectation within the *'ohana*. Members of the *'ohana*, or extended family, worked together to support one another. To the old Hawaiians, family included not only the father, mother, and children, but also relatives by blood, marriage, and adoption. Members of the *'ohana* were grandparents, aunties, uncles, cousins, and sisters and brothers of aunties and uncles. The *'ohana* was the basic foundation for survival on the Hawaiian Islands.

The Hawaiian monarchy tried to help the Hawaiians maintain their way of life and still keep positive international relations. However, many White men— **haoles** as they are currently referred to—held positions in the Hawaiian government and wanted to see the Hawaiians adapt to the new Western culture. Missionaries came over to convert the sinful, heathen Hawaiians to Christianity. They changed the Native Hawaiian dress to more modest clothing. The White men and their Western culture began to crush the Hawaiian traditions of religion and government. Oppression and colonization describe the plight of the Hawaiian people.

By the reign of King Kamehameha III (1824–1854), Hawaii was caught between two cultures. During this period, Western customs took over. The traditional value system of *aloha aina* was weakening under the pressure for private land ownership. King Kamehameha III gave in to the *haole* advisors and formed the Great *Mahele*, the division of the lands. With this act, the land was no longer distributed by *aloha aina* but by private land ownership and title. The Hawaiian value system was not congruent with this type of land holding. Originally the land was divided in three ways: one to the king or the crown, another to the chiefs, and the third part to the commoners. However, by 1850, non-Hawaiians were able to purchase property, and the communal, *kokua*-style government and its economy came to an end. By 1888, 75% of all arable land was controlled by the *haoles*. Individual ownership and capitalism prevailed, and the *haoles* began to form their Western-style economy and government in order to support their monetary goals. The land was no longer governed by *aloha aina* or the Hawaiian people; the basic roots of the Hawaiian people and their culture were now part of history.

At the time of Captain Cook, it is estimated that there were 300,000 Native Hawaiians on the islands; by 1876, the population had declined to 3900 Native Hawaiians. Within 100 years after the first contact with the Western world, the Native Hawaiian population declined by 90%. High mortality rates resulted from diseases introduced by foreigners, to which the native population had no immunity. Tuberculosis, syphilis, gonorrhea, smallpox, and other diseases brought both death and infertility to the Native Hawaiians. Disease, poverty, and the diminishing existence of the traditional culture took their toll.

Colonization, Statehood, and Cultural Renewal

Like Native American Indians, Aboriginal Hawaiians are not immigrants to the United States but are indigenous to the land. Hawaii and its people were recognized by the United States and the world as a sovereign nation. Hawaii has internationally recognized treaties with a number of powers, including France, England, and the United States. The Native Hawaiians never surrendered their political rights through treaties, nor did they vote for annexation. They are considered a "non-self-governing people" by the United Nations. Hawaiians are different from other immigrants on the islands, such as Asians, because those other parties voluntarily gave up the nationality of their homelands. The Aboriginal Hawaiians were forcibly changed within their own homeland.

In 1893, Queen Lili'uokalani, the last queen of the Hawaiian monarchy, attempted to return Hawaii to the Hawaiian people by writing a new Constitution. On January 17, 1893, Queen Lili'uokalani and the Hawaiian monarchy were overthrown by American businessmen and government officials. She was later tried and convicted for treason. They confiscated her lands and imprisoned her in her own palace. It was in that place that she wrote the song "*Aloha Oe*, Farewell to Thee." The Hawaiian flag was taken down and the American flag raised—the ultimate symbol of triumph and domination of Western culture, and the final defeat of the Hawaiian monarchy. On July 7, 1898, President McKinley signed the annexation resolution, and Hawaii became a territory of the United States without a vote from the Native Hawaiian population. Hawaii became the 50th state in 1959, signifying the end of the Hawaiian nation. But it did not signify the end of the Hawaiian family or culture—nor were the Hawaiian spirit and identity extinguished.

The 1970s brought a revival of the Hawaiian culture. By examining their own cultural heritage, Hawaiians began a renewed interest in and commitment to their traditional language, music, dance, arts, and crafts. The Hawaiian population looked deeper into their own culture, their religion, and their ancestors' way of life. Beyond the *hulas* (dances) and the *ali'i* (chiefs) ornamentation at the hotels of Waikiki, the native population returned to the sacred sites of the old Hawaiians and the chants that preserved the legends of the Hawaiian people.

Groups were organized to represent Hawaiian interests, such as ALOHA, Aboriginal Lands of Hawaiian Ancestry, and the pro-sovereignty organization PKO, Protect Koho'olawe' 'Ohana. In 1978 the state Office of Hawaiian Affairs (OHA) was created, run by and for Hawaiians. The OHA manages Hawaiian assets, including the 1.8 million acres of the nation's crown and government lands that were taken illegally from the monarchy in 1898. Programs and services the OHA provides to the native population include education, economic development, planning, grants, research, and housing. These organizations are committed to returning the land to the Native Hawaiians. Hopefully once again the land will prosper under *aloha aina*, and *pono* (balance) will be maintained. In 1993, Congress passed a resolution apologizing for the overthrow of the monarchy, with President Clinton's signature.

On September 11, 1996, Hawaiians voted on their sovereignty: Of the 30,423 eligible voters, 26.72% (8129) voted no and 73.28% (22,294) voted yes. In a press release, Lulani McKenzie, Executive Director of the Hawaiian Sovereignty Elections Council, announced:

> This is a victory for Hawaiians: 73.28% of those who voted want to move forward and elect delegates to a convention. Today, 103 years, 7 months, and 24 days after the overthrow of the Hawaiian monarchy, we are at the Dawn of a New Age. It is time for our people to stand together, join hands, and put our differences aside. As we move toward the year 2000, Hawaiians have the opportunity to make significant changes. This is our time in history. The path to rebuilding a sovereign Hawaiian Nation is before us; the opportunity to uplift our people and improve all of their lives appears clearer.

Traditional and Emerging Family Systems

Native Hawaiian families are best viewed in a historical context; from this perspective, we can more fully appreciate and understand the meaning of the contemporary family as one bridging with its past. Like all Polynesians, Native Hawaiians adopted the existence of a superhuman force they refer to as *mana*. As mentioned at the beginning of the chapter, *mana* represents the primordial force in the universe that animates or gives life to all things. In this context, the Native Hawaiians believed in *polytheism*, the worship of many gods in the universe. Because they were accepting of different gods, they were also tolerant of other religions. They were able to take different strains of religious thought from other sources and blend them with their own. Implicit in valuing tolerance was the willingness to allow others to "do their own thing"—to be free. Tolerance and freedom are two important values that Hawaiian families can trace to their religion.

Given the centrality of religious and spiritual beliefs to Native Hawaiians, a principle emerges in the context of family life: Hawaiians believe that their gods and the well-being of the family, and Hawaiians in general, are interdependent; for better or worse, they need each other. The family is not a slave to God; rather, it represents a symbiotic relationship, in which both parties mutually benefit from living and working together. Underlying this relationship are two principles at the heart of the Hawaiian value system: reciprocity and the mastery of one's destiny. Reciprocity is like a gigantic spider web, whose threads represent the mutual obligations that each member of society bears toward others. As long as each person fulfills his or her responsibilities, the web holds together in beautiful symmetry.

While Native Hawaiians and their families share both geographic and cultural distinctions, the contemporary Native Hawaiian family must make an informed choice about which ethnic identity it will embrace for guiding their lives and particularly for raising their children. Evidence from research indicates that a strong identification with one's Native Hawaiian ancestry is prevalent even in families where the actual Native Hawaiian blood percentage is minimal (McCubbin, McCubbin, Thompson, & Thompson, 1995). The critical defining characteristics that distinguish a Native Hawaiian are traceable blood of Hawaiian ethnic ancestry, and personal and public affirmations of such identification.

The family must decide to be an identifiable member of the Native Hawaiian community. With this perspective in mind, the Native Hawaiian family will be portrayed as a distinct ethnic group with shared values and beliefs rooted in its rich Polynesian history.

Relatively few pure Native Hawaiians remain, and most of them have only a small percentage of Hawaiian blood to trace back to—a situation created by marriages across ethnic groups. It is appropriate to characterize the people and families in the Hawaiian Islands as a "melting pot," a mixture of families of different ethnicities. Yet portraying Native Hawaiian families as a "diluted" or "mixed-race" ethnic group would not be accurate.

There is another group of Native Hawaiian American families. Aboriginal Native Hawaiians, including those with a small percentage of Hawaiian blood, have an ethnic identity that is clearly defined and embraced, and reflective of the Polynesians who established their home in the Hawaiian Islands sometime between A.D. 500 and 800. The first to see, to settle in, and to thrive in the islands, these Native Hawaiians developed a stable culture and lifestyle that flourished until 1778. An alternative portrayal of Native Hawaiian families emphasizes the rich history and cultural heritage of this aboriginal Polynesian group, and points to the importance of ethnic identity and beliefs as defining factors in describing and studying this unique group of Native Americans.

In general, Polynesian family systems, including Native Hawaiian family systems, are very different from the nuclear family systems typical of European American societies. Three key features distinguish Polynesian families:

1. Multiple caretaking or parenting.

2. Sharing the care of children within the extended family through adoption or foster care.

3. Early indulgence of infants, followed by distinct and rapid initiation into a system of sibling caretaking.

From an ethnic perspective, modern Hawaiian American families are a very heterogeneous group. Cross-cultural marriages, a continuous influx of visitors and immigrants, and children born to parents of diverse ethnic backgrounds have all transformed the identity of Native Hawaiians. While their ancestors were unified politically, religiously, socially, and culturally, contemporary Native Hawaiian families are highly differentiated in religion, education, occupation, politics—and even in their claims to Hawaiian identity. Notable Hawaiian scholars have predicted that there would be few commonalities to bind Native Hawaiians together; in 1982, they were as diverse in their individual and collective character as any other ethnic population in the United States. The next century will witness historic and deep commitment on the part of Native Hawaiians to revive the ancient Hawaiian language, traditional music, and dance, along with a national movement for the Native Hawaiians to lay claim to their heritage, land, and right to self-determination. The next two decades will establish a new future for the Native Hawaiian family.

Household Size and Composition

When estimating the number of Native Hawaiian households, particularly in the state of Hawaii, we must consider the different results of various data sources. For example, U.S. census data are based on the ethnic self-identification of the respondents (U.S. Bureau of the Census, 1990). The census reveals that Native Hawaiians and part-Hawaiians constitute 12.5% of the population in Hawaii. According to the census, the largest population is Caucasians (33.4%), followed by Japanese (22.3%), Filipinos (15.2%), Chinese (6.2%), and all others (10.4%).

In contrast, if we estimate the number of Native American Hawaiian households on the basis of health surveillance sampling, we have different results (Hawaii State Department of Health, 1992). In this survey, the ethnicity of the respondent is based on the ancestry of the parents. The estimates place the Hawaiian and Native Hawaiian population at 18.8%, or 6.3% larger than the 1990 U.S. census. From these data, Caucasians still represent the largest population, but only at 24.1% (versus 33.4% according to the census). Next largest are all others (20.6%), followed by Japanese (20.4%), Filipinos (11.4%), and Chinese (4.7%).

To project the size of future Native Hawaiian populations, we can use the age distributions from the 1990 census. Individuals 18 years of age and younger constituted nearly half (42%) of the Native Hawaiian population. This age group comprises only 10–20% of those in the other major ethnic groups. The number of Native Hawaiians of childbearing years is increasing. With nearly half the Native Hawaiians in this young age group, we can estimate an increase in the number and percentage of Native Hawaiian families in the future.

The name Native Hawaiian refers to both pure-Hawaiian and part-Hawaiian individuals and family systems. Against the backdrop of the fact that in 1778 the population of pure Native Hawaiians was 300,000 and that in 1878, one century later, the population declined to 57,985 (a decline of nearly 80%), we have witnessed a dramatic increase in the number of people of Native Hawaiian heritage, predictably of part-Hawaiian ancestry. Understandably, pure Hawaiians are small in number; only about 8000 full-blooded Hawaiian descendants remain. In 1990, the number of Hawaiians (pure and part Hawaiians combined) reached a high of 211,014 (Office of Hawaiian Affairs, 1994).

In spite of these historic cataclysmic changes, accompanied by increased diversity in religion, social ties, education, politics, occupations, and economics, it would be erroneous to imply that the Hawaiians have little or no familiarity with their ancient culture. Although contemporary Native Hawaiian families may be somewhat heterogeneous and amorphous, the current resurgence of claiming Hawaiian identity and values presents an emerging profile of families who are far more rooted in their history and traditional culture than was the case 5–10 years ago.

Within the *'ohana*, the functional unit is the household. Family members who are not kin by blood or adoption are called *ohua* (signifying passengers on a canoe or ship exclusive of crew). Through the head of the household, the *ohua* integrates with the *'ohana*. The household includes members of the family proper of all ages, plus unrelated dependents and helpers. The *to'o*, or functional head of the household, was not then and is not now necessarily the senior member; it was and is specifically the member who assumes responsibility and makes the decisions.

The average household size for Native Hawaiians (3.7 people for owner-occupied and 3.1 for renter-occupied) is larger than all other ethnic groups except for Filipinos (4.3 for owner-occupied and 3.3 for renter-occupied) (Office of Hawaiian Affairs, 1994). Children account for the higher average household size in both Native Hawaiian and Filipino households. Native Hawaiian families are overrepresented in households with 4, 5, 6, and 7 or more people; over half live in owner-occupied and renter-occupied units housing 4 or more individuals. Native Hawaiian families are also overrepresented in:

▲ Married couple families with their own children under 18 years.

▲ Groups of families with female-headed households.

▲ Female-headed households with their own children under 18 years.

▲ Households on public assistance.

▲ Households with no telephone.

▲ Owner-occupied housing units below the poverty level.

The Socialization of Children

Contemporary Hawaiian Americans measure accomplishments by the efficient and effective use of time. In the traditional Hawaiian family, however, time had a different meaning. Most important was what a family member or the *'ohana* (the whole family) was doing, not when a task was started or how much time it took to finish, or how much total time was invested in the task; the task or event itself was the important matter. Life was not measured in hours, minutes, days, or years, but in terms of *'ohana* activities, individual experiences, in memorable and climactic events.

This concept of family time brings into focus the importance of quality time with children within the Hawaiian family. Because the experience and the event are what matters most, Hawaiian families emphasize the value of children and the family-related activities in which they participate; these are considered to be life-affirming experiences. This is the real meaning of time for the Hawaiians—the degree to which they can shape its quality.

The Hawaiian family acknowledges the belief that the mind and body, along with nature, influence the perception of time. Pleasurable and enjoyable events, if they are experienced and affirmed, are accompanied by a quickening in time. Boring, sensory, bland experiences tend to create the feeling of delayed time. In Hawaii, for example, the warm weather creates a lethargic feeling and the perception of a slowing of the pace of time, in contrast to family experiences and behaviors in the context of the invigorating gusty trade winds. Even today, it is not uncommon to note the family's belief that the pace of time is determined and shaped by the quality of the experience. Parenting and investing in children are less an issue of time management and more a matter of commitment to invest in the development and shaping of quality and meaningful experiences for the next generation.

Hawaiian families are often criticized for socializing children to be laid back, happy-go-lucky, and carefree, and not to plan for tomorrow—a lifestyle that the dominant culture believes makes Hawaiians and their families less competitive and able to respond to the demands of modern life. This stereotype is also a natural outgrowth of the traditional value that Hawaiians place on the use of time. As already noted, the Hawaiian family underscores the importance of present experiences in order to ensure quality parenting and child raising.

Contrary to stereotypes, this investment in the present supports the Hawaiian family's planning for the future. The primacy of today is based on a sensible future expectancy, not on the belief that there must be immediate satisfaction because tomorrow will never come. In fact, in traditional Hawaiian culture, there was little tolerance for carefree, happy-go-lucky family members who did not hold up their responsibilities to the 'ohana and the community.

It is interesting to speculate on how resiliency in children is cultivated and nurtured (Werner & Smith, 1989, 1992). Following this line of reasoning, we can focus on family attributes that help foster a child's ability to recover from and move past adversity (Thompson, McCubbin, Thompson, & Elver, 1995). Families, and particularly parents, who take the time to observe, identify, and affirm even the most minute of their children's capabilities and strengths increase the child's potential for developing personal abilities and resiliencies. By taking the time to engage with their children, to nurture their behaviors and feelings, parents and adults in parenting roles increase the child's self-worth, confidence, and belief in future possibilities—what scholars have called a child's islands of competence. The Native Hawaiian family's focus on the present, and their commitment to understanding children and their behaviors, have great potential for promoting resiliency in their offspring.

A contradiction to this child-focused view of time and parenting is sibling-focused child care, which characterizes the Native Hawaiian family. While both parenting and sibling child care may obviously coexist, the long-term consequences of this parenting strategy have yet to be determined.

Prolonged contact between two cultures will inevitably result in some changes for at least one of the cultures, and usually the process involves some degree of alteration in both cultures. In the case of Hawaiians, much of the Hawaiian culture has been lost in the process of **acculturation**. The Hawaiian culture was systematically suppressed, and some argue that this was the result of a conscious colonization process. The history of the Hawaiian people shows the unjust abrogation of their lawfully constituted government, the unlawful seizure of ancestral lands without compensation, the stripping away of their sovereignty, and the imposition of a more dominant Western culture. A sad feeling of hopelessness and powerlessness followed, and the demoralization and disintegration of Native Hawaiians and their families is clearly demonstrated by today's social, economic, health, and educational statistics.

The rapid loss of their culture is considered a significant factor in individual and family stress. According to Marsella (1979), there are seven areas in which Hawaiians experience stress at both individual and family levels: conflicting values; social change (urbanization and modernization); acculturation;

life events (divorce, joblessness, etc.); goal striving (overly high aspirations); role/status discrimination; and role conflict. Interestingly, these stressors appear to take their toll on children at about the sixth grade, the year prior to junior high school, when they begin to express doubt about their abilities, particularly their academic skills.

The connection between culture loss and children revolves around the issue of child-rearing practices. Howard (1974) found that Hawaiians who scored low on cultural knowledge also tended to score lower on measures of self-esteem and on the effectiveness of their coping strategies. Other indices of "Hawaiianness" (e.g., percentage of Hawaiian ancestry, ethnicity as defined by spouse, and cultural self-identity) cultivated in the family environment show a positive relationship between self-esteem and social competence. Knowledge of, and pride in, ethnic heritage is an important if not critical element for the development of social competence among contemporary Hawaiians.

Intimate Relationships

The Hawaiian language reflects the importance of social and interpersonal relationships extending far beyond the immediate biological family. For example, the term *kupuna* signifies grandparents and the relatives of the grandparents' generation, as well as forebears and related folk who have died, or distant forebears in genealogy or legend. Husband and wife are designated simply by the words *kane* and *wahine*, meaning male and female. In this context, the family is considered to consist not only of its living members, but also its forebears.

Intimacy for Hawaiians is not given special consideration or treatment because the concept and practice of communicating love, affection, and caring are very much an open part of the *'ohana* way of life. Not only is intimacy communicated openly and demonstrably, it is fostered as a family value, underscoring the importance of sharing, commitment, and the value of touch. Hawaiians physically embrace others, even casual or new acquaintances, characterizing their openness in accepting others into the community or the *'ohana*. This is part of the spirit of *aloha* (love and caring), *lokahi* (togetherness and belonging), and *kokua* (working together).

The courtship process follows Western norms and expectations; relationships are shaped by love and affection, accompanied by a commitment. Parental permission for marriage is the norm, but there are no absolute rules of parental control over mate selection. In the Hawaiian culture, it is the quality of the relationship that prevails throughout the courtship and marriage process. Men and women are both free, but women are expected to be pure. Infidelity or the lack of sexual restraint are frowned upon for women.

The open and accepting nature of Hawaiians to people of different ethnicities increases the probability of interracial marriages (Adams, 1937). With the rapid decline in the number of pure Hawaiians, the prospect of marriage within the group also declines, adding to an increase in cross-cultural unions.

Work Relationships and the Family

Work and family life in contemporary Hawaii remains linked to the past. Between households within the *'ohana*, there was constant sharing and exchanging of food, utilitarian articles, and services. *'Ohana* living in one community raising taro, for example, would take a gift to some *'ohana* living near the shore, and in return would receive fish or whatever was needed. The fisherman needing *poi* would take fish, squid, or lobster upland to a household known to have taro and would return with his taro. In other words, the *'ohana* constituted the community within which economic life moved. In contemporary Hawaii, while this exchange of goods is not based on survival through mutual exchange, there remains an element of sharing openly and of exchanging goods across households—carrying on the tradition rooted in Hawaiian and Polynesian history.

The *'ohana* also emphasized the value and importance of communal labor. When the fiber used for fish nets was to be harvested, scraped, and spun, all the *'ohanas* joined forces in the shed to work together. Similarly, a family building a new dwelling was aided by the *'ohana*. And the *'ohana* functioned as a unit in external economic and social affairs. The taxes levied by the chiefs during the period of collection fell not upon individuals or single households, but upon the *'ohana*.

Today, we continue to witness the endurance of this practice of communal labor. But instead of being a fundamental part of family survival, it emerges in the form of shared responsibilities for major family celebrations such as the family *luau*, or feast, for special events. Families not only bring items from their *'ohanas* to share, they also share the work involved in putting on the event.

Traditionally, the pivotal individual of the *'ohana* was the **haku** (master / director), usually the eldest male of the senior branch of the whole *'ohana*. The *haku* divided the catch among the households, presided over family councils, and in general had authority over the members of the households in such matters as entertaining strangers, supervising work and worship, and planning communal activities. Because both men and women were of strong character in the *'ohana* and were extremely independent in speech and action, the *haku* was no dictator; he was subject to the advice and opinions of the householders and of all other members of the *'ohana*.

Women in contemporary Hawaiian households have an important functional role in the broader society. Women continue to be viewed as homemakers and men the breadwinners. But this traditional and functional distribution of responsibilities does not fully reveal the dynamic roles women of Hawaiian ancestry played in history and still play today. In the tradition of American farm families, Native Hawaiian families were also rooted in the land, with both men and women making critical contributions to the well-being of the family unit. Although the emphasis on farming has obviously diminished in importance, particularly as Hawaii's economic base became rooted in the tourist industry, the role men and women play in contemporary society and in Hawaiian families has not shifted substantially. In urban areas, the high cost of living demands dual employment for most Hawaiian families, and the importance of each member contributing time, money, and effort to the family remains constant.

Certain women of Hawaiian ancestry were far from traditional in their roles and responsibilities—and in their impact on future generations of Native Hawaiians. Some of the prominent leaders of the Hawaiian monarchy were women, and they held major roles—including the queenship. Two major trusts that today serve to ensure the preservation of the Hawaiian culture and provide services to the children and families of Hawaiian ancestry were established by, or in the name of, prominent women leaders of the Hawaiian Islands. The Bishop Estate, established by and in honor of Bernice Pauahi Bishop, a princess and direct descendant of King Kamehameha I, is the most prominent. Valued at well over $8 billion, the Bishop Estate serves to educate the children of Hawaiian ancestry, to make them good and industrious men and women. Thousands of children of part or full Hawaiian blood or ancestry have been beneficiaries of Mrs. Bishop's vision and dream for tomorrow. The Queen Lili'-uokalani Estate serves the poor, by providing social services and programs to Native Hawaiian families and children in greatest need.

Even in the contemporary society, women whose role and influence extend beyond the family household and into the Hawaiian community are common. The sovereignty movement has been guided to a major degree by women in leadership roles. The emphasis on the preservation of Hawaiian lands, and the commitment to reviving Hawaiian culture, have been fostered in part by women of Hawaiian ancestry.

Life-Cycle Transitions

According to the Office of Hawaiian Affairs (1994), among Native Hawaiians 15 years of age and older, nearly half (48%) are married, but a notable percentage (36%) are single. The divorce rate of Native Hawaiians is among the highest of the major ethnic groups, at 50–60%. This divorce rate contributes to the large number of Native Hawaiian female heads of household with children, and possibly to the large number of Native Hawaiian mother-child subfamilies (mother and child living in a household and related to the head of the household). One out of every three newborns (33%) is Native Hawaiian. Among Native Hawaiian newborns, slightly over two-thirds (67%) are born in the urban areas of Hawaii. As already noted, Native Hawaiians are the fastest-growing ethnic group. This population analysis reveals that the Native Hawaiian population will have an annual growth rate of approximately 2%.

Native Hawaiian families are overrepresented in the low-income group (annual income under $15,000; 18% versus overall population of 10.3%), and slightly underrepresented in the high-income group (annual income over $50,000; 34.7% versus overall population of 41.7%). Native Hawaiians are in the largest ethnic group with families below the poverty level, the largest ethnic group with families on public assistance, and the largest ethnic group with individuals 200% below the poverty level (Office of Hawaiian Affairs, 1994).

Modern life for the Hawaiian family in the homeland is a challenge, given the high cost of living. Government assessments of budgets for middle-income urban families identified Honolulu to be the nation's most costly city. It takes an estimated $9000 more per year to live in Honolulu than in Dallas, Texas, for example. To survive in Hawaii, the Native Hawaiian family usually has dual incomes. Two-thirds (67%) of all people over the age of 16 are in the labor force—the highest percentage of any other state except Alaska and Nevada. Nationally, slightly less than two-thirds (62%) of all people over age 16 are in the labor force. In Hawaii, well over half (57%) the women over age 16 are in the labor force (Office of Hawaiian Affairs, 1994).

Historically, Native Hawaiians are strangers in their own land. They face acute housing difficulties; few are new home-owners, and few can afford to be home-owners in the near future. According to the Office of Hawaiian Affairs (1994), in 1990, only one in 10 householders was Native Hawaiian, while four in 10 were Caucasian. With over 4899 Native Hawaiian households on public assistance and 3925 Native Hawaiian families with incomes below the poverty level, many live in public-housing projects. The vast majority either share living quarters with parents and / or relatives, or live in crowded rented housing units with virtually no hope of home ownership. Even with improved rental housing rates and declining prices of houses to buy, the outlook for Native Hawaiians remains gloomy.

The clear pathway for economic and social improvement for Native Hawaiian families is through education. Educational improvement results in increased income possibilities. According to the Native Hawaiian Educational Assessment Project (1983), the majority (64.2%) of Native Hawaiian children are clustered in elementary school (grades 1–8) and in high school (26.2%). Furthermore, there has been a steady increase (about 11%) in the number of Native Hawaiians attending the University of Hawaii, in contrast to the 0.1% attending in 1987. In general, Native Hawaiians are underrepresented among the populations obtaining college and advanced university degrees. Compared to the total population (two in 10, or 20.3%), fewer than one in 10 (8.3%) Native Hawaiians older than 24 completed 4 or more years of college. It is estimated that slightly less than 30% of adults of Native Hawaiian ancestry are identified as functionally illiterate. Efforts to bring Native Hawaiians into the five top job categories—officials and administrators, school administrators, professional and technical, teachers and secretarial/clerical—have proven to be ineffective, and they remain notably underrepresented in these occupational areas.

Native Hawaiian families are perhaps the ethnic group with the highest health risk in Hawaii. This risk profile results from the high levels of stress in their lifestyle and behaviors, and their late or lack of access to health care. Thus, it is not surprising to find among Native Hawaiians and family members a high incidence of disease, ailments, early disability, and premature death. To summarize, according to the Office of Hawaiian Affairs (1994), Native Hawaiians are overrepresented among those who:

▲ Have been diagnosed with lung cancer, thyroid cancer, and uterine cancer.

▲ Have died from heart disease and malignant neoplasms (cancer).

▲ Have heart disease (ages 36–65), 1.3 times higher than for any other ethnic group.

▲ Have hypertension (ages 19–65).

▲ Are Asian and Pacific Islanders with AIDS; nearly half (41%) of all Asian and Pacific Islander AIDS cases are Native Hawaiians.

▲ Have respiratory diseases, including asthma, bronchitis, and hay fever.

▲ Have diabetes; Native Hawaiians age 35 and older comprise nearly half (44%) of all cases in the state of Hawaii.

▲ Are pregnant women who do not receive any prenatal care (36%).

▲ Are mothers under the age of 18 (50%).

▲ Are mothers with newborns having low birth weight (25%).

▲ Have died a premature death; of deaths among those less than 1 year old, nearly half (40%) are Native Hawaiian children; of deaths among those ages 18–19, more than half are Native Hawaiians.

▲ Have health-risk profiles: 42% are overweight, 60% have a sedentary lifestyle, 32% are smokers, and 22% suffer from hypertension.

▲ Receive government aid; the highest concentration (73%) receive AFDC.

Ethnic groups at the lower end of the economic ladder have an increased probability of resorting to violence and crime. As a result, they comprise a large segment of the inmate population in state and federal prisons. Among the ethnic groups in Hawaii, Native Hawaiians make up a major portion of the local inmate population. According to the Office of Hawaiian Affairs (1994), in general Native Hawaiians are overrepresented among:

▲ Those arrested for property crimes (burglary).

▲ Those arrested for violent crimes (robbery).

▲ Sentenced felons (highest, at 37.6%).

▲ Inmate populations in prisons (highest, at 40.1%).

▲ Inmate populations in jail (highest, at 31.1%).

Family Strengths and Challenges

Traditionally, Hawaiians viewed salvation to be more of a family than an individual matter. Because the family was the dominant social unit, values associated with elders were also closely linked with the concept of salvation. Elders, the beloved family guardians, were often also selected to become deified and referred to as *amakuas* after their death. In the Hawaiian family, while everyone was granted immortality after death, a select few, usually elders, were given special *amakua* status because of their deeds while they were alive. Although there are no written records confirming the criteria for selecting *amakuas*, their roles were passed on from generation to generation through oral histories (Kanahele, 1986). *Amakua* roles included:

▲ Manager of the spiritual affairs of the temporal family.

▲ Provider of comfort and council.

▲ Disciplinarian.

▲ Advocate of causes for both individuals and the *'ohana*.

▲ Avenger of wrongs done to family members.

▲ Guide in the afterlife.

▲ Protector and savior in time of need.

▲ Patron.

Pukui, Haertig, and Lee (1972) describe *amakuas* in this way:

As gods and relatives in one, they give us strength when we are weak, warning when danger threatens, guidance in our bewilderment, and inspiration in our arts. They are equally our judges, hearing our words and watching our actions, reprimanding us for error, and punishing us for blatant offense. (p.123).

In understanding the roles and importance of *amakuas* in family life, we can also begin to identify those important values in the family context that were not only held in high regard but also revered. Kanahele (1986) offers the following synopsis of these characteristics of family leadership:

▲ Knowledge and understanding of the personalities, desires, aspirations, and problems of family members.

▲ Ability to relate well to the family unit.

▲ Ability to mediate in family disputes.

▲ Taking charge of family activities.

▲ Seniority in the *'ohana* hierarchy.

▲ Recognition and acceptance by the family.

▲ Possession of a high level of *mana*, along with the ability to use it wisely.

The relationship between the *amakua* and the family was that of a partnership, a working family alliance. The *amakua* provided protection, warning, council, healing, forgiveness, and discipline, and in return the family members did good deeds, appeased the *amakua*, provided nourishment, and paid homage. The *amakua* and the family members had joint and separate responsibilities.

Given the high value Hawaiian families attached to the eternal family, one of the important roles of the *amakua* was to ensure the preservation and honor of the family. The *amakua* served as a guide, a safeguard into life after death; there was no need to fear death or the hereafter, for one's soul would be warmly received and safely guided by the *amakua*. Death became a welcome package to the Hawaiian mystical sea of *Po*, where guardian and kindred spirits dwell.

Even in contemporary society, remarkable affinity prevails and endures among Hawaiians for their *amakuas*. One of the reasons for this continuity is the prominence that family values continue to have in the Hawaiian community and culture. When coupled with the hope of being together with loved ones in the afterlife, the residual imprint of *amakuas* remains alive and well.

Beneath the ceremony reflecting the integration of the Native Hawaiian family system into the mainstream dominant culture, and contrary to popular perception, a constant struggle remains between the family's identity and ethnic identification and **assimilation** into Western beliefs and practices.

Aboriginal Hawaiian families continue to struggle with minority status in their own lands, trying to find an identity and sense of meaning in a rapidly changing, technology-oriented society. The hurdles of being socially, economically, and psychologically challenged add to the complexity of the Hawaiian family's efforts to carve out a future that will preserve and reinforce their heritage, and at the same time will empower them to have a secure foothold on their destiny. These challenges have been presented throughout this chapter—not to create an image of a "down-and-out" cluster of native families, but to accurately depict the daily realities.

Native Hawaiian American families are survivors, resilient in their own ways, and adaptive without fully compromising their identity. Obviously, adaptation involving changes in the family, as well as changes in the society in which they live, has necessitated sacrifices and compromises—some positive and some negative. The loss of culture has enduring and possibly devastating effects on the health and well-being of the *'ohana* system and the Hawaiians themselves. Yet as the numbers of Native Hawaiians, albeit in families of mixed ethnic heritage, increase, this change is accompanied by a resurgence in Hawaiian ethnic identity through language, ancient practices, and a commitment to the revival of a culture once oppressed.

Family strengths related to this resiliency have also been emphasized throughout the chapter, particularly in presenting the cultural values *aloha* (love and acceptance) and *kokua* (sharing) passed on from one generation to another (Kanahele, 1986), as well as the family values of caring for elders and social support, which have served families well in the face of adversity (McCubbin & Thompson, 1992).

Hawaiian values form a supportive framework for the Hawaiian families even in contemporary society. Family life typically encompassed the values of generosity, spirituality, dignity, humility, hospitality, cooperation, creativity, and respect for genealogy, close family ties, mediation of disputes, and respect for elders. While the Hawaiian family system cannot claim uniqueness in emphasizing these values, when combined with other traditional and modern Hawaiian practices, which are unique, these values take on added importance.

There is no question about the Hawaiianness of the *hula, oli* or chant, *haku hulu* or feather-craft, *kahanalu* or body surfing, *ho'oponopono* or way of mediating family problems, *kahuna lapa'au* or Hawaiian medical practitioner, nor the *hanai* or adoptive system. The oft-cited spirit of *Aloha*, for example, has universal applicability as do dedication to family, appreciation and support of one's peers, placing consideration of others before consideration of self, and a strong conservation ethic.

If Hawaiian families are to play any role in the future of Hawaii, they must retain their identity. It is the collective total of the family's qualities, attitudes and values, their customs and traditions, and their history that makes Hawaiian families unique as a people, and as a great resource. Hawaiians and their Hawaiianness give Hawaii its strongest sense of identity to which all island people—Chinese, Japanese, Filipino, Portuguese, Korean or Caucasian can relate in a meaningful way, be it through Hawaiian music, dance, canoeing, surfing, food, words and beliefs, land and sea.

Recent studies of Native Hawaiian American families under stress reveal the importance of ethnic heritage to the durability and survivability of family life. In a survey of the stressors affecting Native Hawaiian American families with preschool-age children (McCubbin, Thompson, Thompson, Elver, & McCubbin, 1994), the great importance these families place upon their Hawaiian heritage is evident:

▲ We worry that the family will not be able to take care of the elders in the future (43.2%).

▲ We worry that parents are not able to spend time with children to encourage learning (43.3%).

▲ We worry that we are losing our ethnic values (44.8%).

▲ We worry that our ethnicity/roots are dying (45.4%).

▲ We worry that the land we were promised will never come to us (45.4%).

▲ We worry that children will join groups abusing alcohol/drugs (45.4%).

▲ We worry that the family cannot pay for health insurance in the future (50%).

▲ We worry that jobs will not be available for children in the future (53.1%).

▲ We worry that our native language will fade away (55.4%).

▲ We worry that the family will not have enough money for the children's education (60.8%).

The theme of affirming the importance of Hawaiians' ethnic heritage surfaces repeatedly. In another study of Native Hawaiian families under stress, five family strengths emerged as important protective factors against family dysfunction (McCubbin, Thompson, Thompson, Elver, & McCubbin, 1994):

1. Family problem-solving communication.

2. Family sense of coherence.

3. Family hardiness.

4. Family schema.

5. Community social support.

The most important protective factor is a family's ability to effectively communicate to solve problems. Families in which members communicate respectfully with each other are healthier. Families having a strong sense of coherence, including a sense of trust and predictability about the world they live in, are less dysfunctional. Families who have developed an internal strength, or hardiness, are also healthier. The study also demonstrated the importance to Hawaiian families of their ethnic identity, or what is called family schema—the degree to which they believe in and respect their Hawaiian heritage. Families with a strong ethnic identity are not only less dysfunctional, but also more effective in their problem-solving communication, have a greater sense of coherence accompanied by trust and predictability, and have a stronger sense of family hardiness. The fifth factor in predicting family well-being is a strong network of community social support—belonging to a larger group of people for sharing help and understanding. Hawaiian families with greater community support are also more likely to have a strong sense of confidence, challenge, commitment, and control, and also a deeper degree of ethnic identification.

Misconceptions and Stereotypes

Native Hawaiians are often characterized as being conflict-avoiders, lazy, shiftless, irresponsible, dumb, and also hostile. All **stereotypes** have some element of truth, for one can always find situations or incidents to confirm them. This is particularly true of how people and families of ethnic groups are often seen and judged. Positive stereotypes of Hawaiians include being good singers and entertainers, and being loving, positive, and generous. But these portrayals can also be considered negative because they imply the inferior capacity of people unable to compete academically and socially in a competitive Western culture.

In a study of student attitudes toward their own and other ethnic groups in Hawaii, Finney (1961) reports:

> There was a high agreement in what people of various groups (including Hawaiians themselves) thought of Hawaiians. A large number of favorable opinions were expressed. Hawaiians as a group were described as warm, friendly, and pleasant to know; as being frank in expressing their true feelings; as being fun-loving and not serious; and as being happy. On the unfavorable side they were described as being dependent; as working no harder than they have to; and as not being ambitious; as not being conscientious in carrying out responsibilities or fulfilling duties and obligations; and as being lax in disciplining their children, with sporadic severity. (p. 80)

In general, the Hawaiian people are distinctly different from members of the dominant American culture in terms of their cultural heritage, background, and values. The pervasive negative stereotype of the lazy Hawaiian has made it difficult for Hawaiians to attain the levels of achievement that might have come more easily, had they not faced such preconceptions. Contrary to these stereotypes, historians and serious students of Hawaiian culture attest to the capacity of Hawaiians and their families for hard work, especially when it involves a worthwhile goal and work with others in a group (Kanahele, 1982). The lazy Hawaiian stereotype emerged out of the early days of the sugar industry, when *haole* planters were faced with Hawaiians who refused to do routine ground-breaking work in poor conditions for low pay. The Hawaiians refused to be exploited.

The "entertaining and loving people" stereotypes have emerged in the context of tourism and the entertainment industry of the Hawaiian Islands. Hawaiians are glamorized as purveyors of this *aloha*, or welcome-all, spirit representative of the native people's good will, and of the tourist industry's desire to portray Native Hawaiians as lovers of music, dance, play, surfing, fishing, and swimming—exotic stereotypes that lure visitors to the islands. As Kanahele (1982) notes, although these stereotypes are abstractions, they are potent realities when they shape the behavior and attitudes of the dominant population toward Hawaiians in general.

Another important stereotype that has profound implications for the education of young Native Hawaiians is that Hawaiian families do not have educational aspirations for their children, that Hawaiians do not value education as do the Japanese, Chinese, and Caucasians. Studies by Alu Like (1976) offer another perspective:

> The problem is not that the Hawaiian parents do not value education; almost unanimously they feel it is most important for their children to graduate from high school and important for them to go to college as well. Hawaiian parents do, however, have mixed feelings about the effectiveness and responsiveness of the public school. (p. 42)

Burrows (1947) observes that Hawaiians may present themselves as having a front—such as playing the role of having a carefree life, basking on the beach, renouncing the pursuit of worldly goods—to mask a deeper withdrawal. Hawaiians may exhibit a marked reserve toward people of other cultures. They trust only those who have demonstrated enough sincere friendliness, enough respect for them as individuals, to deserve it.

Another prominent stereotype is the conflict-avoidance coping strategy Aboriginal Hawaiians have adopted and evolved over time. This pattern is apparently focused on avoiding conflict, shame, or any form of social disruption. In this way, Hawaiians avoid unpleasant situations and potentially divisive issues, even though their input might be vital to the group's best interests. This behavior is accompanied by a tendency to accept arbitrary decisions rather than to "make waves" by raising questions or challenging the issues or facts presented. Howard (1974) observed Hawaiians in work groups who would follow instructions they knew to be incorrect or inefficient because they did not want to confront the leader of the group with an alternative course of action. This coping mechanism is related to the reluctance of Native Hawaiians to attend clinics and to avoid seeking legal assistance or other forms of help with establishment figures.

Avoiding conflict and confrontation is a generic Hawaiian American family strategy that may suit the goals of family affiliation and social group harmony. But it may be ill-suited for competitive success in Western society, with its emphasis on directness, open exchanges, and questioning of the status quo. Confrontations are necessary in dealing with the commercial, political, health care, and legal institutions of contemporary society.

The behavior pattern of avoidance may also be linked to Hawaiians' expression of hostility, frustration, and anger. When facing situations that bring culturally based conflict into play, Native Hawaiians may experience deep feelings of frustration or anger, particularly if the family was frustrated for a long time suppressing their feelings, holding back truths, and looking the other way to avoid conflict.

If Hawaiian American families are to play any role in the future of Hawaii, they must retain their identity. It is the collective total of the family's qualities, attitudes, and values, their customs and traditions, and their history that makes Hawaiian families unique as a people and a great resource. Hawaiians and their Hawaiianness give Hawaii its strongest sense of identity, to which all island people—Chinese, Japanese, Filipino, Portuguese, Korean, and Caucasian—can relate in a meaningful way, through Hawaiian music, dance, canoeing, surfing, food, words and beliefs, land and sea.

The burden of dealing with Hawaiianness should not be a major obstacle for contemporary Hawaiian American families. They live in an entirely new era of ethnic pride and multicultural **pluralism**. There is a sense of pride and honor in being Hawaiian or of Hawaiian ancestry, and thus being part of an elite or special group of people.

Personal Interview

Caroline is a Native Hawaiian who was born on the Island of Oahu. She has a family of four children, two boys and two girls (the old-

est boy died unexpectedly 3 years ago). Her husband is also a Native Hawaiian, born on the Island of Maui. They have six grandchil-

dren, all of whom lived with them for several years before moving on to their own homes or apartments when they could afford to do so. Theirs has occasionally been a four-generation household, but at present, it consists of two generations: Caroline's mother, Caroline, and her husband, who is retired. They are the regular caretakers of the grandchildren. It is common in the Hawaiian family to have such caretaking arrangements and to have multiple generations living under the same roof.

What are some of the stereotypes about Native Hawaiian American families?

Caroline: Hawaiians have many labels attached to them. The most common are that they are lazy, on welfare, have too many children, are uneducated, are delinquents and criminals, unmotivated to work or to improve upon themselves, and overweight. They eat and party a lot. To some degree these stereotypes are accurate. Hawaiians are truly health risks, due to being overweight and stressed. This is, however, not a very fair way to characterize a racial group. Not only is this offensive, but it reinforces a negative self-image. The old Hawaiians were very hard-working and fit people. In actuality, there is little truth to these characterizations; the negative stereotypes are stated to offend the Hawaiians and make them feel less about themselves.

What can you say about Hawaiian American families—their customs, beliefs, values, and practices?

Caroline: We have many positive values. I remember a story told to me about food and how Hawaiians value their food. A friend tells the story of his purchasing a McDonald's hamburger and taking it to his *tu tu*, his grandmother's house. There she was eating *poi* and raw crab. He commented how "gross"

the food was and how she was eating it (using both hands, one for the *poi* and one for the crab). His grandmother responded with calm and wisdom: "Never belittle the food you eat, for someday you will starve." Hawaiians had great respect for the food they grew, harvested, and ate. We were always taught to eat some of everything we were served.

I can remember attending a workshop on Hawaiian values. We were asked to draw a picture of a heart and select the most important family value we shared. We were then asked to share our drawings and values with each other in the group. Common to everyone was the Hawaiian value of *aloha*, which translates into love, being kind to one another, and making things right. This was linked to the Hawaiian value of *lokahi*, or working together, and *pono*, the value of making things right for everyone. These values are all related and taught to us from a very young age. The Hawaiian values are interconnected to promote good will, sharing, and kindness among family members and the community.

My deep commitment to Hawaiian values comes to me through how I was raised and my education. Even though my family was of mixed ancestry—Hawaiian, Japanese, and Caucasian—the Hawaiian values were prominent and emphasized in my family. I attended the Kamehameha Schools, a special school for children of Hawaiian ancestry, where we were taught Hawaiian customs and values. We were taught to appreciate and value our Hawaiian music, respect for our elders and those senior to us in age and status, respect for God, and self-discipline. We had many rituals and ceremonies to remind us of our heritage and the respect we needed to show for them. Even while our education pushed Western values, our heritage and respect for our ethnic roots were also affirmed.

Even though we were criticized as an ethnic group, we knew no prejudice. We were taught to be respectful and accepting of other races and beliefs. Loving and valuing of others of different beliefs and backgrounds were taught and emphasized in our education. Stereotypes were not part of our teachings or beliefs; it was not until after I graduated from high school that I came to realize the pejorative labels used and conflicts among people and races. I appreciated my upbringing and type of education.

Should the Hawaiian community and families be an independent nation and have their lands restored under their control?

Caroline: I believe that things should remain the way they are. Sovereignty is not the answer to everything. We need to respect our *kupunas*, our ancestors, and move forward. The ceded lands should be returned to the Hawaiian people as promised, but this does not mean sovereignty. The Hawaiian family is different today than in the past, and we cannot turn back the clock and restore what is lost. We must move forward, building upon what we have now. This push for sovereignty may be a popular position in the islands and among the Hawaiian people and families, for many believe that sovereignty is the right way to go; we must reclaim all of what was rightfully the Hawaiians'.

Discuss the pros and cons of Hawaiian families socializing their children to identify with their Hawaiian heritage and ancestry.

Caroline: It is very, very important to teach the Hawaiians their heritage and values. All races and cultures do this to some degree. The *lauhala* making (making mats from the leaves of the lauhala tree), for example, should be taught from one generation to another. Not

only will we lose our culture, but future generations will be deprived of a rich heritage, which helps them develop their self-identity. There is so much beauty in the Hawaiian culture and language to pass on. For example, Hawaiian quilt making is an important expression of our culture; making *poi* (food for eating); *hula* dancing, *kahiko* and *auwana* (ancient and modern *hula*), and chanting, are all parts of who we are, and we need to keep focused in shaping our identity. Western teachings and values pull us away from our heritage, so we need to take special care to ensure that this heritage is passed on to all Hawaiians, no matter how small a blood quantum of Hawaiian exists. Thankfully, there is a renaissance or revival of the Hawaiian culture which will move into the twenty-first century.

What are your feelings about three- and four-generation households, with parents and grandparents carrying a large share of the parenting responsibilities for the grandchildren and great-grandchildren?

Caroline: It is difficult to do, but it is wonderful. We can all learn from one another. This is common practice among Hawaiian families. Part of this is out of necessity; it is too costly to buy or rent in Hawaii. We *kokua*, or chip in together, to help each and to learn from one another. We can pass on values and beliefs. We can pass on wisdom from one generation to another. There are more adults to care for the children and to help with tasks and opportunities for education of the young. The problem-solving method of the Hawaiians has a greater chance of working. This problem-solving, more commonly known as *ho'oponopono*, a family method for solving family and individual problems, emphasizes the value of family members working together, through discussion, to address and work through issues and conflicts.

I don't want to say things are rosy all the time. It is difficult to have so many people and generations together. Conflicts and misunderstandings also have a greater chance of emerging. I can remember my own childhood included three aunts and two uncles and our five cousins, as well as grandmother and grandfather. It was a wonderful experience, I recall. We continue to be close, even though we all now live in different parts of the United States.

The Hawaiian parenting style of sibling care is somewhat controversial. Discuss the pros and cons of this Hawaiian family socialization process.

Caroline: Well, I don't believe in this. I realize that this is part of our Hawaiian practice, but I am troubled by the responsibilities placed upon the older children to care for the young. Maybe it is because I was the oldest in the family. Because both of my parents worked, this became a problem for me. I am not sure I was equipped to do this. It is easy for children to get out of hand, and I could not manage all the problems; it is too much responsibility. I had to grow up, too. This may be one of the reasons why Hawaiian children drop out of school, miss so many classes, and do poorly in school; family responsibility for caring for younger children increases with age, and so does schoolwork. Something has to give, and because we are rewarded for family work rather than schoolwork, we run the risk of hurting our education and our future.

Questions for Discussion

1. What are some of the negative and positive stereotypes of Native Hawaiian families described in this chapter?

2. Describe how contemporary Native Hawaiian American families have been shaped by their history.

3. Review and discuss the values and beliefs of Native Hawaiian families. In what ways are these values and beliefs problematic for these families in contemporary society?

4. How can Native Hawaiian families best preserve aspects of their heritage and at the same time adapt to Western ways and values? Is it possible?

5. Discuss the revival of the Hawaiian culture and practices. Will they have a positive or negative impact on family life?

6. What are the pros and cons of the current efforts of the Hawaiians to achieve sovereignty, to regain control of their lands and implement greater self-governance? Will this be better for the Hawaiian families? Worse?

Suggested Resources

Readings

Budnick, R. (1992). *Stolen kingdom: An American conspiracy.* Honolulu: Aloha Press.

Dudley, M. K., & Agard, K. K. (1990). *A call for Hawaiian sovereignty.* Honolulu: Na Kane O K Malo Press.

Gallimore, R., & Howard, A. (Eds.). (1968). *Studies in a Hawaiian community: Na Makamaka O Nanakuli.* Honolulu: Bishop Museum, Department of Anthropology.

Jarves, James J. (1847). *A History of the Hawaiian Islands* (4th ed.). Honolulu: Government Press.

Office of Hawaiian Affairs (OHA). (1994). *Native Hawaiian data book.* Honolulu: Office of Hawaiian Affairs.

MacKenzie, M. K. (1991). *Native Hawaiian rights handbook.* Honolulu, Office of Hawaiian Affairs.

Pukui, M. K., & Craighill Handy, E. S. (1953). *The Polynesian family system in Kau, Hawai'i.* Wellington, New Zealand: The Polynesian Society; and Rutland, VT and Tokyo: Tuttle, 1972.

Trask, H.-K. (1994). *Light in the crevice never seen.* Corvallis, OR: Calyx Books.

Videos

Keith, V. (Producer). *Hawaiian soul.* (Available from Namaka Oka'Aina, 3020 Kahaloa Drive, Honolulu, HI 96822.)

Namaka Oka'Aina. (Producer). *Contemporary Hawaiian artists.* (Available from Namaka Oka'Aina, 3020 Kahaloa Drive, Honolulu, HI 96822.)

Namaka Oka'Aina. (Producer). *Faces of the nation.* (Available from Namaka Oka'Aina, 3020 Kahaloa Drive, Honolulu, HI 96822.)

Namaka Oka'Aina. (Producer). *Makua homecoming.* (Available from Namaka Oka'Aina, 3020 Kahaloa Drive, Honolulu, HI 96822.)

Namaka Oka'Aina. (Producer). *Na Wai e Ho'ola i na Iwi (Who will save the bones?)* (Available from Namaka Oka'Aina, 3020 Kahaloa Drive, Honolulu, HI 96822.)

Namaka Oka'Aina. (Producer). *Waimanalo eviction.* (Available from Namaka Oka'Aina, 3020 Kahaloa Drive, Honolulu, HI 96822.)

Namaka Oka'Aina. (Producer). *West Beach story.* (Available from Namaka Oka'Aina, 3020 Kahaloa Drive, Honolulu, HI 96822.)

References

Adams, R. (1937). *Interracial marriage in Hawaii*. New York: Macmillan.

Alu Like, Inc. (1976). *Analysis of needs assessment survey and related data*. Honolulu: Native Hawaiian Project.

Burrows, E. G. (1947). *Hawaiian Americans: An account of the mingling of Japanese, Chinese, Polynesian and American cultures*. New Haven, CT: Yale University Press.

Finney, J. C. (1961). Attitudes of others towards Hawaiians. *Social Process, 25,* 78–83.

Hawaii State Department of Health. (1992). *Health surveillance program,* special tabulation.

Howard, A. (1974). *Ain't no big thing*. Honolulu: University of Hawaii Press.

Jordan, C. (1976). *Maternal teaching modes and school adaptation*. Honolulu: Kamehameha Early Education Program, Kamehameha Schools / Bishop Estate.

Kanahele, G. (1982). *Hawaiian values*. Honolulu: Project Waiaha.

Kanahele, G. (1986). *Ku kanaka stand tall: A search for Hawaiian values*. Honolulu: University of Hawaii Press.

Marsella, A. (1979). Cross-cultural studies of mental disorders. In A. J. Marsella, R. G. Tharp, & T. J. Ciborowski (Eds.), *Perspective on cross-cultural psychology* (pp. 1–26). New York: Academic Press.

Marsella, A. J., Oliveira, J. M., Plummer, C. M., & Crabbe, K. (1995). Native Hawaiian (Kanaka Maoli) culture, mind and well-being. In H. McCubbin, E. Thompson, A. Thompson, & J. Fromer (Eds.), *Resiliency in ethnic minority families: Native and immigrant American families. Vol. 1* (pp. 93–114). Madison: University of Wisconsin System.

McCubbin, H., & Thompson, A. (1992). Resiliency in families: An east-west perspective. In J. Fisher (Ed.), *East-west connections in social work practice: Tradition and change* (pp. 103–130). Honolulu: University of Hawaii, School of Social Work.

McCubbin, H., McCubbin, M., Thompson, A., & Thompson, E. (1995). Resiliency in ethnic families: A conceptual model for predicting family adjustment and adaptation. In H. McCubbin, E. Thompson, A. Thompson, & J. Fromer (Eds.), *Resiliency in ethnic minority families: Native and immigrant American families. Vol. 1* (pp. 3–48). Madison: University of Wisconsin System.

McCubbin, H., Thompson, A., Thompson, E., Elver, K., & McCubbin, M. (1994). Ethnicity, schema, and coherence: Appraisal processes for families in crises. In H. McCubbin, E. Thompson, A. Thompson, & J. Fromer (Eds.),

Sense of coherence and resiliency: Stress, coping and health (pp. 41–70). Madison: University of Wisconsin System.

Native Hawaiian Educational Assessment Project. (1983). *Final report*. Honolulu: Kamehameha Schools/Bishop Estate.

Office of Hawaiian Affairs (OHA). (1994). *Native Hawaiian Data Book*, Honolulu: Office of Hawaiian Affairs.

Pukui, M. K., Haertig, E. W., & Lee, C. A. (1972). *Nana I Ke Kumu (Look to the source)*. Vol. 1. Honolulu: Hui Hanai.

Thompson, E., McCubbin, H., Thompson, A., & Elver, K. (1995). Vulnerability and resiliency in Native Hawaiian families under stress. In H. McCubbin, E. Thompson, A. Thompson, & J. Fromer (Eds.), *Resiliency in ethnic minority families: Native and immigrant American families. Vol. 1* (pp. 115–132). Madison: University of Wisconsin System.

Trask, H. (1995). Native sovereignty: A strategy for Hawaiian survival. In H. McCubbin, E. Thompson, A. Thompson, & J. Fromer (Eds.), *Resiliency in ethnic minority families: Native and immigrant American families. Vol. 1* (pp. 133–142). Madison: University of Wisconsin System.

U.S. Bureau of the Census. (1990). *Detailed population characteristics: Hawaii*. Washington, DC: U.S. Department of Commerce.

Werner, E., & Smith, R. (1989). *Vulnerable but invincible: A longitudinal study of resilient children and youth*. New York: Adams, Bannister & Cox.

Werner, E., & Smith, R. (1992). *Overcoming the odds: High risk children from birth to adulthood*. Ithaca, NY: Cornell University Press.

Glossary

acculturation The process of adapting to patterns of a different culture.

aloha (Hawaiian) Affection ranging from extending a greeting to a new person to embracing a loved one.

aloha aina (Hawaiian) The value of ensuring the preservation of the balance between life, land, and sea.

amakua (Hawaiian) An elder given special status after death.

assimilation The process in which a smaller ethnic group adopts the characteristics of a dominant culture and loses its original identity.

barrio (Spanish) A subdivision of a city, a neighborhood, or a suburb occupied primarily by Hispanics, often having a high rate of poverty.

caste A hereditary social division in Hinduism; caste membership restricts a person's choice of occupation and social group.

chain migration A process by which previous immigrants facilitate the migration and settlement of subsequent individuals and family members.

compadrazgo (Spanish) Godparents who have a moral obligation to act as guardians, provide financial assistance in times of need, and substitute as parents in the event of death.

Confucianism The ethical teachings formulated by Confucius and introduced into the Chinese religion, emphasizing devotion to parents, family, and friends, ancestor worship, and the maintenance of justice and peace.

conjugal relationship A relationship formed through marriage.

consanguineous relationship A relationship formed by common blood lines.

culture The collective concepts, habits, skills, art, instruments, and institutions of a group of people.

curanderismo (Spanish) A form of healing using natural and herbal remedies.

curandero(ra) (Spanish) Folk healers who use herbal remedies and practice faith healing.

discrimination Making a distinction in favor of or against a person on the basis of prejudice.

dual heritage A heritage that represents or includes characteristics of more than one ethnicity.

endogamy Marriage within a particular group.

enmeshment An extremely high level of family closeness, resulting in a lack of individualism.

267

espiritismo (Spanish) A faith-healing method common in Puerto Rican and Cuban communities.

eternal progression The practice in the Mormon community of perfecting individuals within the context of the family.

ethnicity Common ancestry and social and cultural heritage that is passed down from generation to generation.

ethnocentrism The belief that one's own ethnicity and its characteristics are superior to those of other ethnic groups.

exogamy Marriage outside a particular group; also known as out-marriage.

extended family A family unit consisting of parent(s), child(ren), and other close relatives.

familialism A pattern of social organization which emphasizes family relationships, loyalty, traditions, and strong feelings for the family.

family ethnicity The way in which a family defines itself in terms of common ancestry and social and cultural heritage (race, religion, or national origin).

feudalism The economic, political, and social system in which land, worked by serfs attached to it, was held by vassals in exchange for military and other services.

fictive kin Unrelated individuals who are treated as if they were related.

filial piety A child's obligation to and respect for ancestors and parents.

free agency The sense of responsibility for personal choices, actions, and consequences in the Mormon community.

gender role The culturally defined role a person is expected to perform based on being male or female.

genealogy An account of the descent of a person or family from an ancestor.

glass ceiling effect The illusion that one can reach the top in one's career, but in reality an invisible ceiling prevents it.

haku (Hawaiian) Master or director; usually the eldest male in the family.

haole (Hawaiian) A White man.

Hinduism A 2500-year-old religion forming the basis of Asian Indian psychology and philosophy.

Hispanic Of Spanish or Latin American origin or background.

ie The basic family unit in traditional Japanese society, consisting of past, present, and future members of the extended family and their households.

illegal alien A person who has entered the United States without authorization.

Jim Crowism A practice or policy for segregating or discriminating against Blacks.

joint family A type of extended family that includes the married couple, their unmarried children, and their married sons with their spouses and children; three or more generations may live together in a joint family.

kinship system A social organization of the family that defines rights and obligations based on an individual family member's status.

kokua (Hawaiian) Help or aid to the extended family; giving without expectation: the foundation of Hawaiian civilization.

lineality A direct line of descent or kinship from an ancestor.

machismo (Spanish) In Hispanic cultures, the concept of masculinity, characterized by bravery, courage, self-defense, responsibility, respect, altruism, pride, protection, steadfastness, individualism, androgyny, and honor. In the United States, the concept is based on the belief that the male is virile, aggressive, and accountable only to himself.

mana (Hawaiian) The spiritual force and power shared by all living things.

marianismo (Spanish) In Latin American Catholicism, the idealized mother role, as represented by the Virgin Mary.

matriarchy A social organization or family in which the ultimate authority is vested in women; the head of a matriarchy is called a matriarch.

matrilineality A line of descent or kinship through the mother.

migrant worker A farm laborer who moves from place to place to harvest seasonal crops.

model minority myth The belief that Asian Americans have high levels of educational attainment, low crime rates, and an absence of juvenile delinquency and mental health problems.

nuclear family A family consisting of mother, father, and at least one child.

'ohana (Hawaiian) The overarching value system of the Hawaiian family; the extended family.

out-marriage The practice of marrying outside one's own ethnic group; also known as exogamy.

patriarchy A social organization or family in which the ultimate authority is vested in men; the head of a patriarchy is called a patriarch.

patrilineality A line of descent or kinship through the father.

pluralism A social condition in which several distinct ethnic, religious, and racial communities live in harmony and appreciate one another's similarities and differences.

polygamy The practice of having more than one spouse at a time.

polygyny A form of polygamy in which a man has more than one wife at a time.

polytheism Belief in more than one god.

prejudice A judgment or opinion formed without closely examining the person or group you are evaluating.

racism An active expression of prejudice or discrimination based on inherited characteristics of ethnicity or cultural group membership.

Reconstruction The period of reintegration of the former Confederate States into the Union after the Civil War, 1867–1877.

religiosity The quality of being extremely religious.

respeto (Spanish) A special respect given to family elders, the foundation on which the entire Puerto Rican family system is based.

rite of passage A ceremonial or formal observance or procedure in accordance with proscribed rules or customs.

Santería (Spanish) An African-Cuban religious and folk-healing method.

small-producer family A family of entrepreneurs or laborers who own and operate a small business, such as a laundry shop or grocery store.

social identity The way an individual perceives the world based on social, physical, economic, and cultural characteristics.

split-household family A family arrangement in which income earning is separated from the main household and carried out by a member living abroad, while keeping the family home, socializing children, caring for the elderly, and maintaining family graves are the responsibility of wives and other relatives.

stem family A family arrangement in which retired parents live with a child who inherits the leadership role; those families who can afford to may have a separate but adjoining house or wing of the family residence for the elders.

stereotype An oversimplified set of beliefs and generalizations about an individual or group of people.

xenophobia Fear or hatred of foreigners or strangers.

Index